W9-CEL-896

From Dark Night to Gentle Surrender

On the Ethics and Spirituality of Hospice Care

From Dark Night to Gentle Surrender

On the Ethics and Spirituality of Hospice Care

Patricia Kobielus Thompson

University of Scranton Press
Scranton and London

© 2010 University of Scranton Press
All rights reserved.

Library of Congress Cataloging-in-Publication Data

Thompson, Patricia Kobielus, 1949-
   From dark night to gentle surrender : on the ethics and spirituality of hospice care / Patricia Kobielus Thompson.
      p. ; cm.
   Includes bibliographical references.
   ISBN 978-1-58966-194-3 (pbk.)
   1. Hospice care--Moral and ethical aspects. 2. John of the Cross, Saint, 1542-1591. 3. Hospice care--Religious aspects--Catholic Church. I. Title.
   [DNLM: 1. John of the Cross, Saint, 1542-1591. 2. Hospice Care--ethics. 3. Catholicism. 4. Religion and Medicine. 5. Spirituality. 6. Terminal Care--ethics. 7. Terminally Ill--psychology. WB 310 T475f 2009]
   RT87.T45T56 2009
   362.17'56--dc22

                                                        2009042834

Distribution:

University of Scranton Press
Chicago Distribution Center
11030 S. Langley
Chicago, IL 60628

PRINTED IN THE UNITED STATES OF AMERICA

In memory of my parents

John and Carolyn Kobielus

CONTENTS

PREFACE

Almost ten years in the field of hospice nursing and a lifelong love of theology and spirituality have been synthesized in this study. Today's medical milieu is a complex one, which includes major technological advances as well as alternative forms of medicine. These elements, which build upon the traditional ideals of the practice of medicine and the healing arts, often cause distress and spur spiritual questioning because of the increasing number of choices they offer to patients and families. Various types of treatment abound which include approaches never before imagined. Options offered frequently confuse not only those seeking treatment for their illnesses, but also the practitioners who offer them. Ethical concerns have arisen because of these new options, and currently we face a continuing evolution in the art of biomedical decision-making.

From the early attempts to synthesize philosophical and theological approaches, to the reconsideration of the theory of virtue ethics, the field has evolved rapidly and continues to do so today. Included in this evolution are signs of a spiritual hunger in both patients and health care professionals. Despite the tremendous advances in technology, we remain aware of the natural limits of human life. At the same time, we recognize technology's ability to prolong it beyond all prior expectations. This tension has challenged practitioners to face ultimate questions with their patients and families. In this profoundly sensitive end-of-life period, both sides come face to face with the inevitability of human death—and ultimate questions are raised.

What is to be done? What is not to be done? Who are we as moral agents? And what can we do to strengthen our spirits in the midst of it all? These are the questions that prompted me to begin the exploration into the spirituality of St. John of the Cross as it might be applied in the ethics and spirituality of hospice care. I sought a spirituality which could not only help me as a practitioner in the field of hospice and palliative care, but could also be something shared—primarily by example and not by preaching—with those whom I cared for professionally.

Throughout the six chapters of this study I have examined the hospice movement itself, several of the philosophical and theological approaches which contributed to the evolution of the field of biomedical ethics, and the spirituality of St. John of the Cross with its implications for both practitioners and patients. Finally, I have mentioned several selected resources for modern practitioners which offer the support of a particular religious tradition—that of the Roman Catholic Church. Because I write from the Judaeo-Christian point of view and am of the Roman Catholic faith, it is the tradition with which I am most familiar. I am aware also of the plurality of religious traditions, however, and have profound respect for their views on the sanctity of life.

For me, this study is only the tip of the iceberg. What is suggested here is one approach to a spirituality which appreciates the mystery of God-given life. Likewise, having sat at the bedside of dying patients for nearly ten years, I know there is a mystery surrounding each individual patient's manner of death. I also know that, as practitioners, we are not privy to the inner spiritual journey of those to whom we minister. But as professionals who hold that life itself as sacred, we seek a spirituality which frees us from desperate clinging to the familiar "proven" elements in our lives. Such a spirituality may enhance our ability to walk with those facing imminent death. St. John of the Cross gives us one way to discern our best approach to this.

Many people have supported me in my journey to this point. I thank the faculty of the Theology Department of Duquesne University, first of all, for providing support throughout my years in the doctoral program. This work was the culmination of that period of study. Secondly, I thank my colleagues at Forbes Hospice in Pittsburgh for ten years of teamwork as we dealt with the concerns of our patients in the program there. I thank the patients themselves, who gave to all of us much more than they could have imagined. We, who supposedly cared for them, received a depth of spiritual insight we could not have predicted.

I thank Jeffrey Gainey, Director of the University of Scranton Press, who received this work and has supported it from the beginning with an enthusiasm that would boost anyone's creativity. His belief in the message of the work has been a strong impetus for me to share it with others in this way.

Finally, I thank my husband Dr. William Thompson-Uberuaga, my best friend and constant support for thirty-three years, and our daughters Carolyn and Stephanie and their families, who provide us with inexpressible joy and hope at every turn. Without them, this work would not have come to pass.

INTRODUCTION

Significant changes in the health care system, as well as my almost ten years in the field of hospice and palliative care nursing prompted this study. I first envisioned it as a way to combine two separate courses of study—Nursing and Theology. Over time, however, the research showed me that the nature of nursing practice, and of medical practice in general, calls for much more than mere technical skill on the part of practitioners. It demands an integration of one's spiritual life with one's professional practice.

Questions have arisen in the last several decades which were unheard of in the earliest years of the medical and nursing professions. These questions, both ethical and spiritual, seek to reach beyond what *can* be done in a given situation toward reflective consideration of what actually *should* be done to foster the ultimate well-being of both patients and practitioners.

Because of technological advances, human life is now being prolonged far beyond what early medicine ever envisioned. Now the questions arise regarding the most beneficial treatments, addressing as well the spiritual and psychological aspects of being human and facing one's own death. For this reason, there seems to be a great need to integrate into professional practice a viable spirituality. This will not only carry practitioners through the increasingly difficult decision-making surrounding end-of-life care, but it will also translate into effective, sensitive patient care. In the case of terminal illnesses, practitioners with such a spiritual grounding may find it easier to "walk with" their patients through very distressing emotional times.

In Chapter One, I have examined the development of the hospice concept through history. From the earliest hospices designed to assist travelers, down through the centuries and into the twentieth century where Cicely Saunders began in England what we know as hospice care, I explore the roots of today's hospice and palliative care. By including the modern Hospice Code of Ethics, I attempt to focus specifically on the serious ethical concerns surrounding end-of-life issues.

In Chapter Two, selected aspects of the philosophical and ethical background of modern biomedical ethics have been addressed. The pertinent thoughts of Aristotle, St. Thomas Aquinas, and several early twentieth-century philosophers are examined—as is the intense development of the field in the past three decades. Likewise, I have included the concept of biblical covenant responsibility, as well as the recent re-integration of virtue ethics in the medical professions.

Chapter Three reflects on St. John of the Cross, a sixteenth-century mystic whose *apophatic* approach was expressed in *The Ascent of Mount Carmel* and *Dark Night of the Soul*. A spiritual director and Carmelite friar, he was asked to describe his prayer life to his own directees. He admitted, however, that he felt he could not adequately convey the depths of his own spiritual experience. Nevertheless, his teaching on the giftedness of God's love in all unexplainable circumstances may very well provide an applicable model for today's medical practitioners. The "dark night" of human end-of-life experience may find itself brought "into the light" through the spiritual letting-go which St. John advocates.

Chapter Four brings the considerations closer to home, addressing several health care professionals' experiences as they attempt to translate spirituality into action within the modern medical milieu.

In Chapter Five, the end-of-life journey of a scholar-theologian captures a bit of both worlds. A man whose life work was academia found himself thrown back on the spiritual resources which had formed the basis of his career—in a way he had never imagined. The integration of both his academic knowledge and his gut-level experience of his own terminal illness provides a vivid picture of the emotional and psychological issues surrounding terminal illness.

Finally, in Chapter Six, several Roman Catholic resources are mentioned which serve as additional points of grounding for modern professionals. Noting that in all religious traditions there are aspects of the "dark-night journey," I emphasize the fact that each practitioner must find his or her own spiritual roots in a unique way and in specific life circumstances. But the Roman Catholic tradition out of which this study grew continues to evolve, and offers tradition and community support for a spiritual integration of one's professional life.

Though such a study is merely a beginning, all spiritual seekers will evolve as they personally respond to the grace of God. Perhaps, for families and patients facing end-of-life decisions, this book will provide insight into the reasons for choosing hospice care.

CHAPTER ONE

HOSPICE CARE

ORIGINS OF TODAY'S MODERN HOSPICE CONCEPT

An overview of what we know today as the hospice concept begins as far back as Greek and Roman times. The many excellent resources available provide a detailed history of the origins and growth of this concept, which has been thoroughly described by Madalon Amenta and Nancy L. Bohnet in their book *Nursing Care of the Terminally Ill*.[1] These women were instrumental in founding the first hospice in Pittsburgh, Pennsylvania, in the late 1970s. They begin with Greek and Roman times, where travelers in Greece were believed to be protected by the god Zeus Xenios (derived from the Greek *xenos*, meaning guest friend), and Roman travelers by Jupiter Hospitalis. The Latin term *hospes* may designate either host or guest, with the understanding that there was a contract of sorts between them, consisting in care and feeding, more particularly care in illness and infirmity. The pilgrimage of life joined everyone. In the midst of this journey people shared the goal of mutual care, one human for another, in institutions known as *aesculapia*, or healing sanctuaries.[2]

With the influence of Christianity, institutions known as *xenodochia* were formed. Within the walls of these establishments were dedicated (and often, ordained) deaconesses who provided the earliest institutional care for the ill and infirm. One of the more famous of these deaconesses was Fabiola, whose hospice was formed in about the year 400. Hers was one of the earliest prototypes of today's hospitals.[3] Her institution cared not only for healthy traveling pilgrims, but also for those who were ill, and for those whose illness was terminal.

Fabiola had been a wealthy Roman matron who converted to Christianity, and her activities were noted by the Emperor Julian the Apostate in some musings dated around 361. He reflected on the activities of the new group known as Christians. Noting the inability of the Roman powers to stamp out the group by any apparent means, including torture, he nevertheless deeply respected their care for the sick and the poor, and urged all Roman citizens to begin immediately to imitate them.[4]

About 475, the Hospice of Turmanin came into being. Located in Syria, this institution was renowned for its care of travelers. At that time, these travelers (known as *peregrini,* from the Latin phrase *per ager*, or "through the field") counted on the people in these institutions to take them in, to care for their bodily needs, and sometimes to treat their illnesses. It was a responsibility taken quite seriously, with the community aspect being the glue holding people together and prompting loving, caring actions toward fellow human beings.

Proceeding to the Middle Ages, we see that the care of the sick was taken over by religious orders specifically dedicated to the merciful care of the sick and dying. One of the foremost groups was the Knights Hospitallers of the Order of St. John of Jerusalem in the twelfth century. These men were specially trained to care for the sick. Again, it was a religious dedication, with the focus on each life as a spiritual journey. The final goal of this journey was union with God, the Ultimate Being. God was the basis of their dedication and the source of their strength in carrying out their mission.

If one needed professional care during an illness, these were the people who were sought out. Unfortunately, the political and military powers attempted throughout the history of the Knights Hospitallers to squelch their activities and to surround military encampments "with banners and jewels." The Order itself acquired many gifts and much wealth, and was eventually driven out of its last great outpost, the Island of Malta, in 1798. As Stoddard notes, this was two hundred years after King Henry VII took most of its English holdings.[5]

Philippe Ariès writes of the fifteenth century: "Despite all the conventions he had to observe, the testator of the later Middle Ages expresses a feeling that is close to that of the *artes moriendi*: awareness of self; responsibility for one's destiny; the right and duty to make arrangements for one's soul, body, and property; the importance of those last wishes."[6] The *artes moriendi*, or "arts of dying," included icons which depicted people at home, in their own beds, surrounded by family, and often with heavenly figures somewhere in the picture. Most often the Blessed Virgin and Christ Crucified were included in the scene.[7] Thus, the religious aspects were depicted, giving solace to the bereaved and hope of better things to come.

In London, around 1538, a petition was presented to the king for a place where those who were dying could be taken. This included the supposed "dregs of society." The petition described a place where people could be "lodged, cheryshed and refreshed."[8] The citizenry held a very negative attitude toward those who were dying in a most visible way in the streets of London—and to whom little care was formally given. Hospitality was still being sought for those *in extremis*, but as Stoddard has noted, it was not to be had from the government.[9] Rather, the attitude toward these desolate poor and sick was one of self-righteousness and contempt. They were things to be removed from sight.

Although various hospitals existed at the time, their policies often expressed the desire of that particular society for "order, efficiency, and social discipline."[10] Hospitals were places where one went to be "mended," although often it was known that it would be one's very last journey. During this time, hospitals began to be an arena for teaching and research. Thus, people became guinea pigs and sought sponsors who would recommend them to the institution and guarantee their funeral expenses. This first tinge of a "business mentality" foreshadowed our more modern institutions. In the fifteenth century, with the development of the study of anatomy and the practice of surgery, the components of medical care began to be divided into "curing" and "caring" as two different mindsets.[11] This division has continued, becoming more pronounced as new technologies and medical specialties have developed through the centuries.

To search for the compassion which was speedily being trampled by the growing industrial focus, we might revisit the era of St. Vincent de Paul and the Sisters of Charity, the order he founded in the seventeenth century. These women were trained to care for the sick wherever they found them. Again, it was the castaways and downtrodden who received their attention.[12] Hospices were formed throughout France by these nursing sisters.

As Stoddard notes, the ambiance of their institutions remained throughout the eighteenth century. In the beginning of the nineteenth century, seen through the eyes of Baron von Stein in Prussia, their hospices inspired the founding of Kaiserswerth—one of the first Protestant hospitals with an order of nursing sisters—by Pastor Fliedner in 1836.[13] These women were both nurses and teachers, working both in prisons and with the poor. The idea was also carried into Ireland, where in Dublin, Sister Mary Aikenhead, of the Irish Sisters of Charity, founded the first institution formally known as a hospice, for the care of terminally ill patients.[14]

In a reference to St. Christopher's (the hospice founded by Dame Cicely Saunders after her studies at St. Luke's Hospice in London), Philippe Ariès notes the difference between the emphasis on curing which was so evident in the modern hospitals, and that on caring, the prime focus of the hospice movement: "In some countries there is a movement to keep these patients in places that specialize in painless death and preparation for it, places where they could avoid the disadvantages of a medical organiza-

ily reasons for such actions, but they frustrate the true hospice concept, where, as much as possible, facts are addressed openly. The patient and family are given tools to deal with the normal process of dying and bereavement. The open awareness system is such a view. Here it is possible to address many issues directly, truthfully, and often productively. The resolution of many personal and familial issues is possible in such a system.

With the advent of St. Christopher's Hospice in London in the late 1960s, the first working model of today's hospices was created. A "space" was given for individuals and families to travel the journey together with other patients and families, providing support, encouragement, and "community" to bolster the spirits and hopes of all involved. This community aspect is all but lost in the bustling society of today's world, especially in the cities where apartment living isolates people in small cubicles of life. (In one author's view, modern society is typically a mass of "atomized individuals."[19])

Thus, we see the historical progression of the modern hospice movement from the earliest places of refuge for pilgrims, through the era of the dedicated religious orders, and on through the last few centuries where death went from being a natural part of one's life to something hidden away behind closed doors. The industrial age, with all its technological progress and new discoveries, could not make the dying process any more acceptable to those who now in some ways expected quick answers to all medical "problems." Within the walls of the developing hospitals, there were still wards where the incurables were placed. There they found their calls for assistance increasingly ignored by staff rushing to "cure" those for whom there was still hope. In fact, the industrial age was instrumental in distancing caregivers even more from their patients. "Professional" and "scientific" distance further limited personal interaction and kept patients compartmentalized in safe informational boxes.

CICELY SAUNDERS AND THE FIRST MODERN HOSPICE

The twentieth century saw even more individualization of care. The specializations constantly evolving in the medical field divided ailments into ever more specific subdivisions. Formerly, there had been a more global approach to the disease process. Now the understanding of the most minute details of cellular biology, virus structures, anatomical systems, and specific medical interventions led to the compartmentalization of people according to categories. Medical science all too often isolated persons from the caring, attentive ministrations of the physicians people had previously known as their "family doctors."

They found themselves in a system of clinicians dedicated to one specialty or another. From none of these specialists—or rather, from a rare few—came the attention to one's "person" that Cicely Saunders's Hospice of St. Christopher strove to put back into the process. Her interaction with particular patients led her to focus on the idea of a modern hospice as "a collection of ideas and attitudes informing an array of services based on a holistic philosophy of living and dying."[20]

With her own experience and understanding of hospital regimens, she deliberately made the goal of hospice care "to prolong meaningful living where personality is not warped or obtunded by social isolation, drugs, treatments, equipment, or the environment."[21] Saunders's description of hospice care included the phrase "a place of meeting." Frequently the modern hospital seems more like New York's Grand Central Station. Patients are transported back and forth for repeated tests, diagnostic explorations, resident and intern conferences, and all the trappings of the fast-paced medical community.

In many teaching hospitals, troops of residents and interns follow attending physicians in large groups into patients' rooms, placing lab charts up on walls and speaking to one another as if the patient were not present. The patient is "the liver in 1025" or "the gall bladder in 456." It is a dehumanizing experience. The patients often feel a total loss of control over their own lives. The system is perhaps efficient, but it is not inclusive of the human and personal aspects of each patient.

In such a hospital atmosphere, Cicely Saunders's goal of creating a place where a person might approach death "in a conscious and forthright way" and have the opportunity to "examine the dimensions of meaning, relatedness, forgiveness, and transcendence that this powerful life event inevitably brings to the fore"[22] is highly unlikely to be achieved. Realistically, in such a situation, their emotional, spiritual, and psychological needs will be lost in the flurry of diagnostic activity. They will be left to face the prospect of death, loss, and family bereavement in the darkness of the night.

In a quotation from Shirley du Boulay's *Cicely Saunders: Founder of the Modern Hospice Movement*, Amenta and Bohnet provide a description of what a group of social work students observed in 1960 as they toured St. Joseph's Hospice. The most striking points were these:

1) absence of pain and drowsiness; 2) liveliness and peace-
fulness; 3) an indefinable atmosphere which left one feeling
that death was nothing to be worried about; 4) integration—
patients, staff and visitors were all of equal importance; there
seemed to be no dividing barriers; 5) simplicity of approach
to the problem of pain; 6) lack of narrow-mindedness which
might so easily be present in a place run by a particular order,
e.g., agnostics, atheists or nonthinkers [*sic*] are helped to accept death in a way most suitable to them as individuals, besides those who already have strong Christian faith.[23]

An atmosphere such as the one just described is almost impossible
to achieve in today's hospitals. There is intense activity, myriads of tests
and medical procedures, and demands for "results" and "outcomes." All
these elements combine to form a barrage of information "bytes" that are
certain to move too fast past the beds of terminally ill patients. The advent
of the teaching hospital created this situation, and while the focus of such
institutions is important, it overlooks the slower elements of living which
need to be fully addressed.

The patients are people for whom the procedures, cures, rehabili-
tation, and cure-all mentality are no longer appropriate. This lessening of
aggressive treatment was addressed early on by Elisabeth Kübler-Ross as
she studied in Chicago. She met with great resistance from the senior staff
in her quest to develop a new approach to the dying. But her dogged determination brought about changes that today are receiving new and perhaps
more focused attention. It is to this woman that we now turn, to explore
what she added to Cicely Saunders's work in England.

ELISABETH KÜBLER-ROSS

The work of Elisabeth Kübler-Ross fostered the growth of the hospice concept in the United States. Through her work with dying patients,
this insightful, persistent physician was able, after several years of fighting
the prevailing system, to bring about an attitude of reform toward the care
of the terminally ill.

During her residency training in Chicago, she discovered that patients who had terminal illnesses were hidden away in back rooms. She observed that the modern society had determined somehow that, because of
all the technological advances, the prevailing impression was that a "good"
life should be free of discomfort and pain. Death had become hidden, talked

about in hushed tones, and patients facing death were left alone—their call bells unanswered, conversations clipped and superficial—to ponder their condition without the support of the people who could possibly have helped them the most.

Kübler-Ross considered the situation from the point of view of the physician. Most of her colleagues expressed little about the process of dying. She observed that physicians did not wish to admit that any of their patients were in a terminal state, and the lectures she offered in the hospital were very poorly attended.[24]

One of the first important sources of insight for her was a black cleaning woman whose interactions with the patients produced a tremendous change in their attitudes. She had experienced the death of her son through a terrible mismanagement of medical care. To her, death was not a stranger. Rather, it was something she had had to embrace, and from that point on she was no longer afraid of it. Thus, in her interactions with the dying patients she was able to approach them, listen to them, touch them, and be present to them. As Kübler-Ross then says, "All the theories and science in the world could not help anyone as much as one human unafraid to open his heart to another."[25]

To do the "opening up" required of caregivers called forth from each one personally something that was not, and still is not for the most part, taught in medical schools. "In order to be able to create a foundation for that encouraging climate (of communication), caregivers had to learn how to acknowledge to themselves their own repressed, intense, and painful feelings, often very near to the surface."[26] Dealing with these feelings does not come easily to many young physicians and professional caregivers, especially in a fast-paced hospital atmosphere.

One of the first realizations caregivers must have is an awareness of their own ability or inability to deal with what society has deemed difficult or unapproachable. Sandol Stoddard remarks in *The Hospice Movement* that "each society chooses its own outcasts. Ours demands health and beauty, talent and power."[27] When we are faced with something lacking those qualities, we often refuse to acknowledge its presence because it calls forth from us something yet undeveloped in ourselves. Elisabeth Kübler-Ross recognized this in her colleagues in Chicago.

She set about deliberately to highlight in her weekly conferences—with their permission—selected terminally ill patients. Colleagues were invited to participate, while the patients spoke and answered questions. It was a long, involved process, fraught with resistance from physicians who continually refused to admit the terminal status of some of their patients. What she found was a situation described in these terms: "The classical deathbed scene, with its loving partings and solemn last words, is practically a thing of the past; in its stead is a sedated, comatose, betubed object, manipulated and subconscious, if not subhuman."[28]

Into this picture, Kübler-Ross chose to bring her experience of dealing with the close-to-the-surface emotions of some of her patients. These emotions were the unscientific, "unable-to-be-proved" elements of disease. There were no set formulae telling physicians what to do in the face of such emotions; thus, the situations were often avoided. It was this avoidance that needed to be addressed and transformed by an intense focus on the unique characteristics of each person. Within the confines of a teaching hospital there was, and is, very little time to do this reflecting, especially on "non-scientific" aspects of disease. These aspects are not easily captured by the "elitist medical jargon" of the laboratory.[29] Values fostered in such a laboratory include detachment, rationality, scientific accuracy, and an unemotional outlook. Such values are totally inappropriate in dealing with a human person in a terminal state.

THE AVOIDANCE OF DEATH

It may be helpful at this point to address what Philippe Ariès describes as the present attitude toward death in our society. We have already seen the attitudes in the previous centuries. The "journey" motif was very strong in ancient times, and this is one element now being revisited in the new approach to hospice care. Today's medical culture, however, as well as the broader culture, fails to allow for the time needed to appropriate the reality of death. There are tremendous expectations, beginning with the physicians, who are taught to "cure" above all else, and with patients and families themselves, who in the face of bereavement are expected to accept the reality and then move on quickly with their lives.

Ariès notes, "If death is too noticeable, too dramatic, and too noisy, most especially, if it is also dignified, it arouses in the staff an emotion quite incompatible with their professional life, still less with hospital routine. For death has been brought under control in order to reconcile an accidental, sometimes inevitable phenomenon with the psychological security of the hospital."[30]

The prevailing culture will not allow those involved in practicing health care, and even less those experiencing that health care, to remain one moment too long in something that cannot easily be categorized and labeled. Rather, it forces the raw human emotions into the businesslike atmosphere of the modern-day hospital routine. Ariès focuses on this reality in an entire chapter, "Death Denied." Death is seen as a failure of the medical profession. More than that, it is seen as "business lost."[31]

Specifically, the reality of death, while it must be faced as a practical matter—what does one do with the body?—does not enjoy the front-page exposure of the newest transplant or viral technologies. Ariès states, "A heavy silence has fallen over the subject of death. When this silence is broken, as it sometimes is in America today, it is to reduce death to the insignificance of an ordinary event that is mentioned with feigned indifference. Either way, the result is the same. Neither the individual nor the community is strong enough to recognize the existence of death. This attitude has allowed the old savagery to creep back under the mask of medical technology."[32]

Within this extremely sterile atmosphere lives the patient—and the patient's family. Acceptable forms of emotional expression are those remembered on the face of Jacqueline Kennedy on the day of her husband's funeral. Completely stoic, "brave" countenances are de rigueur. Such an appearance allows all who are involved in the care of terminally ill patients to go about their business without the inconvenience of having to face intense emotions or uncertainties. These elements have "no place" in the scientific, antiseptic world of modern medicine. Again, Ariès states, "Death must simply become the discreet but dignified exit of a peaceful person from a helpful society that is not torn, not even overly upset by the idea of a biological transaction without significance, without pain or suffering, and ultimately without fear."[33]

THE PRESENT RE-AWAKENING

There seems now to be a transformation occurring in the approach to the dying, once again, furthering Kübler-Ross's earlier efforts which found great support but which still today are extremely difficult to fund. The demand for more focus and understanding on the last stages of life is again acquiring a life of its own. Documentaries and books abound in which the difficult issues are addressed in various ways, forcing both medical professionals and laypersons to take serious stock of their approach to this final stage of living. Surprisingly, even though hospices have been in the United States since the middle and late 1970s, many consumers are totally unaware of them, or if they are aware, they keep the images in a vague and "safe" place. Many have visions of dark rooms where dour, serious practitioners operate in a subdued, morbid atmosphere. Even with the earliest examples in North America, such as Connecticut Hospice in New Haven, St. Luke's in New York City, and Dr. Balfour Mount's Royal Victoria Palliative Care Service in Canada, almost medieval pictures still exist in some people's minds about what really constitutes modern hospice care.

A film was made in 1976, directed by Michael Roemer, called *Dying*. People were observed both in clinical situations and in their homes. Honesty about disease and prognosis is apparent in all the encounters highlighted in this film. Episodes include the more traditionally attended death at home as well as a situation which Ariès describes as having "a complete absence of emotion."[34]

What seems to be apparent in this documentary film is that even with different styles of acceptance of death and the dying process, there is a universal need to face squarely all the emotional aspects included in the experience. One's total aloneness is paramount. Support is often not there for families who have lost loved ones. Silence is frequently what greets persons suffering terminal illnesses. Silence even from those closest to them. What we have not thus far been able to eliminate has now been placed like an old book onto the highest shelf in the bookcase, where it does not even have to be dusted, much less read.

NEWER DEVELOPMENTS

Perhaps the most insidious effect of this removal of death from immediate sight is the appearance of the growing public demand for euthanasia and assisted suicide. Again, the technological advances are both boon and curse. Although it is true that physician-assisted suicide and euthanasia have been realities practiced secretly, away from the glare of the public lights, the increasing public demand speaks volumes about the society's attitude toward one's "right" to control the uncontrollable. The focus is on the ultimate end rather than the process, which up until now we have not been able successfully to control.

Our need to encapsulate things, to wrap them in a safe container and place them away from closer examination, is a strong, driving force in these public movements toward legalization of assisted death. So it would appear that in order to slow down what seems to be an uncontrollable momentum toward public policies on these matters, we must come face to face with what both Cicely Saunders and Elisabeth Kübler-Ross saw in their practices: the intense, raw human emotions surrounding terminal illness.

We must also address what has been done, and what continues to be done, in the field of palliative care. The technology which runs rampant over humanity in other areas can also be employed successfully in treating the symptoms—physical, spiritual, psychological, and emotional—experienced in terminal illness.

GOALS OF HOSPICE CARE

For this next section, I will combine information gleaned from almost ten years in hospice work with my research on the professional goals of this area of medical and nursing practice. Some of this information—for example, the description of the training given hospice personnel in interpersonal skills—was part of my daily routine and thus is not specifically referenced to outside sources. I have tried to integrate that experience into the overall focus of the study.

Cicely Saunders and Elisabeth Kübler-Ross both envisioned the care of the terminally ill taking place in an atmosphere open to addressing four specific aspects of any human person. These aspects, as previously noted, are the physical, psychological, spiritual, and emotional—all elements in a holistic approach to medical care. In order to facilitate such an atmosphere, hospice staff members and volunteers are carefully taught to include all possible elements of a patient's life in their consideration of that particular person. Not only the disease itself, but each person's family, friends, background, outlook, attitudes, and perceptions are all considered as parts of his or her own unique "puzzle."

Sandol Stoddard makes a very important statement about this focused approach to the care of the dying:

> Nothing that is human is excluded from the premises, or from the consciousness, of hospice life. Beauty here is not a matter of tidy appearances, logical proprieties, or even of physical prowess. Rather, it pertains to those exchanges between people, living and dying, who value one another as vessels of a purer and more lasting force, who look beyond present turmoil and incapacity, to the realization that our entire planet has now become one village seeking to be healed. With the spread of the hospice concept in our culture, many of us may discover that we are learning from the sick how to be well again, and from the dying, how to live.[35]

Within such an atmosphere, the hospice personnel are taught to be present to the patients and families with definite goals in mind. These goals include the initial acceptance of a terminal diagnosis, education about what might specifically be expected as the disease progresses, spiritual and psychological support during the dying process, and bereavement counseling for the family members who are left behind when the patient dies.

An important element to remember is that this sort of care is medical care with a very focused expertise. It demands a serious dedication on the part of those who practice it, drawing not only on intellectual talents and textbook knowledge, but also on the deep reservoir of personal character and commitment of each health care professional. It is a focus on a very different sort of "healing." This healing does not include the recovery of full bodily capacity. Rather, it encompasses the entire personhood of each individual patient. It is a healing in an entirely different dimension, far beyond bodily limits. This is the sort of healing that for the most part can neither be documented nor proved.

This sort of healing is also something that demands of the health care professional an ability to move beyond mere task-orientation. In today's modern hospitals, intensive care units have become bastions of machinery, constantly blinking, beeping, pushing fluids in and pulling fluids out, with personnel rushing around pushing various buttons in order to monitor the bodily functions being so closely watched. In hospice care, generally, most machines are gone. There are no blinking lights, no readouts on cardiac monitors to which one must attend. Perhaps there is a machine delivering pain medication, but essentially there is only the patient. In this situation there is more to be addressed. In the words of Sandol Stoddard, "The work of a hospice is to give patients the attention they need; it is a job equally as demanding as that of a more conventional hospital but involving different skills, more personal. But it's good hard medicine all the same."[36]

It would be appropriate here to consider some of the characteristics observed in hospice nurses in general. The specific emphasis of hospice care demands that practitioners exhibit a certain ability extending beyond the technical. Some of these characteristics are described by Amenta and Bohnet, in a study done for the *Journal of Clinical Psychology*: "They were more forthright and spontaneous; more confident, assertive, and strong willed; more imaginative and creative; more freethinking and independent, not only than their colleagues working in traditional settings, but in many cases, more so than normal women in the general population."[37] This description highlights the strengths of the hospice nurses studied in that particular survey, and now would also include the many men who have chosen hospice nursing as well. These men exhibit like characteristics, but it may also be added that many of them have moved beyond male stereotyping and are far beyond the "macho" or "executive" image that bespoke success in the business world. Rather, they have a significantly developed sensitivity of expression and care which is absolutely necessary in the field of hospice work.

What then are these professionals all about, and what is the goal of hospice? Paraphrasing the work of Amenta and Bohnet once again, the goals of hospice can be seen in this way. There is a strong emphasis on holistic care. This encompasses the totality of the patient as a human being within a surrounding family and culture, with specific psychological, spiritual, emotional, and physical concerns. Such an emphasis eliminates a primary focus on monitoring machines or body functions. It accepts that a "cure"—which means the elimination of the disease process—has now become impossible.

The "cure" or "healing" sought in hospice care is of a broader nature. Treatment elected in hospice care has as its goal the comfort of the patient: freedom from pain, as well as freedom from anxiety and other symptoms of both the disease process and the dying process itself. By this I mean the dying process as a "leave-taking"—*from* what is known in the present, and moving forward *into* what is ultimately unknown. This entire process is the focus of hospice care.

Within this process lies an emphasis on utilizing all possible strengths of the patient. The entire family is the "unit of focus" for hospice workers. That is to say, a great significance is placed on observing everything that goes on around each patient, as well as what goes on within. Patients are asked what is most meaningful to them, how they wish to spend their last months, weeks, or days, and efforts are made to facilitate these desires. There is a hospice team involved in such care. Physicians, nurses, social workers, chaplains, and volunteers called from many arenas of life all contribute to the complete care of a patient who has chosen hospice.

A primary focus in a hospice plan of care is pain control. Unfortunately, within the medical world there is still the fear of addiction to narcotic drugs. It is true that in many circumstances the fear is warranted. Many of these drugs are indeed misused by unscrupulous individuals. But in the care of a person suffering intractable pain, whether in an isolated area or throughout the body, as with bony metastasis, the idea of addiction is absurd. It was shown long ago that even when heroin was used as the drug of choice, as was the practice in England, that if the pain disappeared, so did the desire for the drug.

As Dr. Ira Byock notes, "With severe pain, there is no maximum dose of pain medication; the right dose is the one that works."[38] Byock relates the story of a young woman in Montana who was diagnosed with kidney cancer. The young woman went through an agonizing process of accepting the disease, a process made worse by the fact that she was the mother of a young toddler. Family support was there, but as the disease progressed the pain became increasingly intolerable. The young husband often cried himself to sleep at night, in frustration at not being able to help her.

Dr. Byock initiated a thiopental drip, which put the patient into what was called "twilight sleep." This allowed the family to experience some peace. This procedure was done with the full consent of the patient herself, who at that point had come to accept the inevitable and wished only to be at peace, surrounded by her family. The story illustrates further that the patient's choices, and the availability of highly specialized pain-relieving medications, allowed her to be freed from the intense, debilitating pain the disease was causing her. In this way the other needs of both the patient and her family could be peacefully addressed, in the now quiet atmosphere of her own home.

Perhaps one of the most difficult aspects of hospice care is allowing patients who have terminal illnesses to work through their dying in their own way and in their own time frame. This is not possible in the fast-paced hospital world. The ideal situation for a hospice patient is to be able to remain at home with support in place from available family, friends, church, and neighbors. Into this picture then comes the hospice team. All available resources are enlisted.

Essential to this process is a nonjudgmental attitude. There is no place in hospice work for personnel to enter another's home and make judgments about lifestyle, housekeeping, choice of companion, faith expression, or any of the elements that combine to make each patient a unique individual. Again, this calls forth from hospice staff at all levels a very serious awareness of their own mind blocks which could prevent them from giving the person the best care possible. Negative attitudes are, realistically speaking, parts of each individual, but in the face of a patient with a terminal illness, and in the presence of that patient's family, a hospice worker is called to have a clear focus on the goal of hospice care, and not to impose his or her own beliefs and attitudes on anyone there.

For example, if hospice personnel find themselves increasingly irritated or bothered by a patient or family member, it is essential that this reaction be honestly addressed by the hospice worker in consultation with other team members. One's own needs for a certain orderliness or organization, for example, must not be allowed to overwhelm the patient and family as they struggle within their own unique circumstances to make the best of a very bad situation.

Pain, often the most oppressive of the symptoms with which dying patients have to cope, comes not only from the physical aspects of the disease, but also from the emotional component inherent in any leave-taking. This can also be overwhelming to the caregiver. Today's pharmacological resources are immense, however, and there is truly no reason why pain should go unattended. Combinations of drugs may be safely and sensitively used to provide the patient with freedom from debilitating pain.

Palliative care, that is, the focus on complete symptom control, is gaining more intense application today. Persons engaged in palliative care, the essential element in symptom management for hospice workers, have as their primary responsibility the assessment of all possible causes of pain. With careful scrutiny and sensitive inquiries, most pain can be and often is controlled. For those persons experiencing the most difficult symptoms, all possible interventions should be tried. The cases where pain cannot be controlled, if the work is done in this way, should be extremely few and far between.

In their book *Pain Management Handbook*, Evelyn Salerno and Joyce Willens differentiate between the two types of pain which may be considered intractable. Intractable pain "can be defined as 'stubborn,' 'persistent,' or 'difficult to alleviate, remedy, or cure.'" The two types of pain are acute and chronic pain, both of which are experienced by persons in a terminal state.[39] Acute pain in this sense is categorized as pain which has a "well-defined temporal pattern of onset usually associated with a clearly identifiable etiology."[40] This sort of pain, since it is associated with a particular injury to a particular organ or tissue, can often be reversed. Radiation therapy is frequently employed to shrink tumors and relieve pressure on specific organs, thereby alleviating some of this acute pain. Acute pain also causes both physical and emotional distress, which, when combined with the emotion involved in facing a terminal prognosis, can complicate treatment in these patients.

Chronic pain, on the other hand, "persists longer than several months, and tends to progress in concert with the natural evolution of the disease."[41] At times, because chronic pain does not cause the same sort of immediate physical symptoms as the acute pain, these patients "are often apathetic, withdrawn, non-communicative, sleepy, and depressed," even to the point of denying any pain at all.[42] This can lead to misunderstandings between patient and caregiver, and calls for a sensitive assessment of each individual patient's situation. The complications of such states include "a self-perpetuating cycle of pain, insomnia, depression, and fatigue, to the extent that some look to early death or suicide as the only way out."[43]

Providing complete pain control is one of the primary goals of hospice care. This entails a process of accurate assessment of the causes of the pain, thorough knowledge of appropriate medications, and the constant reassessment of the effectiveness of any chosen therapeutic regimen. According to studies cited by Salerno and Willens, intractable pain can theoretically be reduced to "between 1% and 5% of the total population at risk."[44] Additional studies indicate that certain of the population (5% to 25%) will only obtain total pain relief through profound sedation.[45] The good news is that studies continue in this area, with the hope that more effective means will be discovered and implemented for this very serious concern.

Because emotional and psychological concerns often exacerbate the physical symptoms, they make hospice work all the more challenging. Untangling the web of symptoms, possible causes, and areas of treatment is a complex process. Concerns range from a person's body image to concerns about relationships, sexuality, saying good-bye to those closest to them, and family and friends' resistance to being involved due to their own fears of loss and death. Appropriate referrals and consultations from the fields of psychology and social work are often utilized in these instances.

Spiritual issues often resurface during the days and months prior to a person's death. It often seems that one searches for meaning in everything when it is all seemingly being taken away. It is in this area that hospice personnel must tread very carefully. Awareness of the big picture of religious issues and personal spirituality is essential. Again, there is no room for the imposition of one's own personal outlooks on anyone. Seeking "deathbed conversions" is totally inappropriate. The situation does allow for gentle communication in this area, however, taking the lead from the patient, and from the family. Often one simple statement or reflection can allow further expression of spiritual concerns to a sensitive and caring person, be it the nurse, the social worker, or the hospice chaplain. What is important in this matter is to realize that such spiritual care falls under the larger umbrella of holistic care, that which encompasses the total person and not just the physical elements.

Hospice care, done properly, provides for the atmosphere necessary to combine care from different fields in a directed focus on the whole humanity of each dying patient, within the circle of his or her family and community. The goal is one of fostering one's ability to live as completely and fully within the boundaries allowed by the illness itself, making use of the opportunities present in each unique situation. It was seen early on in the evolution of hospice care that the dying process was made a little less onerous when the patients and families themselves experienced certain elements of control over the situation. Although the inevitability of their deaths never moved from their awareness, a more positive direction of their available energy was emphasized.

This direction included the ability to focus on whatever concerns existed for them, whether financial, relational, spiritual, or any other life issues pressing upon them. Attempts to balance the control of pain with whatever level of alertness was possible have always been a main focus of the medical care in hospice work. In this way, the concerns at hand could be addressed as thoroughly as possible. If the patient was not able to participate directly, hospice workers were enabled to access resources not only from family but also, if necessary, from community and government sources. The advent of the Medicare hospice benefit in the 1980s assured government support of such care. These initial support measures are now receiving even more focus in the light of the many health maintenance organizations now in operation.

Thus the progression in the focused care of the dying has continued in our country through the last thirty years. There is still much to be done, practically, in obtaining funding for the unique situations which occur as someone undergoes the terminal stages of a disease. But the essential elements of hospice care have never changed. They transcend the technological wizardry and move practitioners back into the realm of their own personal resources. There is no hiding behind machines in this field.

The field of medicine has all too often been one in which the physicians were treated as "gods." Their opinions were taken at face value, with very little questioning on the part of the recipients of their care. In the field of hospice care, however, such an approach can only be detrimental. When patients and families are prevented from exercising all possible ways of participating in their treatment, there is a notable decline in their quality of life. Patients who exercise an active role in their decisions and who feel their physicians and allied health personnel are communicating honestly and openly with them are able to collaborate in their own care to a much greater extent.

Although the disease itself may ultimately claim the person's life, hospice care—delivered with empathy, sensitivity, warmth, and understanding—allows the personal journey to be the primary emphasis. Within this framework, the hospice caregivers themselves can experience growth as persons and as professionals. As fellow journeyers, they fully collaborate with their patients to make the dying process a more natural and less to-be-feared part of the journey.

PRINCIPLES OF HOSPICE CARE

The field of biomedical ethics has been and continues to be an evolving science. But more than a science, it needs to be an art practiced by dedicated individuals who have not lost sight of the patients for whom they care. Hospice care makes use of very specific principles in its focus on the dying process. The field of biomedical ethics, which will be examined more closely in the next chapter, has undergone a shift in focus and is expanding its emphasis to include other approaches, such as virtue ethics. These go beyond the initial use of the four specific principles which were the primary focus at the beginning of the evolution of the field of biomedical ethics. This approach, formally known as *principlism*, while very necessary in the initial stages of development of the field, tended to be somewhat limited, and is now being combined with the other approaches. This makes the biomedical-ethical field more encompassing.

For hospice, then, this shift is a freeing one. Self-determination, otherwise known as *autonomy*, is a basic premise of hospice care. Principles of informed consent are paramount in medical treatment today, and it is especially important with end-of-life issues, where all other control has been lost to the disease, and all that remains to the patient is the surrounding environment. Autonomy and self-determination in this instance demand that the patient be given as much control of his or her circumstances as possible.

One's "self" in any given instance is ultimately all that it is possible to care for. The losses that terminal illness dictates are immense, and as Daniel Callahan states (in regard to illness), "Its ultimate terror is that it reveals our final fate, which is to lose control of our lives, to see the self that is our deepest possession, the center of our being, as perishable."[46] For the patient in the midst of such terror, the principle of self-determination, or autonomy, needs the ultimate respect from the health care professional.

There have been a number of instances in my own professional career where I have heard stories about a person's choices having been glossed over in favor of more aggressive treatment. The specter of failure is a very real one to many physicians educated to "cure" their patients, and who come face to face with the reality that not all illness can be so easily dismissed. How many terminally ill patients have been directed to undergo "just one more" treatment, in the hope that this one will prove successful?

On the other hand, palliative care ethics, which is really the touchstone of the hospice philosophy, seeks to encompass all areas of the patient's life. In doing so, it involves the physician not just as a scientific practitioner, but as a human being with definite moral responsibilities, not only to the patient, but to himself or herself as a moral agent in relation to another human being.

"Palliative care needs well developed, wise, and compassionate people, whose common sense is combined with professional knowledge; it does not need people who lack these characteristics but are trained to appear as if they possess them."[47] What is proper to the practice of such individuals is that they are deeply aware of the boundaries which must not be crossed in dealing with each unique personal situation of patients at the end of life. Part of this awareness is a consciousness of the effects of living with terminal illness.

No one in this situation can be his or her "normal self," because all normalcy is removed when one faces death. In the modern culture, it has been thought that all negatives should be controlled, the very thought that this is not possible puts patients and families in an immediately defensive posture. In an ideal situation, however, practitioners at all levels now have the opportunity to exercise a high level of collaboration among themselves and with the patients and families.

Balancing the four major ethical principles in such a situation is extremely challenging. These principles are autonomy, beneficence, nonmaleficence, and justice. The three latter principles fall mainly in the realm of the practitioners, especially beneficence and non-maleficence, which are, respectively, the responsibility to do what is good for the patient, and the responsibility not to do harm to the patient.

Justice encompasses both the practitioner and the patient. It is the responsibility of the patient to place himself or herself in the larger picture, as far as distribution of care is concerned. This might be somewhat difficult if seen in relationship to one's experience of dying, but acceptance of a terminal prognosis and the realistic approach to what is beneficial can assist a person in making a decision either to pursue or not to pursue various treatments. On the part of practitioners, a realistic approach to the benefits available through certain treatment modalities can assist them in helping patients and families make appropriate decisions, with a view toward what is just for all concerned.

Earlier approaches to the concept of autonomy fell into two categories. One was the *rational* category, which focused on the intellectual component of decision-making. Another was the *preferential* approach, noting that decisions made were expressive of the preferences of the individuals concerned. These came from Immanuel Kant and John Stuart Mill, respectively.[48] Basically these two approaches have melded into what is today known as one's "informed consent." Such consent encompasses many more aspects of one's personal being than just mental functions or personal preferences.

In today's medical culture, the most important element of this transaction between physician and patient is trust. Too often this is not present. Finding a physician who will take the time to sit down in a protected environment to honestly and openly present all the facts of the situation is a valued discovery. Such physicians are vital participants in hospice care, and even prior to hospice care, because it is such a person who can demonstrate the sort of open communication that is the very cornerstone of end-of-life care.

Autonomy and self-determination, then, are vital components of decisions in hospice. But these principles extend much farther than the patient and the family members. In palliative care, it is essential that the practitioners also retain a sense of their own personal autonomy and self-determination. Any interaction with patient and family, on a level such as that demanded in the face of terminal illness, calls forth from the physicians, nurses, social workers, chaplains, and volunteers in a hospice program the deepest levels of awareness not only of the values and goals of their patients, but also of their own in the larger picture of treatment.

"Does palliative or any kind of health care mean that painful emotions, loneliness, guilt, and anxiety should all be extinguished by the right sort of drug treatment, or by a learned stereotyped response on behalf of the professional?"[49] This rhetorical question suggests that no surface treatment of the issues is appropriate in the care of the dying. This work demands a courageous plunging into the bare facts of human life in its closing stages. Because of the intensity of such interactions, the concept of the team approach in this sort of health care is very important.

Within such a team, difficulties can be shared and somewhat diffused through the open exchanges between team members. The autonomy and self-determination so important to each patient also applies to the practitioners, and the discernment of what can or cannot be done, and more precisely what should or should not be done, is well accomplished within the bounds of a well-functioning hospice team. They become accountable to one another in their professional capacities. Respect is critical to the process, especially the respect of one competent professional for another.

Without the strong support of the team system, each individual practitioner is left to his or her own strengths in determining the best method of treatment. A situation like this can lead to quick burnout for the professional and must be avoided as much as possible in palliative care casework. In any case, before entering into any patient-caregiver relationship, the boundaries of autonomy and self-determination must be clearly defined, and must be continually re-evaluated during the course of care. It is only when each partner in the relationship senses that the other holds him or her in a respected position that the fullest confidence is obtained in the decisions to be made.

Truth-telling is another important element in a palliative care relationship. From the very first diagnosis and prognosis, the approach of the health care practitioner to the patient either makes or breaks the subsequent encounters between them. In some cultures and societies, there are definite hierarchies of relationship, often with the physician at the pinnacle of the information pyramid. In such cultures, a breakdown in trust occurs when anyone other than the physician breaks the news to the patients and families. In other cultures, the oldest male in the family is the information-bearer. To destroy these boundaries severely limits the trust level obtainable in further encounters.

Randall and Downie have indicated two positions in regard to what sort of "truth" is to be told to terminally ill patients. One position is that patients should be told "all that they are able to comprehend." The second is that patients should be told only "the amount of information which patients indicate that they want."[50] In either one of these approaches, there are rather negative effects, due to the fact that the emotional component of each situation varies tremendously. What would work in one situation might fail in another.

Regardless of one's ability to comprehend a certain level of knowledge, the ability of any given patient or group of family members to appropriate the entirety of the situation can only be determined by a careful, unhurried assessment of the whole picture on the part of the professional. It falls to the professional, then, to choose appropriately the extent of the delivery of information. In the face of family pressure, it may not always be easy. In fact, some families in hospice programs insist that patients not be told about their terminal status.

Caregivers faced with such demands on the part of families best serve the needs of their patients by honestly telling family members that they will not lie to a patient if he or she should ask them "Am I dying?" In fact, it has been noted by many professionals that patients usually know the extent of their illness. What happens is that a cat-and-mouse game develops over bits of information. The patient does not wish to offend the family, the family does not wish to upset the patient, and the entire picture is one of dancing around the central issues. Such a picture does not allow for the presentation of the truth as such. It in some ways prohibits a smooth passage through the end-of-life stages of the disease process.

The manner of presentation of the facts is also a very important one in end-of-life issues. Sensitivity and compassion must be present. Professionally, one's responsibility is great. The information known to the health care professional must be presented to the patient and family in a manner that takes into account all aspects of the family situation. In today's hospital culture, the speed of events often precludes a full entering-into the family situation. It seems it is a rare physician who is able to carve a time niche into a very over-scheduled day in order to communicate peacefully with his or her patients. But this time set aside for open, truthful conversation between physician and patient is constitutive of the formation of a trustful working relationship throughout the course of treatment. It requires on the part of palliative care and hospice physicians a willingness to answer difficult questions in a forthright, sensitive manner.

This demeanor is difficult to maintain when the emotional level of the discussion is such as that involved in acceptance of a terminal diagnosis. Many physicians are not capable of such interactions and fail badly in their attempts to communicate on this level. Again, the pressure of surrounding family members can be overwhelming. Each hospice practitioner must foster within himself or herself the strength and insight necessary not only to come to a wise and prudent decision about truth-telling, but also to face directly any difficult and highly emotional personal interaction. The development of highly sophisticated communication techniques is vital.

Randall and Downie include three "standards of disclosure" in their treatment of the concept of truth-telling. The first is that of "professional practice." They name it as the only legal standard in the United Kingdom.[51] It takes into account the professional responsibility of each practitioner, but in the minds of the authors does not go deep enough into the specifics of particular patients. They also express the opinion that it does not cover the moral aspects of each situation adequately.

The authors move from this standard to that of the "reasonable person." In a hypothetical situation, the amount of information garnered would correspond to that which most people would "consider relevant and essential" in making decisions about treatments and procedures. Again, specifics are lacking. There are varying "lists" of information about any one disease, and particular situations call for particular applications of available information.

Finally, the authors mention the "subjective standard," which is the amount and type of information a specific patient requests. While this is directly applicable to a particular patient, the authors feel that it does not take into account a particular practitioner's responsibility to deliver certain types of information. All in all, the three standards are not enough to form a comprehensive picture in a particular case for the delivery of information and "truth." So once again it falls upon the hospice (or palliative care) worker to develop an astute moral sensitivity which can be applied in the discernment process so necessary in hospice work. Taking each case as the unique entity it is, each hospice caregiver summons all the insight, wisdom, technical knowledge, and interactive ability he or she possesses to approach the truth-telling so integral to hospice care.

Two other principles important in hospice care are beneficence and non-maleficence. The overall good of the patient and the family provides the motivation to hospice workers. A peaceful, dignified dying process is the ideal goal. What occurs in the interim depends greatly on the ability of the patient and various hospice team members to move through the "journey" with insight and sensitivity.

Each stage of the cycle of life has its particular focus. Kübler-Ross first delineated the five elements of the dying process in her book *On Death and Dying*. She listed them systematically as 1) denial and isolation, 2) anger, 3) bargaining, 4) depression, and 5) acceptance.[52] Each of these stages presents itself in a totally unique manner in each patient and family. It is the responsibility of every staff member to discern where along the emotional continuum they see the patient and family members. A sensitive approach to the overall well-being of the family calls for accurate reading—free of personal biases as much as is humanly possible—of the emotional and psychological states of all concerned. The attitude of beneficence calls for an honest appraisal of each staff person's ability to handle and face what he or she sees in any given patient or family member. True team cooperation will always entail open "ability exchanges" between staff members. That is, territoriality and possessiveness must be avoided. Proper hospice care fosters the strengths of the practitioners toward the overall good of the patient and family members.

The practice of the principle of non-maleficence is vital in hospice care, especially in light of the modern medical culture. This practice calls for a deep awareness on the part of each health care worker of what is right and wrong, good and bad, in today's health care world. The vast array of available technologies and treatments is highly confusing to families. Again, an honest look at the situation of each particular family will assist professionals in their discernment of the best approach to treatment in end-of-life cases.

First, the physical status of each patient needs to be determined. What might work for one patient (for example, the use of intravenous fluids) would be a totally inappropriate choice for another patient (due to the physical side-effects of additional fluids). What for some would be both physical and psychological comfort would for others be totally detrimental, adding negative side effects to the patient's overall condition. The focus on physician-assisted suicide and euthanasia confuses families, who are torn between watching their family member suffer physical and emotional distress, and wanting to alleviate their own distress at the loss they will be incurring.

Non-maleficence in any of these cases indicates that each professional is seriously responsible for a proper level of assessment of the situation. Disease process, prognosis, physical manifestations of disease and distress, and the emotional-psychological status of both patient and family are all elements that enter into the picture for analysis. A sensitive and caring practitioner looks not only within himself or herself for the proper approach, but also feels secure enough to consult with other team members in the effort to secure the most positive and least harmful approach to care.

In this period of growth in the field of biomedical ethics, especially with the expansion into new applications which build upon the initial emphasis on principlism, speaking of the basic principles of hospice care lays the groundwork for an overview of the basic Hospice Code of Ethics. This code was set forth by the National Hospice Organization in 1995 in a special publication and will be examined here in its entirety.

THE HOSPICE CODE OF ETHICS[53]

Because hospice involves several levels of interdisciplinary service, it was important to delineate the primary ethical focus of the organization. Fully aware that hospice enters people's lives at a very difficult point in the family life cycle, in 1995, the National Organization set out five primary principles for the delivery of hospice care. These are: autonomy, beneficence, conscientious objection, nonmaleficence, and justice. Through this code, the Organization encourages its members to subscribe to four primary precepts:

- to meet the hospice care needs of clients and their families;
- to act in good faith; to be honest, truthful, and fair to all concerned;
- to instruct both local and national communities in the tenets of hospice philosophy; and
- to maintain the highest level of skill and expertise of the staff and volunteers in the delivery of care.[54]

Within this general framework, the Organization encourages each hospice program to form its own particular process and format which will be applicable in the situations where conflicts and disagreements arise, because of conflicting ethical principles.

We will now examine the specific recommendations within each precept more closely.

The first precept, "To meet the hospice care needs of clients and their families," includes eight specific recommendations for hospice practitioners:

- to remain sensitive to and be appreciative of the ethnic, cultural, religious, and lifestyle diversity of clients and their families;
- to ascertain and honor the wishes, concerns, priorities, and values of the clients and their families consistent with the law and the organization's values as stated in its policies;

- to support, affirm, and empower the families as caregivers;
- to acknowledge and respond with sensitivity to the interruption of privacy that is necessitated by hospice care at home; to enter no further into family life and affairs than is required to meet goals of the hospice care plan;
- to respect and protect the confidentiality of information concerning hospice clients and families;
- to provide quality hospice services in a timely manner to all who qualify, regardless of race, religion, sexual orientation, ethnic background, or ability to pay;
- to recognize the vulnerability of those who receive hospice care, and thus refrain from accepting personal gifts of significant value; and
- to recognize the vulnerability and privacy needs of the hospice client and family, thus displaying extraordinary sensitivity in offering opportunities to promote hospice care.[55]

This first precept, with its eight explicit points, calls for the best assessment skills of every hospice professional involved in the care of a particular patient. Addressing the first point—remaining sensitive to and appreciative of the ethnic, cultural, religious, and lifestyle diversity of clients and their families—each caretaker finds that he or she must dig deep into personal inner resources. Besides one's own personal resources, there are many sources of information available to practicing health care providers which increase the knowledge base necessary for dealing with culturally unfamiliar situations, religious differences, and choices of lifestyle.

The level of resistance we encounter in ourselves may be surprising when people or situations present us with a reality drastically different from our own. Professionals engaged in the care of the terminally ill must be called upon to address this resistance within themselves with extreme honesty and openness. Whatever prevents them from engaging themselves professionally with these patients and families must be eliminated from the total picture of the health care encounter. A tremendous impairment in one's ability to interact positively with another human person ensues when obvious biases and prejudices prevail. It is only in the serious appraisal of the humanness of another individual, one in very difficult circumstances, that professionals are able to assess the real needs of each patient and family.

Along with the openness required of professionals in the face of different cultural, religious, or lifestyle choices comes the desire to ascertain each patient's true wishes, concerns, values, and priorities. This is the second point mentioned in the analysis of the first precept of hospice care. Dialogue is vital here. Listening skills need to be developed which will provide the opportunity for patients and family members to express what lies deepest within their own feelings about life—and about the end of life. Time, set within the often hectic hospital situation, must be set aside for such dialogue. Without such dialogue, in the face of terminal disease, patients are unable to form coherent statements of what they desire—their goals, ideals, and personal needs—as they confront their own end time.

The third point under the first precept of hospice care is that of support, affirmation, and empowerment of the families as caregivers in the hospice situation. Too often in the medical culture, it has been noted that the physician "holds all the cards." This is entirely inappropriate in a hospice setting. Overemphasis on intellectualism or technical expertise is of no practical use, ultimately, when all medical interventions have been tried and all have reached their limits. At the point of the choice for hospice care, hospice caregivers, from the admissions coordinator through the ranks of the nurses, social workers, and chaplains, focus primarily on the ability of each family member—along with and in conjunction with the patient—to handle the issues inherent in any terminal illness.

Admissions coordinators assess the overall situation prior to a patient ever being received into a hospice program. Upon admission, the nurses assess the physical needs of the patient, and pass along to the social workers and chaplains information collected about the family situation, interactions, the patient's frame of mind, conflicts, areas of support, and possible future needs. In turn, these social workers and chaplains call upon the strengths of their fields to complete a total plan of care.

Within this plan of care are the "players," those professionals and family members capable of being the most helpful in the situation. Involving family and community resources, the ideal goal of hospice care is to facilitate the optimal care of the patient. Empowerment in this situation means that at each encounter the talents and strengths of the family and community members—as well as those of the patient—are fostered, nurtured, and called upon for the transition through the dying process.

Any medical situation puts a patient in the awkward position of submitting to intimate encounters, bodily examination, technical procedures, and conversations with strangers which would not normally be met in a "regular" encounter. The fourth point in the first precept of hospice care calls on professionals to "acknowledge and respond with sensitivity to the interruption of privacy that is necessitated by hospice care at home." In this area there is a great need for each professional to respect the family and personal boundaries of each unique situation.

The overall goal of hospice care is to facilitate the smooth transition of a person from a vital, active participation in his or her life situation to one in which he or she slowly loses control of normally routine activities, submits to the help of others who are increasingly needed for assistance, and reaches the end of life in the most peaceful, dignified manner possible. Here there is no room for probing further than is necessary into people's personal lives. There is no need to delve into the more personal, private areas which may or may not be revealed willingly to the professionals. Professionals must seriously question themselves if they find themselves entering too deeply into others' lives.

Here, it is vital that one's own personal needs for engagement take a back seat to the needs of the family. Although it is flattering to have families and patients confiding in them, the hospice professionals must use extreme discretion in these encounters. Becoming enmeshed with families may be a serious detriment to the proper delivery of hospice care. Honest sharing among hospice professionals can help to offset such enmeshment, and allow both professionals and clients to keep sacred the boundaries of the human encounters so necessary in hospice care.

Confidentiality is the focus of the fifth component of the first hospice precept. This area is one of the most important in any medical encounter, not just in the hospice setting. It ties into the element of trust that is one of the most important in any interaction between health care professionals and their patients. There are several frameworks of reference which may guide professionals in their understanding of the elements of confidentiality.

"Duty-based frameworks, which underlie most codes of nursing and medical ethics, will include a duty to protect information acquired within the clinical encounter. Right-based theories will emphasize the client's right to privacy and the confidential nature of communications and records pertaining to his or her care. Goal-based theories like utilitarianism will base this presumption on the negative long-term effects of arbitrary disclosure of information given in confidence."[56] These frameworks provide a basis for discernment as to which concerns, if any, should be shared with others, be they family members, physicians, or other members of a medical team.

What is shared between hospice professionals and their patients, along with their families, is understood to remain totally confidential, with the exception of information which could protect a person from a potentially fatal decision, made out of desperation or depression. In the case of families dealing with terminal illness, there are many aspects of one's entire life which are shared with nurses, social workers, chaplains, physicians, and volunteers. Our human nature sometimes urges us to share information with others which will make us look good. Personal situations, positions in life, perceived prestige, or other elements of a client's life can sometimes lead professional caregivers to divulge to others the situation of the family or person with whom he or she is involved. In any medical situation, not only hospice care, this sort of behavior is not only unprofessional, it is unethical. It demands from each professional an honest analysis of his or her own motivations and values. This is part of any professional role, especially in the case of hospice care, because of the ultimate nature of the concerns voiced in such situations. The sorts of things that are shared with hospice professionals are deeply serious in nature, due to the nature of the situation. Therefore it is of the utmost importance that all hospice workers consider the confidences and concerns shared as if they were their own.

At times it is extremely difficult to maintain confidentiality, especially when friends of the patient who may be involved in the person's care ask professionals for information. There must be a conscious effort, presented gently yet firmly to these friends, to divulge only the information necessary for the best of care to be provided, and only after presenting the situation to the patient and obtaining permission to involve the persons in the first place. Superfluous details need not be shared. It falls to the hospice staff to find a balance of information to provide to others about the status of their patient.

With an eye to the good of the patient, as well as to the highest level of care to be given, each staff person must weigh the level and depth of information which is to be provided to those surrounding each patient. Trust flourishes or dies with the perception of the patient and family that their unique situation is being treated with the same care that the professionals would want for their own lives.

In addressing the issue of confidentiality, one may approach it with an eye to who is entitled to any information. Several groups may be included: 1) those who must know; 2) those who should know; 3) those who could know; and 4) those who shouldn't know.[57] Because hospice functions in a team framework, it is understood at the outset that the members of the team—the medical director, nurses, social workers, chaplains, and ancillary workers—are all privy to personal information. But it is also understood that these team members will keep confidential information private, sharing it only among themselves as is appropriate to advance a person's care. Each patient is apprised of this at the onset of care. Professional behavior then dictates that all staff persons act in a highly professional manner in maintaining the confidentiality of this information.

Providing quality hospice services in a timely manner to all who qualify is the subject of the sixth element in the first precept of hospice care. Discrimination on the basis of race, religion, sexual orientation, ethnic background, or ability to pay is absolutely forbidden in a hospice program. This seems obvious on the surface, and indeed it is the subject of laws, but in one's professional life there are areas in which it is essential that each hospice professional have a strong, honest appraisal of his or her own attitudes toward patients and families who practice beliefs and lifestyles unlike their own.

One incident comes to mind: A Caucasian nurse, in explaining the care she was attempting to provide to an African-American patient, said "I assumed there might be a knowledge deficit, so I tried to explain in the simplest possible terms." That attempt resulted in the patient's family members feeling insulted, and telling other staff members that they wanted no further dealings with that particular nurse. Their anger was almost palpable. It would have been helpful for the nurse to have been aware of her own not-so-subtle prejudice.

On the subject of ability to pay, fortunately, most hospice programs have some sort of funding which allows patients who are unable to pay to receive outside funding for their end-of-life care. Not only government sources, but private funding comes in handy in situations such as this. Again, however, it is incumbent upon the hospice professionals to purge themselves of any attitude of looking down on individuals who have limited financial resources.

Likewise, the religious preferences of patients and families can cause misunderstandings and periods of awkwardness between staff, patient, and family members. There are many resources available to hospice workers which explain religious outlooks, attitudes, practices, and beliefs. There is no excuse for hospice staff to be ignorant of the patterns of religious and cultural treatment of the end of life.

The climate in today's culture seems to be tending toward greater tolerance of alternative lifestyles. For example, in each person there are basic, gut-level feelings of either acceptance or rejection of the lives of homosexual individuals. Awareness of one's own deep-set prejudices is vital. One may or may not approve of another's lifestyle, but hospice patients are to be seen as unique persons, human beings suffering terminal illnesses. Every effort must be made to rise above one's own sometimes close-to-the-surface prejudices and provide sensitive, compassionate care to each patient who comes to a hospice program for care. Too often these people have already undergone years of obvious discrimination regarding their sexuality, so it seems at the end of their lives they should be granted respect for their humanity, and for the concerns every human being faces at the end of his or her life.

The same openness, finally, applies to those of varying ethnic backgrounds. Misunderstandings, long-held biases, fears, and prejudices rear their heads in the intense situation that is hospice care. Within each hospice caregiver there are resources which will enable a smooth pattern of interaction between patient, family members, and hospice professionals. Calling forth these resources in one's own unique way will facilitate the optimal provision of care for the patient and families.

The seventh point under the first precept calls each professional to "recognize the vulnerability of those who receive hospice care" and to avoid accepting any personal gifts of significant value. Needless to say, the circumstances at the end of life make patients and families dependent upon the care of professional caregivers, and thus could create a situation where they feel they must express their gratitude with more than a token. Accepting such gifts is inappropriate, and they must be sensitively and gently returned.

The final point in the first precept of hospice care is that of the recognition of the vulnerability and privacy needs of each hospice patient and family. Each hospice professional is called to "display extraordinary sensitivity" in offering opportunities to provide hospice care.[58] Here it is again an indispensable element in one's professional demeanor to be an approachable, sensitive person who is fully aware that each patient in a terminally ill state has been stripped of all former sources of identity gleaned from a particular profession, state in life, or rank in society.

There is before each hospice staff person someone who—because of the invasive nature of much of medical care, allowing unknown people into his or her most private realm, forced to share the most intimate details of life—is totally vulnerable to the professional caregiver. In a sense, hospice workers "ask permission" time and again to enter into the care of their patients. Utter respect for each person as a singular human being, experiencing the end-of-life process in his or her own unique way, is the hallmark of dedicated hospice professionals. The Code of Ethics offers this point to emphasize the vital importance of such respect in any approach to a terminally ill patient. Without it, the fullness of the hospice concept cannot be realized.

The first precept of hospice care, with its eight specific points, encompasses every aspect of open, ethical relationships between hospice professionals and the people for whom they care. It sets up demonstrable expectations, on which patients and families may depend, as well as the responsibilities, professional and personal, of every staff member who works with them.

The second precept outlined by the National Hospice Organization in its Code of Ethics is this: "To act honestly, truthfully and fairly to all concerned."[59] Under this second precept there are seven specific points:

- to fully disclose to patients and families information regarding cost, services, and complaint policies, as well as any policies regarding discontinuation of hospice service;
- to honestly and conscientiously cooperate as an agency in providing information about referrals, and to work with other agencies to ensure comprehensive services to clients and families;
- to be truthful and accurate in public advertising and information dissemination;
- to make and accept referrals solely in the best interest of the clients;
- to refrain from giving or accepting gifts of value or monetary compensation for the purpose of obtaining or making referrals;
- to make every effort to honor the intent of benefactors and donors supporting the hospice program; and
- to ensure that hospice services are not diluted for financial reasons.[60]

The first point in this second precept concerns full disclosure of all information regarding costs, services, and complaint policies. It also speaks of the policies regarding the discontinuation of hospice services. First and foremost, each patient and their family members must be made aware of the entire spectrum of services available to them as they enter into the hospice program.

In the changing world of health maintenance organizations and insurance company mergers, it is difficult at times for even the hospice admissions coordinators to be fully up to date on the latest coverage available for end-of-life care. Too often, coverage stops when "skilled nursing" is no longer needed. It is at this time that families sometimes panic, because it is all too easy for someone's life savings to be consumed with hiring caretakers and companions, should immediate family members not be able to take full charge of a patient's care.

Inability to pay is never a proper reason for discontinuation of hospice services. Foundations and funds are available for such instances. Likewise, personality or family "difficulties" are not sufficient reasons to discontinue care. Every effort must be made to work out such difficulties and to continue to provide optimal care for patients, in open and honest interaction with all family members concerned. It should also be clear to all who enter into a hospice program that they have an open door to managers and coordinators should they feel they are not receiving the care to which they are entitled.

Point two under the second precept concerns referrals to other agencies. It follows that in today's medical culture there may be choices made which transfer the care of patients from one agency to another, beginning with the hospital referrals. Often, regular home care agencies claim that they are able to provide "hospice" care as well as their regular home care visits. With properly trained staff, this is indeed possible, but all too often these claims are made only to keep the patients under their care so as not to lose the funding they receive. In fact, this is depriving patients of a true opportunity to participate in hospice care. Regular home care nurses are not necessarily trained in the specifics of hospice. Thus they are unable to enter into the overall concept, unless they themselves have an acute sensitivity to the issues surrounding death and dying.

Referrals to other hospices as well must be conscientiously made. Transfer of care must be done with the good of the patient in mind. If it seems another agency would be better able to provide that care, ethics require that the transfer be made. Competition is at the forefront of medical culture today, with large hospital mergers and buyouts, as well as many smaller, independent agencies vying for patients. Unfortunately, these agencies are sometimes less than forthcoming in what they actually do provide to patients. Standard practices must be carefully examined and unethical practices weeded out so that patients will be able to receive the care they deserve.

The third point under the second precept concerns being truthful and accurate in public advertising and information dissemination. Again, sometimes it is what is *not* said that is the most deceiving. One agency recently advertised itself as "the first inpatient situation in the Pittsburgh area where you can live out your last months in a peaceful surrounding, with specially trained hospice staff." Unfortunately, some vital information was left out. Payment methods are strictly governed, especially with the Medicare hospice benefit, and standards of care are carefully delineated. Patients and families entering into what was advertised could very easily be confused, and end up privately paying very large costs because of denials of payment from Medicare. In the medical culture that exists today, it is a struggle to maintain agencies, and people are easily overwhelmed by the raft of information spilling forth, leading to less informed choices regarding their health care.

Making and accepting referrals solely in the best interests of the client is a self-explanatory point under the second precept. Admissions coordinators must weigh the facts in each situation, and even if it should mean losing a particular referral, honest appraisal of the patient's true needs is essential in an ethical acceptance of a case. Referring someone on to another, more appropriate agency follows on this honest assessment.

Gifts and monetary compensation for the purpose of obtaining or making referrals is strictly prohibited in the Hospice Code of Ethics. It amounts to bribery, and must not be tolerated in any program of hospice care.

There are many foundations and wealthy benefactors supporting long-standing hospice programs. Keeping the practices of any one program in line with the original ideals and goals of their benefactors is of vital concern to all managers in hospice agencies today. These goals and ideals are formally set out in the agency's mission statement. Providers of care, the hospice team, must always strive to keep their professional practice in line with these original goals. An honest appraisal between team members of the effects of their program is also an essential element. Professionals exert checks and balances on one another in their open, honest dialogue in team meetings and appraisals.

Finally, hospice services must not be "diluted" for financial reasons. All efforts must be made to provide care using every available resource. Care cannot be deficient because there is a perceived lack of funding. Providing optimal care entails using all staff resources available to encompass the totality of the hospice concept—the care of the physical, psychological, emotional, and spiritual welfare of each patient, and of his or her family members.

The third precept of the Hospice Code of Ethics, "To instruct both local and national communities in the tenets of the hospice philosophy," contains six separate elements. Because of the tenor of the medical culture today, it is paramount that the message of hospice be placed before the public in a timely and informative manner, touching on all the elements of the program of hospice care:

- to encourage dialogue about hospice in all appropriate public forums;
- to encourage inclusion of hospice care in all federal, state, and commercial health care plans;
- to provide the consumer with sufficient information about hospice, to enable true informed consent;
- to act as a liaison in consumer discussions concerning decisions regarding end-of-life care;
- to assume a leadership role in ensuring access to hospice care for all terminally ill patients; and
- to serve on committees or in groups concerned with policy-making decisions which will affect health care in this country.[61]

The first point in this precept encourages hospice programs to promote dialogue in all appropriate forums. Speaking out wherever possible, hospice directors and managers must take every opportunity to widen the vision of physicians and physicians' organizations to include participation in hospice care. Too often it begins with the ignorance of the physicians about what hospice care entails, reflecting the predominant "cure all" philosophy of the medical community. Terminal illness is too often seen as a *failure* of medical science, so the dialogue needed to widen this vision must be promoted.

Dr. Ira Byock, a physician who began a residential hospice program in Missoula, Montana, began speaking out in recent years about the necessity for federal, state, and commercial health plans to include hospice care. Previous efforts to include end-of-life concerns in health care plans have not always been successful. Having one of their own members speaking out openly around the country has allowed more focus to be placed on funding for hospice programs. Little by little, inroads are being made so that the financial burdens of health care at the end of life are lifted as much as possible.

Intense marketing must be done to awaken the public to the possibilities of hospice care for themselves and their loved ones. This is the subject of the third point in this precept. Too often, family members tell staff members, "I didn't even know this existed." (This comment was overheard in a particular hospice inpatient unit that had been in existence for almost twenty years!)

Our culture avoids discussions of death. Note the hushed tones funeral directors sometimes employ when speaking with their customers. It is important to provide people with enough information so that they can make informed decisions. They must be given accurate facts about what their options and choices are.

The fourth point urges hospice providers to act as liaisons in discussions about hospice care. Again, those making choices for themselves and family members must be given accurate facts about what their options and choices are. Communication skills are vital in such discussions, with confident presentation of the facts of hospice care, as well as sensitive attention to the heavy emotional burdens and vulnerabilities of the decision-makers.

Hospice care providers are encouraged to take a leadership role. Without competent, trained professionals who speak out regularly, the concept of hospice care will continue to remain under an informational shadow. At the same time, the committees and groups responsible for making policy decisions need to be open to the participation of hospice professionals. Here these professionals will find access to those in power who can speak about these end-of-life issues in government arenas where funding originates. Realistic, well-prepared individuals must participate in these committees for any progress to be made in the continued growth of hospice care.

The fourth precept in the Hospice Code of Ethics—"To maintain the highest level of skill and expertise of the staff and volunteers in the delivery of care"—includes five points on the professional development of hospice staff (a comprehensive team comprising physicians, nurses, social workers, home health aides, and volunteers):

- to recruit, select, orient, educate, and evaluate each staff person and volunteer to ensure competency based on identified job requirements;
- to remain sensitive to and be appreciative of the ethnic, cultural, religious, and lifestyle diversity of staff and volunteers;
- to support, affirm, and empower the staff and volunteers in the delivery of care;

- to recognize the unique stressors inherent in hospice work and provide access to ongoing support for all staff and volunteers; and
- to ensure that contracted providers are properly trained and quali-
fied, and that they provide care consistent with the values and philosophy of hospice.[62]

Point one in this precept focuses on the recruitment, selection, orientation, education, and evaluation of each staff person and volunteer. Continuing education programs are available throughout most health systems;
for agencies not specifically affiliated with a larger system, programs
around the country and in local communities abound which focus on all
elements of hospice care. Today there is increasing involvement of spiritual
leaders in promotion of hospice care, especially in light of the focus on
physician-assisted suicide and euthanasia in today's larger culture.

Within each educational program, there need to be checkpoints for
all staff and volunteers where they can measure their abilities against the
standards of hospice care. For nurses, for example, there is a separate pam-
phlet on the Standards of Hospice Nursing Practice. There is no doubt about
the level of care required of these nurses. It goes far beyond mere technical
knowledge and demands—from the professionals themselves—dedication
to this field, encompassing the total picture of the care of patients who are
terminally ill.

Remaining sensitive to and appreciative of the ethnic, cultural, religious, and lifestyle diversity of staff and volunteers is the subject of the
second point in this precept. This follows upon the very same awareness
and sensitivity needed in any patient and family encounter. Wise placement
of those staff and volunteers—who are of varying cultures, religions, and
lifestyles—with patients whom they will be especially able to help is a
great advantage in a hospice program. Likewise, making use of the resources these staff and volunteers provide to the entire program is a step
management should take. Fostering and nurturing the skills and talents of
those not specifically in management situations can only add to the fullness
and richness of the entire program.

Without support, affirmation, and empowerment of their skills and
talents, staff members and volunteers lose energy and sometimes withdraw,
seeking to use their skills elsewhere. It is not that they come into the work
first and foremost to enhance themselves (although many say they obtain
rewards they never imagined from the work), but it is imperative that man-

agers and supervisors be intensely aware of the strengths of each of their staff members. Unfortunately, with the growth of the large agencies through mergers and acquisitions, the size of the organization can sometimes inhibit this awareness.

If managers find that they are not able to keep in touch with their personnel, it would be advantageous for them to employ methods which will allow for the employees' strengths to be noticed and fostered. Basically, there is no place for managers who are threatened by the strengths of their employees, fearing they may be overshadowed. It can only benefit the entire program to capitalize on the strengths they see before them. If this is not done, there is a strong drain of talent and energy, and the full potential of hospice care is never fulfilled.

Support staff needs to be utilized to the full in any hospice program of care. The work itself is personally and professionally demanding. The fourth point in this precept focuses on the "unique stressors" involved in hospice work. Group and individual counseling and feedback are essential to the successful continuation of professional involvement in hospice. Within each program, then, resources need to be made available to staff and volunteers to "debrief" after particularly stressful and draining encounters. Not only does this foster stronger communication among staff, managers, and volunteers, but it also provides professionals with a source of continued insight and strength as they carry out their hospice work, working to reduce the intense burnout prevalent in this field.

The final point includes the proper qualifications and training for contracted providers of hospice care. As always, the goals, values, and philosophy of hospice must be communicated to the agencies with whom the parent hospice agency contracts. Reliability is essential. It reflects badly on the entire hospice program if agencies employ unreliable personnel. Many an on-call nurse has received telephone calls from frustrated, angry families when personnel from an outside agency have failed to show up at a home. For the good of all concerned, the dependability of such agency workers must be impeccable, and the overall hospice philosophy clearly understood by all who engage in contracted care.

The entire Hospice Code of Ethics covers each professional caregiver as well as the many volunteers who participate in a hospice program. Especially in the care of the terminally ill, such an ethical base is indispensable. It would appear that people who go into hospice work in the first place have a level of sensitivity and dedication that is at times more encompassing. That is not to say that others' dedication is necessarily less, but hospice care—due to the sensitivity and primacy of the issues faced during the progression of a terminal illness—seems to call forth from the practitioners in the field a strongly spiritual outlook which can give their patients and the patients' families a "safe" place to process their concerns. It will also carry the professionals themselves through many hours of darkness and uncertainty when all aggressive medical treatment has been exhausted and patients are left to the most basic of personal and familial resources.

This spiritual outlook is not necessarily *confessional*, meaning that no specific faith persuasion or denomination is emphasized. But the overall personal spiritual strength of such professionals is an irreplaceable element, and one that must be nurtured, fostered, and respected for the professional to thrive in the work itself.

SUMMARY

An overview of the development of the hospice concept has been necessary as the foundation for exploring *Dark Night of the Soul* as it relates to each hospice practitioner. Likewise, a glimpse of the Hospice Code of Ethics provides grounding in the sort of character expected in any hospice professional. More extensive, detailed histories of the growth and transformation of the hospice concept are available today, so this overview has been done with broad strokes in an attempt to present the most essential elements of this type of medical care, which is involved in the physical, psychological, spiritual, and emotional aspects of persons in the last stages of their lives.

Throughout history, it is apparent that those who cared most often for such persons were especially dedicated groups and individuals, often in religious orders, but more recently in the fields of palliative and hospice care. Today's practitioners are physicians, nurses, aides, social workers, chaplains, and volunteers who have been trained specifically to address the unique problems of end-of-life care. A historical perspective is essential here because of the changing attitudes toward death throughout the centuries, and the shifts and changes in treatment of terminally ill patients spurred by the efforts of Dr. Cicely Saunders in England, Dr. Elisabeth Kübler-Ross in the United States, and Dr. Balfour Mount in Canada.

What is now clear is that much more emphasis needs to be placed on specific applications of the care promoted by these physicians. Dr. Ira Byock is now attempting to speak to the medical practitioners, enlightening them and broadening their approaches to pain and anxiety control at the end of life. As well, the special focus in unique palliative care hospital units is being broadened. The health care environment is often very fast-paced, with little time for interaction on the levels necessary to conduct adequate hospice programs, at least in a hospital situation. But with the new focus, and deliberate efforts to work within the present system, it seems likely that the principles of hospice may yet be able to be borne out successfully. It seems that the lives of dedicated, sensitive, and highly skilled physicians, working in conjunction with prepared staff persons, nurses, social workers, and ancillary staff, will have a continuing transformative effect within the medical world.

The Hospice Code of Ethics, with its focus on four primary precepts and the specific delineations within each of those precepts, highlights the nature of the practice of hospice care. It also points out in very specific ways what is expected not only of hospice staff, but of patients and families within this situation. A certain quality of character is requisite for successful hospice practice. There are great demands on the personalities and the professional abilities of all hospice practitioners. This calls for a certain sort of strength that arises from within the depths of these professionals, and must continually be assessed, nurtured, bolstered by both outer and inner resources, and fostered by an atmosphere of honest, open communication.

This sort of work is not for mere technical wizards. Escaping into the world of flashing lights and cardiac monitors will not be something that is available to these physicians, nurses, aides, and ancillary workers. For this reason, then, what the Hospice Code of Ethics calls for is an attitude toward one's professional practice that is grounded in a high level of respect for persons at all levels of their personhood. Honesty, respect for cultural, religious, lifestyle, and ethnic differences, solid spirituality (not necessarily of the confessional variety), and the ability to assess and communicate the essential elements of each unique patient within his or her unique family and community situation—all these attributes come into play in a hospice program of care.

Because the focus of this exploration is essentially on *Dark Night of the Soul* as a metaphor for understanding the ethics and spirituality of hospice care, the elements just set forth in this chapter form a foundation for the personal and professional development of each practitioner who chooses hospice as a profession. I will note in subsequent chapters similarities of character between such practitioners and those fostering the development of a fruitful spiritual life. The ability to meet other human persons on the in-depth practice of hospice and palliative care is the same ability needed in a personal dialogue and relationship with one's god.

From its deepest roots in early history, and through the centuries past, the approach to death and dying has challenged each professional to untold levels, both personally and professionally. Today's medical culture is awash with the highest levels of technological achievement. But within this culture there exists a state of life, the end-of-life time, which goes far beyond what any technological achievement can "solve." It is this state of life which must be revisited directly, through the development of the character of the practitioners themselves. Their searching, questioning, and courage in addressing the "unanswerable questions" will help those terminally ill patients who are in their care to travel their own journeys with more peace and resolution.

I will now take a closer look at the development of several principles of ethical consideration.

CHAPTER TWO

ETHICAL CONSIDERATIONS AND THEIR DEVELOPMENT

DIRECTION AND FOCUS OF THESE CONSIDERATIONS

This chapter will focus on the growth of biomedical ethics as a subcategory within the larger field of general ethics. Included in this consideration will be several specifically selected sources from the Ancient and Medieval worlds. These are the sources from which modern day ethics grew, and consideration will be given to elements particularly applicable to biomedical ethics.

I will begin with the works of Aristotle, noting the connection between his work and the work of St. Thomas Aquinas. Proceeding, I will mention some of the historical movements and attitudes greatly influencing the content of ethical consideration, and will attempt to envision how the background of the present-day field calls forth from practitioners a serious look at themselves as committed professionals in what has been called a *covenant relationship* with their patients.

A complete description of the ethics of Aristotle or of Thomas Aquinas cannot be attempted here, but I will refer in these beginning sections not only to translations of the works most pertinent to this study, but also to several authors whose insights may help to focus on the ethical elements most applicable to our modern study of bioethics. Further, I will reference a selected number of the more recent scholars in the field of biomedical ethics. Their work in the past forty years has provided a strong foundation for the continual growth and exploration seen in the field today.

As David F. Kelly states in his work which focuses on the development of Roman Catholic medical ethics in North America, "The moralists who wrote the texts . . . came to be interested primarily in applying moral principles to the actual daily professional activity of medical personnel—of doctors, of general practitioners, surgeons, medical specialists, of medical nurses. . . . Most of the North American authors were interested primarily in the practical application of precise moral principles to the ethical issues arising from professional medical practice. This had become their primary principle of selection."[1] This statement applies not only to the Roman Catholic scholars who participated in the initial focus on the biomedical ethical field, but also to others not specifically confessional in their beliefs. The field received impetus from their studies of the earliest ethicists, taking its basic concepts from them and synthesizing elements with the specific goal of applying it to modern medical situations.

CONVERGENCE OF THOUGHT AND DEVELOPMENT OF FOCUS

Through the following overview, my plan is to bring into focus the fact that from ancient reflections on what makes a "person of character" come the theories that make up our modern study of ethics, specifically biomedical ethics. Developed over centuries of practice and continued study, and within the ever-growing medical world, this reflection has provided the statement of a synthesis of thought which provides health care practitioners with a model of character to be adopted in their own practice. Consideration of the earliest studies of ethics inspires further study and enables both theoreticians and practitioners to ground the development of their professional character in solid concepts, translated into action by thoughtful decision.

Principlism, so-called because it centered on four specifically chosen principles of ethical behavior, provided impetus to the initial mid-twentieth-century secular biomedical approach to ethical reflection. This will be further explored in this study. Virtue ethics and narrative ethics, which are more recent re-evaluations and applications of the initial emphasis on principles, provide even more breadth in the field.

The scope of this study prohibits an extended examination of any one of these approaches. Therefore, in this chapter I will give a general overview of the background of today's biomedical ethical study. Subsequently, I plan to consider the elements of spirituality in the work of St. John of the Cross's *Dark Night of the Soul* and show how the circumstances of one's personal and professional life, strongly intertwined with the practice of one's spirituality, will enhance and give a solid foundation to one's professional practice.

ARISTOTLE: *THE NICHOMACHEAN ETHICS*

Born in 384 BC, Aristotle was the son of a physician of the court of Philip of Macedon.[2] His early education therefore included being surrounded by an array of "philosophers, scientists, mathematicians, and politicians"[3] whose focus influenced Aristotle's approach to his own learning. Apparently, he was a brilliant student, engrossed in the search for all types of knowledge, but especially centering on the study of "intellectual virtues"—parts of the makeup of human beings enabling them to be fully human.[4]

His *Nichomachean Ethics* was his second work of this nature, following his *Eudemian Ethics*, an earlier and less mature reflection. The work itself was a compilation of his lecture notes which the author seemingly never worked into a separate text.[5] The system out of which Aristotle operated included emphases on theoretical, practical, and productive sciences. The theoretical sciences included theology, mathematics, and physics or natural science, whereas the practical sciences included the study of ethics.[6] Accordingly, ethics focused on action rather than theory, and it provided a model on which a person could act in order to be a good person.

Aristotle's approach was teleological, meaning that the focus was on the ultimate end of one's actions.[7] To Aristotle, the ultimate good was happiness. This belief characterizes him as a *eudaemonist*, one who holds that happiness is the supreme end of life.[8] He stated it in this way: "Every act and every inquiry, and similarly every action and choice, is thought to aim at some good; and for this reason the good has rightly been declared to be that at which all things aim."[9] For the purposes of this study, Aristotle's further comment provides insight into his view of the medical arts. "Now, as there are many actions, arts, and sciences, their ends also are many; the end of the medical art is health . . ."[10] (*Nichomachean Ethics* 1:1094.6).

Aristotle viewed the subordinate goods encountered along the way as stepping stones toward the ultimate good pursued. In reference to this, Copleston states, "The end of giving a certain medicine might be to produce sleep, but this immediate end is subordinate to the end of health. But if there is an end which we desire for its own sake and for the sake of which we desire all other subordinate ends or goods, then this ultimate good will be the best good, in fact *the* good."[11] As Copleston notes, Aristotle's inquiry sought to capsulize for his students the nature of that ultimate good.

Jonathan Barnes, in his introduction to *The Ethics of Aristotle*, states that Aristotle referred to his work as *ta ethika*, which transliterates to "The Ethics." It translates, however, to "Matters to do with Character."[12] More specifically, it concerned *ethike arete*, or excellence of character.[13] In this sense, Aristotle's focus was upon the sorts of choices made by human beings which made them excellent of character, not merely excellent at performing one or another specific task. The striving inherent in such considered choices drew each human closer to fulfilling his or her essential nature and coming closer to the realization of the ultimate good, which for Aristotle was happiness.[14] This realization was the ultimate fulfillment of what it meant to be a morally good human being—a pattern of considered choices toward a specific end.

Two levels of analysis are applicable to Aristotle's study. First there is the ethical level, that of "substantive moral judgments," which label certain human beings and human actions as either "good or bad, right or wrong, virtuous or vicious, obligatory or impermissible."[15] Following upon this is the level of meta-ethical analysis, which is the "articulation and elucidation of our thought about moral matters."[16] This level enables the scholar or practitioner to understand more about what leads one to choose one or another action in a specific situation. It also provides for judicious balancing of the principles intrinsic to any given consideration, with the exercise of *epikeia* or equity in the choice of which law or principle is most applicable to the situation.

Aristotle seemed to state that "morals cannot by any means be reduced to a set of universal principles; any principle that may be formulated is liable to exception, any universal moral judgment (strictly construed) is false. The most we can hope for is a group of roughly accurate generalizations—principles which will meet most ordinary situations but which are always liable to come unstuck."[17] Aristotle here left the way open for the use of what he saw as a "moral intuition," which provided solid grounds for knowing what was the right thing to do in a given situation.

Having spoken earlier of the excellence of character required by a morally acting human being, it is important to note that Aristotle focused upon two sorts of excellence—intellectual and moral (*Nichomachean Ethics* 1103a.15). He said, "Intellectual excellence in the main owes both its birth and its growth to teaching (for which it requires experience and time), while moral excellence comes about as a result of habit, whence also its name is one that is formed by a slight variation for the word for habit. From this it is also plain that none of the moral excellences arises in us by nature, for nothing that exists by nature can form a habit contrary to its nature."[18] This was not to say that the virtues were not potentially present in all humans, but that "The moral virtues . . . are engendered in us neither *by* nor *contrary to* nature; we are constituted by nature to receive them, but their full development in us is due to habit."[19] This view was later to be explored by Thomas Aquinas in his *Summa Theologica* in his analysis of virtues and habits and the characteristics of each. It also indicates that Aristotle realized that work was entailed in the development of such excellence, grounded in deliberate choice and pattern of action.

Likewise, Aristotle recognized the need for prudence, or *phronesis*, in all moral decisions. He also called this quality "practical wisdom." "Now it is thought to be a mark of a man of practical wisdom to be able to deliberate well about what is good and expedient for himself, not in some particular respect, e.g., about what sorts of things conduce to health or to strength, but about what sorts of things conduce to the good life in general" (*Nichomachean Ethics* 1140a.24).[20]

Not only this, but "prudence is necessary for the virtuous man, a) as being 'the excellence of an essential part of our nature,' and b) inasmuch as there can be no right choice without both prudence and virtue, seeing that the latter secures the choice of the right end, and the former the choice of the right means to its attainment" (*Nichomachean Ethics* 1145a.2–6).[21] Again, this was a foreshadowing of the work of Thomas Aquinas as he analyzed the virtues.

Aristotle followed in the footsteps of Socrates as he spoke of all virtue being a form of prudence, but he enlarged the thought in this manner: "No virtue can exist without prudence." (*Nichomachean Ethics* 1144b.26–28*).* Virtue is not only the right and reasonable attitude, but the attitude which leads to right and reasonable choice, and right and reasonable choices in these matters is what we mean by prudence."[22]

It is clear that Aristotle's work contained much of the thought that has subsequently formed and provided grounding for the application of the study of ethics in general to the specifically medical fields. His view of practical wisdom indicated a belief that within each human being there lies the capacity to "act with regard to the things that are good or bad for man."[23] (Aquinas was later to elaborate this point in *Summa Theologica* I–II, 94, where he spoke of the Natural Law.)

Aristotle recognized that goods differed according to the human beings who desired them. Thus he was aware that different pursuits would ensue according to the goals of the individuals engaged in them. He was aware that human beings were motivated by their passions, "appetite, fear, confidence, envy, joy, love, hatred, longing, emulation, pity" (*Nichomachean Ethics* 1105b.20), and that these provided certain "dispositions" out of which actions came (*Nichomachean Ethics* 1106a). Thus, it was through the development of the "excellence of character" that actions were properly directed toward the fulfillment of the ultimate good. In Aristotle's view, people of good character made good choices, and people of bad character followed their whim, seeking pleasure and avoiding pain" (*Nichomachean Ethics* 1113a.15–20).[24]

Having said this, then, Aristotle went on to explore what Aquinas and subsequent scholars eventually sought to elaborate, such qualities as "courage" (*Nichomachean Ethics* 1116a.16–1117b.20), "temperance" (*Nichomachean Ethics* 1117b.25–1119b.1), and "justice" (*Nichomachean Ethics* 1128b.1–1131b.25). It was this line of inquiry which enabled modern-day scholars in the field of biomedical ethics to attempt a synthesis of ethical thought specifically applicable to medical decisions. Although medical practice engaged these qualities from its earliest days, issues in the more recent centuries called for a workable process to be delineated more formally and specifically in the mid-twentieth century, with the advent of ever-increasing levels of technology and questions the earliest medical practitioners never envisioned. Aristotle's *Nichomachean Ethics* served as a starting point for analysis.

THOMAS AQUINAS: THE MEDIEVAL SYNTHESIS

Thomas Aquinas (1225–74) was a Dominican friar whose prolific work greatly influenced theological scholars in subsequent centuries. His position in history provided him with the setting in which he would reflect, write, and teach extensively. The *Summa Theologica* came about because Aquinas, who at the time was teaching the *Sentences* of Peter Lombard to his students, felt that he needed a book to explain theological concepts to beginners.[25] His mammoth text served as the students' introduction to many fundamental theological concepts. It began with the *Prima Pars*, which focused on the nature and existence of God. It proceeded to the two-part *Secunda Pars*, his consideration of "how men and women who are created by God are to find their way back to God" (this second section dealt in great depth with virtues and dispositions needed along the way). It concluded with the *Tertia Pars*, which spoke of Christ as "the one who shows us the way to eternal life, and the sacraments that are our means of salvation."[26]

Aquinas's "moral views stem from a rethinking of biblical teachings (chiefly the *Decalogue* and the two New Testament precepts of love) in the light of the philosophy of Aristotle, Plato, and the Stoics."[27] Aquinas's ethics were, like those of Aristotle, teleological, focusing on the "natural desire of human beings for the perfect good (God) as their ultimate end, to which all morally good acts must be reasonably conformed."[28]

The shift in Aquinas was due to his view that the ultimate good for which humanity searched was not the "happiness" of Aristotle, but rather a relationship with the ultimate happiness, God. Aquinas begins with a vision of the "end of man" (*Summa Theologica* I-II, 1)[29] which is happiness, an end for its own sake, but which for him consisted of the ultimate union of the soul with the Divine.[30] To this end, human beings were involved in a pattern of deliberate choices and actions, differentiated by Aquinas as *actiones humanae* and *actiones hominis*—that is, human actions and actions of "men" (*Summa Theologica* I-II, 1, 1).[31] The important distinction between the two categories lay in the involvement of the human intellect and will.

For *actiones hominis* (acts of a man) there was little or no deliberate thought, since these actions arose from one's male or female creaturehood itself and did not necessarily engage the process of deliberate thought. For *actiones humanae* (acts of a human), however, the engagement of one's intellect and will, which Aquinas called the "faculty of reason,"[32] made all the difference in one's process toward the ultimate end of humans. This deliberate choice made the path of humanity a voluntary one, then, following a pattern of considered choices and actions toward a specific end.

Aquinas's faith led him to an even more focused view of happiness, however. In *Summa Theologica* I-II, 3, "Happiness," Aquinas went further than Aristotle in his definition. There he stated "God is Happiness by His Essence."[33] To Aquinas, the ultimate end of all human striving was participation in that happiness, humanity's ultimate end, and since God was "happy not by acquisition or participation of something else, but by His essence,"[34] then a human being's participation in the essence of God was a realization of his or her own ultimate happiness. From this concept followed Aquinas's analysis of what it was which would enable human beings to move toward their ultimate end.

For Aquinas, as for Aristotle, the intellect and the will were the primary divisions of a human being's capacity for choice. Most important for moral decisions and choices was the proper use of these faculties. "Aquinas devoted much thought to the inner activities of will, understanding, and emotions (passions of the soul) and gave great importance to practical judgment, the intention of appropriate ends, the selection of right means, and reasonable choice of external (commanded) actions."[35]

Each of these topics was covered in separate sections of the *Summa*, in the *Secunda Secundae*. If one had a clear view of what one's ultimate good, of one's ultimate happiness, actually was, then he or she was enabled to proceed more surely in seeking it. Certain dispositions were required for this journey. These dispositions were "patterns of action to which we tend as individuals."[36] Question 49 of the *Prima Secundae*, the Treatise on Habits, explored Aquinas's vision of what habits were necessarily developed in a human being's quest for ultimate goodness and happiness. Again, it depended on a deliberate choice by an individual to develop consciously a consistent pattern of action based on a view of what was for him or her a "good" to be obtained.

Since people were naturally disposed by temperament to certain qualities, it depended on their conscious choice whether or not a particular "habit" could be developed. "To have a *habitus* is to be disposed to some activity or other—not because one tends to that activity on every possible occasion, but because one finds it natural, readily coped with, an obvious activity to engage in, and so on."[37] For Aquinas, then, the development of habits which drew persons toward the object of their desire was something that was under their conscious choice. Ultimately, their "dispositions," which occurred naturally, were very difficult to change, but habits were "changeable" and thus could be addressed in the actions of their intellects and wills.[38]

As with Aristotle, for Aquinas the proper use of the intellect, or the human ability to reason, was paramount in living fully as a human being. For him, there were two divisions of this power. First, there was speculative reason, dealing with theoretical matters, then practical reason, dealing with moral matters, or how one was to act in given situations (*Summa Theologica* I-II, 57.2ff).[39] The speculative mind understood on a purely theoretical level, with divisions into "understanding (*intellectus*), science (*scientia*), and wisdom (*sapientia*). The practical mind dealt with art (*ars*) and prudence (*prudentia*)."[40]

Each of these divisions lent itself to a particular form of understanding, whether of theoretical matters or the practical everyday matters of moral consideration situated much closer to humans as they lived their day-to-day lives. These categories were later to be considered closely as various historical applications grew over the centuries and were specifically applied to moral decision-making in the medical field as it developed.

Aquinas, then, in his monumental study, goes on to consider "virtue" in its essence and as it was displayed in specific applications, in the *Secunda Pars*, both first and second sections, with Questions 55, 56, 58, and 63. Forms of analysis noted in the following sections draw upon his considerations specifically for the virtues (or principles) of beneficence, prudence, and justice.[41]

Of foremost importance for the emphasis of this study is the focus on virtues as they "dispose us for the vision of God."[42] The virtues, as specific applications and development of naturally given dispositions, were fostered with the goal of ultimate relationship with God, or divine happiness. They take on a new light for us today as they become elements of one's professional self which is a "transfiguration of ourselves, [and] takes practice, commitment, and time, for it is based in the awareness that human wholeness demands becoming so much more than we already are."[43]

Referring back to Aquinas's view of virtue as habit (*Summa Theologica* I-II, 49, 1), it is obvious that both the modern revival of the view toward virtue ethics and the conscious discipline required in the effort stem from the belief that "ultimately we become what we most consistently do because the quality of our actions passes over into ourselves; hence, the quality of the act eventually becomes a quality of the person who acts."[44] Aquinas's view of virtues included those which were "natural and supernatural, acquired and infused, those ordered to the realm of human nature, and those capable of following a law of the Spirit" (*Summa Theologica* I-II, 63, 2).[45] This view bespoke his faith and drew a broader conclusion than that of Aristotle. Therefore, Aquinas "introduced psychology, the innovative psychology of Aristotle, into theology. The medieval theologian distinguished grace from activities in order to let the personality act but also to give that activity a stability, a personal subjectivity in both the orders of nature and of grace."[46]

Aquinas viewed grace as "humanity's participation in the divine nature and the source of all Christian life."[47] For Aquinas, this was a primary factor, in that all of the human responses possible in the form of consciously chosen virtuous acts were in actuality a response to the freely given grace of God. All consciously chosen patterns of behavior, then, were directed to the final goal of union with that Divine essence, which we have already noted was essentially happiness.

Within this framework, though, because of the capability of human beings to exercise their reason, *phronesis*, or practical wisdom, existed.[48] An extremely important quality, it could be developed by responding not only to the grace of God as previously mentioned, but also by paying attention to the naturally occurring "law" which was able to be discerned by all human beings in a conscious manner. Aquinas was to cover this in the *Summa Theologica* I-II, 94, where he spoke of the Natural Law.

"A certain order is to be found in those things that are apprehended universally."[49] Here all human beings exercised their natural capacity to discern what was for them "the good," by virtue of what Aquinas had previously addressed under the categories of speculative and practical wisdom, as well as *synderesis*, which is a naturally occurring human capability allowing one to know what was good.[50] So for Aquinas the combination of the naturally occurring ability to discern what was in the best interests of humanity, combined with the receptivity to the grace of God, allowed each human person to follow a consciously chosen path toward the good. This path allowed persons to participate in the eternal law of God as well as to proceed along the natural path of chosen good (*Summa Theologica* I-II, 91, 5).[51]

Reason being the guiding human capacity, and grace being given by the Divine essence, all human decisions may thus be directed to the ultimate good as well as the smaller goods encountered along the way in various particular instances. Aquinas's work was a testimonial to what he believed was the consummate approach to living a moral life in the light of Christ.

SUMMARY OF ANCIENT AND MEDIEVAL EMPHASES

In reviewing selected elements of the scholarly writings of Aristotle and Aquinas, we see that their trust in the capabilities of human beings to discern the good for themselves was high. Although Aquinas was specifically Christian, his appropriation of the elements of Aristotelian studies served as a structure for his approach. We "locate Aquinas's thought on the virtues within his distinctive theology (a theology of personality and grace where, using Aristotelian terms, grace is depicted as a special quasi-nature whose capabiities are virtues and their acts)."[52] Thus, "Thomas, his theology, moral theology, and spirituality inevitably described grace as a participation in the divine nature and the source of all Christian life."[53] For modern-day purposes, analysis of the "intention" of the morally acting agent is grounded in the work of Aquinas as well. "Intentionality elevated and directed moral action, and the real specificity of an act as well as its impact upon other people lost importance as an action was morally defined largely by the intention of the doer" (*Summa Theologica* I-II, 12).[54]

One can see by these reviews that the analysis of morally acting human agents began long before the advent of modern medical practice and the immense surge in technology. The human agents acting within history still had to deal with their inmost nature, however, and it is this nature which has never lost the need for both inner and outer direction toward a specific goal. Continuing on through history, several selected approaches and methods of moral and ethical thought will now be considered.

THE HIPPOCRATIC WRITINGS: MEDICINE'S EARLY DOCUMENTS

The Hippocratic School of Medicine, named after the Greek physician who lived from approximately 460 to 377 BC, produced a large corpus of documents.[55] The Oath which bears his name may or may not have been written by Hippocrates. Rather, it is possible that Galen, a pioneer in experimental physiology, who lived in the third century AD, was the actual editor and formulator of what has come down to us in repeatedly updated form, but which contained the primary precepts of the practice of medicine of that time.[56]

One version of this oath will be included in this study. This version is thought to have actually been written by "a philosophical sect known as the Pythagoreans in the latter part of the fourth century BC."[57]

I swear by Apollo Physician and Asclepius and Hygieia and Panaceia and all the gods and goddesses, making them my witnesses, that I will fulfill according to my ability and judgment this oath and this covenant:

To hold him who has taught me this art as equal to my parents and to live my life in partnership with him, and if he is in need of money to give him a share of mine, and to regard his offspring as equal to my brothers in male lineage and to teach them this art—if they desire to learn it—without fee and covenant; to give a share of precepts and oral instruction and all the other learning to my sons and to the sons of him who has instructed me and to pupils who have signed the covenant and have taken an oath according to the medical law, but to no one else.

I will apply dietetic measures for the benefit of the sick according to my ability and judgment; I will keep them from harm and injustice.

I will neither give a deadly drug to anybody if asked for it, nor will I make a suggestion to this effect. Similarly I will not give to a woman an abortive remedy. In purity and holiness I will guard my life and my art.

I will not use the knife, not even on sufferers from stone, but will withdraw in favor of such men as are engaged in this work.

Whatever houses I may visit, I will come for the benefit of the sick, remaining free of all intentional injustice, of all mischief and in particular of sexual relations with both female and male persons, be they free or slave.

What I may see or hear in the course of the treatment or even outside of the treatment in regard to the life of men, which on no account one must spread abroad, I will keep to myself holding such things shameful to be spoken about.

If I fulfill this oath and do not violate it, may it be granted to me to enjoy life and art, being honored with fame among all men for all time to come; if I transgress it and swear falsely, may the opposite of all this be my lot.[58]

There are those today who view this oath as "archaic," in the sense that because of the pluralism in both cultural and religious matters, certain of its elements are not applicable in today's society.[59] Vows to the gods mentioned therein are no longer applicable, and the initial focus of the oath as a form of "indenture agreement" between the master physician and his pupil, most likely on the verge of the younger's entrance into independent practice, no longer applies in modern society.

There are certain elements, however, which remain objects of intense consideration even now. Fletcher enumerates them as "1) to make the patient's interests supreme (my work will be 'for the benefit of my patients' and 'not for their hurt or for any wrong,' 2) to refuse to give a 'deadly drug to any, though it be asked of me,' 3) to refuse to terminate any pregnancies, that is, 'aid a woman to procure abortion,' and 4) to preserve professional secrets and the patient's privilege of communication ('whatsoever things I see or hear' in medical attendance 'which ought not to be noised abroad' will be kept as 'sacred secrets')."[60] These four elements remain important, though often extremely controversial, in the modern practice of medicine and in the analysis of biomedical ethics.

A further consideration of the Hippocratic Oath reveals strong elements of *paternalism*. Beginning with the relationship of master physician to student, the medical field for centuries was concerned with the "benefit" of the patients, or what physicians and healers could "do" for them in their time of need. Language of *patient rights* is absent from the Hippocratic Oath. The focus lay in the actions done by the physician for his patient.

Paternalism itself stemmed from the view of "fatherly concern" for one's family, and actions were "assumed to be benevolent, caring, and loving, and the father is assumed to seek the child's best interests."[61] A "paternalist, such as the government or a professional, refuses to acquiesce in another person's wishes, choices, or actions for that person's own benefit, often by using force or controlling information (e.g., by deception or nondisclosure of information)."[62]

Subsequent codes of medical ethics "have emphasized patients' needs rather than their rights," but have "paid little attention to the conflicts that are generated when the neighbor has a different interpretation of those needs and interests."[63] With the development of the concept of *patient autonomy*, to be explored in this study in later sections, the realization dawned that patients could be more than mere recipients of a professional's competent care and compassion. The patients could themselves enter into the healing process by considered choices and cooperation with the plan of medical treatment.

Thus, through the centuries, from the initial caretaking role of the physicians and other healers came the approach so prevalent today. This approach demands much of the practitioners. It demands professionalism, personal integrity, competence, and willingness to listen to what the patients actually want. The problems that the continued development of advanced technology has created were not even imaginable in the earliest days of medical practice. Questions that are asked in modern medicine could not have been fathomed then. But within the profession, then as now, each individual practitioner was expected to be a person of integrity and sound character, honest and true to his word. Today's revival of serious consideration of an ethics of character goes back to the earliest days of the covenant between physician and patient. From this standpoint, then, this study may continue in its overview of selected philosophical movements applicable to the modern study of biomedical ethics.

PHILOSOPHICAL CONSIDERATIONS

Certain objectives spur the development of any particular ethical theory. Each ethical theory "provides an ordered set of moral standards (in some cases simply one *ultimate* moral principle) that is to be used in assessing what is morally right and what is morally wrong regarding human action in general . . . a theory of moral obligation."[64] Certain authors suggest criteria which need to be applied to any ethical theory. These are "the implications of an ethical theory must be reconcilable with our experience of the moral life [and] an ethical theory must provide effective guidance where it is most needed, that is, in those situations where substantive moral considerations can be advanced on both sides of an issue."[65]

These two considerations seem important to any analysis of biomedical issues, since speaking in a highly theoretical manner about the issues of one's health and life can sometimes be a distancing factor rather than a helpful one. Likewise, the pluralism and high technological advancement of today's medical procedures necessitates the application of the second criterion, so that all options are clearly set out in as objective a manner as possible. This affords all parties to the decisions access to as much information as possible.

To this end, then, this study will concentrate on some selected philosophical approaches which provided the groundwork for the modern exploration of biomedical ethics. From this springboard have come the syntheses of ancient and more recent approaches to dealing with today's biomedical milieu.

IMMANUEL KANT: DEONTOLOGICAL OR OBLIGATION-BASED THEORY

Immanuel Kant (1724–1804) provided one of the foremost theories useful for today's biomedical ethical study. Deontology, a theory which can be described as "the science of duty,"[66] seeks to ground ethical decisions in duty, or obligation, to oneself and to others. Such a theory "maintains . . . that the rightness and wrongness of human action is *not exclusively* (in the extreme case, not at all) a function of the goodness and badness of consequences. In accordance with this specification, a theory is deontological (rather than teleological) if it places limits on the relevance of teleological considerations."[67]

Carried further, deontological theories ground themselves in the idea of duty, which Kant specified as "perfect or imperfect" in type, which can be divided into four categories: "1) perfect duties to self; 2) imperfect duties to self; 3) perfect duties to others; and 4) imperfect duties to others."[68] In his view, perfect duties were those which called us to "abstain from certain acts," and to this he saw no exception, stating that they are "binding in all circumstances." Imperfect duties on the other hand, were those which "require of us, in some overall sense, that we pursue or promote certain goals (e.g. the welfare of others)."[69] In his view these imperfect duties were never to take precedence over the perfect duties to self or others.

To clarify this a bit, I will return to a brief analysis of Kant's major theory, the *categorical imperative*. In different formulations of his idea, Kant spoke of the imperative that "I ought never to act except in such a way that I can also will that my maxim become a universal law." Applicable to all other human beings, one's actions should be viewed in the sense that they could be applied in all instances and to everyone, basically "without contradiction."[70] A second statement of the categorical imperative affirms Kant's view that each person is to "act in such a way that you always treat humanity, whether in your own person or in the person of any other, never simply as a means, but always at the same time as an end."[71] In other words, they are not to be used *exclusively* as a means, but rather the respect accorded them as individuals inheres in the fact that they are valued (as an end in themselves) as human beings, and not just, using a biomedical example, as subjects of one study or another.

This consideration of the categorical imperative leads back to the idea of perfect and imperfect duties, then. Kant himself held that there are three very vital perfect duties. These are "1) the duty not to kill an innocent person; 2) the duty not to lie; and 3) the duty to keep promises."[72] Intertwined with his view of duties was Kant's view that respect for one's own person, a valued human being, is a prime responsibility. Likewise, respect for others as valued members of the human race is essential for ethical behavior.

What he considered "imperfect goals" were those more specifically chosen actions, varying with circumstances, elected in order to preserve and promote human welfare. The concept of "beneficence" falls under this sort of action—taking good care of oneself and of one another. Following along in this line of reasoning, and as Mappes and Zembaty have included in their analysis, the duty of beneficence to others is an extension of the idea of beneficence to oneself, that "it is no more permissible to manifest disrespect for one's own person than to do so for the person of another."[73] Solicitous care for oneself precedes care for another; the valuing of one's own life, welfare, and health precedes and in some ways foreshadows one's own attitude toward others.

Immanuel Kant's philosophy echoed in many ways the ancients' views of the ability of human beings to exercise their rational nature. He asserted, "Morality is grounded in pure reason, not in tradition, intuition, conscience, emotion, or attitudes such as sympathy."[74] Thus, he operated from the deontological viewpoint that human beings call upon certain inherent duties to self and others which, seen in the light of their capacity to reason, would by their very nature require them to perform certain morally good actions. He looked to the goodwill of agents acting upon perceived duties as the propelling force in morally good ethical choices. This goodwill did not stem from outside fears and forces, but rather from an inner knowing of what was the "good" in any given situation, based on reasoned reflection.

Beauchamp and Childress note that "Kant has a problem with conflicting obligations."[75] Their example includes the conflicting duties of dealing with an elderly, sick relative and with one's keeping promises to one's children. Especially in modern society, where many obligations call upon people to choose which obligation to follow in a given situation, it falls to the moral agent to have developed practical powers of discernment, or the ability to know which priority calls more strongly. Such choices need not eliminate the validity of Kant's point of view for our reflection. Moral theory, grounded in specific principles, provides the structure for further reflection on the development of modern-day bioethics.

UTILITARIANISM AND CONSEQUENTIALISM IN RETROSPECT

"Consequentialism is a label affixed to theories holding that actions are right or wrong according to the balance of their good and bad consequences. The right act in any circumstance is the one that produces the best overall result, as determined from an impersonal perspective that gives equal weight to the interests of each affected party. The most prominent consequence-based theory, utilitarianism, accepts one and only one basic principle of ethics: the principle of utility. This principle asserts that we ought always to produce the maximal balance of positive value over disvalue (or the least possible disvalue, if only undesirable results can be achieved.)"[76]

Beauchamp and Childress, by this definition, set up an analysis of the theory most notably put forth by Jeremy Bentham (1748–1832) and John Stuart Mill (1806–73). These English philosophers considered happiness—in their view, "the presence of pleasure and the absence of pain,"[77]

—to be the good to be sought. Thus they were also known as "hedonistic utilitarians."[78] Two approaches to the theory are possible. First, "positive utilitarianism," seeks to maximize the good of those affected by one's actions, and second, "negative utilitarianism" seeks to minimize the negative effects.[79]

Various goals are also considered as "happiness" by different people. For instance, several goals leading one to choose a particular manner of acting can be enumerated. These are "friendship, knowledge, health, beauty . . . personal autonomy, achievement and success, understanding, enjoyment, and deep personal relationships."[80] These qualities and experiences of happiness were noted by earlier writers G.E. Moore (in his *Principia Ethica*) and James Griffin (in his *Well-Being: Its Meaning, Measurement and Moral Importance*).[81]

Utilitarianism, as a particular expression of consequentialism, was divided into two distinct applications: act-utilitarianism and rule-utilitarianism. Act-utilitarianism can be defined in this manner: "A person ought to act so as to produce the greatest balance of good over evil, everyone considered."[82] This leads individuals to choose their actions with the view as to which will provide the greatest good for the greatest number. Such choices entail much scrutiny on the part of individuals, who certainly must be grounded in one or another view of what is the maximum good, chosen from the list given above.

In the theory of Bentham and Mill, this would be happiness as the presence of pleasure and the lack of pain. This also leaves individuals with a large array of choices from which to select. Certain authors view act-utilitarianism as a "form of situation ethics," in which certain acts are chosen depending on the circumstances and perceived consequences in any given situation.[83] As opposed to rule-utilitarians, act-utilitarians believe that individual acts take precedence over general rules, which they view as being merely guiding "rules of thumb."[84]

Under these rules of thumb are included the maxims "do not kill," "do not injure," "do not steal," "do not lie," and "do not break promises."[85] Within this area of utilitarianism, it is necessary to have solid principles of discernment, with awareness of one's own selfish interests. Strength in decision-making depends on such integrity of individuals, and one's environment plays a tremendous part in the viewpoint of what is wrong or right for individuals as they choose their actions. Each person, within his or her given situation, decides whether or not a chosen act will maximize a perceived good. These acts, often guided by overarching rules or principles, take precedence over those very rules if an individual believes it does not apply in the given situation.[86]

Rule-utilitarianism can be stated as the theory that "a person ought to act in accordance with the rule that, if generally followed, would produce the greatest balance of good over evil, everyone considered."[87] This appears to be a little less strenuous for each individual. Mappes and Zembaty state it in this manner: "Whereas act-utilitarianism seems to confront individuals with an overly demanding moral standard, placing each of us under a continuing obligation to maximize utility with each of our actions, rule-utilitarianism is far less demanding of individuals. It requires only that individuals conform their actions to the rules that constitute a utilitarian-based moral code, and this requirement accords well with our ordinary moral thinking. Rule-utilitarianism also seems to accord reasonably well with our experience of particular, morally significant relationships."[88] The authors explain their thought by reference to larger categories with a stable grounding in principles which motivate certain people to act in a certain way within familial and societal networks. There would appear to be greater freedom in this outlook without the individual being constrained to analyze each given act in every situation, possibly coming up with different choices as situations changed.

With either act- or rule-utilitarianism, the end point of an individual's choice is the maximization of the "good" for everyone concerned. Looking back to the original teleological approach of Aristotle and Aquinas, one author notes that neither of the ancients had the modern day "utilitarian viewpoint." Rather they were more concerned with the effect of one's choices on one's own self, one's own character, and one's own (not collective) happiness.[89] This difference will come into play later in this study as we address each individual's personal pattern of choice in the biomedical ethical field.

Spiritual grounding, a very individual matter, plays a large part in the direction one chooses in any professional life. A person's carefully thought-out decisions ultimately affect the people in his or her sphere of influence, and this fact is part of the whole picture of any decision-making. But the starting point must always be how a professional person grounds his or her own integrity. Valuing life in general, beginning with one's own, a true professional discerns where he or she stands in relation to all others.

W. D. ROSS: THEORY OF PRIMA FACIE DUTIES

In *The Right and the Good*, published in 1930, W. D. Ross first proposed his theory of prima facie duties. A deontological theory emphasizing the existence of certain obligations recognized at the beginning of any deliberations, Ross's position stated that among those initially acknowledged obligations were some that were in conflict with one another. Such conflicts would inevitably cause anxiety and confusion for the persons responsible for making decisions as they attempted to balance the duties which ostensibly drew them in two or more directions at once.[90] Ross's presentation, in recognizing that biomedical decisions were deeply emotional ones by their very essence, was especially important to the continued development of biomedical ethics.

The term *prima facie* is a Latin phrase which means "at first glance."[91] Thus, as persons seek to determine what decision is to be made in a given situation, certain options present themselves in the form of duties. In Ross's view, "there are no absolute, or unconditional, duties, only prima facie duties."[92] He viewed these duties as conditional; that is, depending on the circumstances, one or another of the duties obvious at first glance might be overturned with the discovery that perhaps another one of the discerned duties ought to take precedence.

Mappes and Zembaty point out that in Ross's theory the Kantian framework and the utilitarian framework did not blend well with what was seen as "the ordinary moral consciousness." In his view, "our conviction that we have distinct lines of obligation to distinct people" was at odds with the strict interpretation of the phrase, *duty of maximizing utility*.[93] Rather than situating the basis for the maximization of utility in the same framework as the Kantian deontologists and the noted utilitarians, Ross placed the determination of the overriding duties in the obligations people had to honor "morally significant relations," which he considered those such as "promisee to promiser, creditor to debtor, spouse to spouse, child to parent, friend to friend, citizen to the state, fellow human being to fellow human being."[94] Thus, for Ross, each decision was dependent in large part on the circumstances surrounding it, which would determine the priority of the duties involved.

Ross divided the prima facie duties into several categories, noted by Mappes and Zembaty in this way: "1) duties of fidelity, which included keeping promises, honoring contracts and agreements, and telling the truth; 2) duties of reparation, which called for the rectifying of previous wrongs done to other individuals; 3) duties of gratitude, which took special note of benefits granted by others to oneself or others; 4) duties of beneficence, which called for actions designed to improve the lot of others; 5) duties of nonmaleficence, calling for restraint in such actions as would cause harm to another; 6) duties of justice, which called for appropriate actions designed to distribute goods to as many as possible without consideration of their 'merit'; and 7) duties of self-improvement, which called forth one's own responsibility to better one's own lot."[95]

The theory of W. D. Ross sheds light on what is also important for any acting moral agent. Again, the power of personal discernment is vital to the proper knowledge and application of ethical principles in a biomedical context. Such a theory depends on a strong foundational awareness of personal responsibility as a human being to other human beings. The pluralism so obvious in modern culture and society demands of each such agent a serious recognition of his or her own responsibility in any given circumstance. The ability to balance recognized principles when faced with serious decisions is essential, calling forth from caretakers all the intellectual and spiritual resources they possess. Consideration of Ross's theory of prima facie duties provides another tool for such insight.

POSITIVE AND NEGATIVE RIGHTS

Before proceeding with an overview of what has sometimes been negatively called *principlism*, I will stop momentarily to mention the language of "rights" which became so prevalent in the mid-to late-twentieth-century vocabulary. It is especially important in the focus on autonomy which has become so clear in the last decades in the medical world. Both positive and negative rights are considered. Positive rights are those which state that a person has "a right to be provided with a particular good or service by others." In other words, positive rights "entail another's obligation to do something for someone." A negative right is one that ensures that a person may be "free from some action taken by others." In other words, "negative rights entail another's obligation to refrain from doing something."[96]

In the light of complex medical decisions both rights are important elements of individuals' options. The distinction addresses both practitioner and patient. Whereas each patient has rights to expect certain actions be done and other actions not to be done, each practitioner, in the light of his or her professional oath, has obligations to each patient in the realm of required professional abilities. In a sense, this medical covenant stands as a sacred trust between those who vow to heal and those who seek to be healed. Respect for persons is inherent in any discussion of patient rights in the medical context, and is a grounding element in the consideration of principles of ethical behavior—which will now be addressed.

MID-TWENTIETH-CENTURY GROWTH IN BIOMEDICAL ETHICS

In his forward to the volume *A Matter of Principles: Ferment in U.S. Bioethics*, Albert Jonsen illustrates the development of the field of ethical application known as *bioethics*. He traces the beginnings of the modern field to the 1960s and 1970s—during which time the field expanded by leaps and bounds—noting that there were immense changes of focus during those years. While making particular mention of the initial emphasis on certain principles, Jonsen writes, "A very few scholars, most fresh out of graduate school, found themselves attracted to the study of moral and ethical questions posed by the progress of scientific medicine. . . . Those of us who were in on the creation were not trained as bioethicists—there was no bioethics; we were educated as philosophers and theologians in the academic philosophy and theology of the 1960s and gradually turned those disciplines to the work that in time became bioethics."[97]

Jonsen also notes that the language employed by these new bioethicists was a fruit of their own training and needed adjustment in the face of the newly emerging field. Referring to the linguistic analysts and metaethicists, he refers to their language as "clipped and dry speech, unmodulated by emotion or passion," and observes that metaethics differs distinctly from normative ethics in that it deals "exclusively with the form of moral discourse [and] not with its substance."[98]

Continuing with his analysis, Jonsen mentions the type of language employed by the theologians at that point in the development of the new field. He states, "Catholic theologians grew skeptical of the rationalistic rules of the natural law and their authoritarian interpretation by the hierarchy; they sought to revive an ethics based on the imitation of Christ and the command of love."[99] The attempt to have a meeting of the minds demanded an integration of two very different approaches to ethical thought. "The philosophical ethics of that era had very little to say about the substantial content of moral decision and action. Theological ethics used terms that were incomprehensible to many who were not believers or were believers of a different sort. We had to find an idiom that, at one and the same time, expressed substantive content and was comprehensible to many listeners."[100] To this end, then, the "embryonic ethicists found some guidance away from the arid land of metaethics and out of the prophetic but parochial land of religion. The guidance was the language of theory and principle."[101]

It was a starting point. Jonsen mentions the *Belmont Report* (originally published in *The Federal Register* in 1976), the result of many meetings between members of a commission which had been formed to grapple with the problem of addressing the myriad new applications of ethics to biomedical situations and to formulate a vocabulary with which to communicate effectively in that field. An initial statement by Congress in 1974 established the National Commission for the Protection of Human Subjects of Biomedical and Behavioral Research. This commission was enjoined to "conduct a comprehensive investigation and study to identify the basic ethical principles which should underlie the conduct of biomedical and behavioral research involving human subjects; develop guidelines which should be followed in such research to assure that it is conducted in accord with such principles."[102]

The findings of this commission were included in the *Belmont Report*, which received its name from the conference center in Maryland, at which it was finalized. Included in the report were three basic principles of ethical behavior: "respect for persons, beneficence, and justice."[103] This document was the first formal statement in the new field of biomedical ethics. Later, the initial three principles were developed into four, adding "nonmaleficence" to the list.

As Tom L. Beauchamp stated, "Principles gave an anchor to a youthful bioethics in the 1970s and early 1980s and contributed a sense that the field rests on something firmer than disciplinary bias or subjective judgment."[104] The newly recognized combination of philosophical and theological vocabulary in the new field provided "a clear framework for a normative ethics that had to be practical and productive. [It] provided a focus for the broader, vaguer, and less applicable general reflections of philosophers and theologians of the era. In [its] simplicity and directness, [it] gave us a language to speak with our new audience, the physicians, nurses, and others in health care. . . . Principlism gave clinicians the vocabulary with which to discuss the previously inchoate moral gut feelings."[105]

In recent years, there has been a growth and reformulation of the initial principles in the light of cultural diversity and pluralism, as well as feminist concerns and a revisiting of the ethics of character and narrative ethics. The field at its inception, however, required a structure upon which it could build in subsequent years. The recognition that principles in and of themselves were not the entire picture of biomedical decisions led to continual attempts to refine and apply the general to the specific. "Principles [were to be] understood less as norms that are applied in the model of 'applied ethics,' and more as guidelines that are interpreted and made specific for policy and clinical decision making. A coherent development of principles and rules, not merely an application, is essential."[106]

Beauchamp recognized that "through progressive specification, bioethics becomes increasingly more practical, while maintaining fidelity to the original principles and rules."[107] In the attempt to capsulize what they believed to be the most applicable principles of ethical behavior within a medical context, Beauchamp and Childress settled upon carefully chosen, familiar principles, well-accepted as "the most general normative standards of conduct." They chose four, ultimately, always with the realization that "neither rules nor judgments can be deduced directly from the principles, because additional interpretation, specification, and balancing of the principles is needed to formulate policies and decide about cases."[108]

THE PRINCIPLES GROUNDING MODERN BIOETHICAL CONSIDERATIONS

I have chosen to emphasize the work of Tom L. Beauchamp and James F. Childress in the review of the principles which were selected as the starting point for the mid-twentieth-century focus on biomedical ethics. Though articles by numerous authors abound on the subject, these two scholars have become the most noteworthy proponents of the principlist approach to the constantly evolving field. Now after several editions, the scope of their *Principles of Biomedical Ethics* has been broadened to include an appreciation of other viewpoints which, as opposed to the total denunciation of the use of principles, serve today to enhance and enlarge the realm of reference for scholars and practitioners.

At one point in the development of the field, the four principles were referred to as "the Georgetown mantra," since the development of the Kennedy Institute of Ethics began at that university.[109] In reality, the use of the principles served as a point of departure for the development of what today continues to evolve in scope and depth as the art of making biomedical ethical decisions.

AUTONOMY

Derived from two Greek words, *autos* (self) and *nomos* (rule, governance, or law), the concept of autonomy originally signified the "self-rule of independent Hellenic city-states."[110] Its later evolution centered on individuals and their capacity for unfettered choice in given situations.

"Often autonomy refers to qualities of persons and their actions. An example of an autonomous person is one who, with the requisite mental capacity, reflects on and chooses his or her own moral framework."[111]

This definition might imply that someone acting within a particular tradition or culture is not autonomous. However, as Childress goes on to say, "Autonomy does not necessarily imply that an individual's life plan is created by that person *de novo*, but it does suggest that the individual has adopted, usually reflectively and critically, a life plan as his or her own, even if it was drawn from a community and a tradition."[112] This has great bearing on practitioners' approaches to their patients, in that as acting moral agents, awareness of the patients' cultural and religious traditions is vital to allowing them the fullest expression of their own autonomous choices in medical settings. "Morality is not a set of personal rules created by individuals isolated from society, and moral principles have authority over our lives by virtue of a social and cultural setting that is independent of any single autonomous actor."[113] Returning to the previously mentioned idea of *paternalism*, the exercise of a one-sided, rather protective stance toward one's patients might very well eliminate their ability to act as autonomous individuals in the choice of their medical care.

Very significant in the consideration of another person's ability to make autonomous decisions are several elements included in the initial medical assessments made as patients present themselves for treatment. First of all, objective assessment of one's mental capacity begins immediately as practitioners come into contact with persons in the medical setting. Children are not considered autonomous individuals, as they have not the life experience or intellectual development to make considered decisions on their own behalf. Even Immanuel Kant and John Stuart Mill, in their own theories of respect for persons, "excluded children and the insane" from full consideration as autonomous individuals, restricting inclusion to "those in the maturity of their faculties."[114] So, in assessment of patients prior to discussion of medical options, it is essential that practitioners know how much of their explanation has been understood, and that outside forces are not contributing unduly to the patient's consideration of his or her options. "We analyze autonomous action in terms of normal choosers who act 1) intentionally, 2) with understanding, and 3) without controlling influences that determine their action."[115]

Respect for another's autonomy calls for a commitment on the part of practitioners to give the time needed for the full assessment of a given individual's status as a competent person. Varying circumstances impinge on any given person's ability to make fully competent decisions with full exercise of his or her individuality. Thus any approach to medical treatment necessitates serious consideration of a patient's ability to take control of his or her medical care, from the standpoint of choice. Practitioners need to exercise positive respect for the autonomy of their patients, meaning that they take positive action in determining a patient's status as acting agent in his or her own behalf. But they also need to exercise negative restraint, meaning that they refrain from any action which might directly impinge upon another's right of self-determination in the choice of medical treatment.

Beauchamp and Childress stress five points in the principle of respect for autonomy. These are 1) tell the truth, 2) respect the privacy of others, 3) protect confidential information, 4) obtain consent for interventions with patients, and 5) when asked, help others make important decisions.[116] These five points illustrate the areas in which it is imperative that practitioners exercise excellent skills of assessment and discernment in their relationships with their patients. Within these areas lie the elements of true healing alliances between those seeking to be healed and those offering to heal.

NONMALEFICENCE

"The principle of nonmaleficence asserts an obligation not to inflict harm intentionally."[117]Beauchamp and Childress indicate that this principle has been closely tied "to the maxim *Primum non nocere*," which means "first, do no harm." The authors state that it was not found directly stated in this manner in the Hippocratic corpus, and that it was a "strained translation of a single Hippocratic passage"[118] (we might note the passage in the Hippocratic Oath quoted previously that the physician vowed to "keep them from harm and injustice"). Nevertheless, for full consideration of this principle I will borrow their analysis, which makes a distinction between the principle of nonmaleficence and that of beneficence (to be considered further on in this study). They include the analysis of William Frankena,[119] which divided the idea of nonmaleficence into four specific categories:

1) One ought not to inflict evil or harm (what is bad).
2) One ought to prevent evil or harm.

3) One ought to remove evil or harm.
4) One ought to do or promote good.[120]

These four divisions have both positive and negative aspects.

The first one states the negative—in the sense that one refrains from doing something. The last three state the positive—in that the acting moral agent actually performs a certain action with the goal of preventing evil or harm and promoting the good in a situation. The authors state that "obligations of nonmaleficence are more stringent than obligations of beneficence; and in some cases, nonmaleficence overrides beneficence when the best utilitarian outcome would be obtained by acting beneficently." Here they include the example of a physician refraining from killing a person on death row with the view of using his organs for donation. Basically, the act would have "the highest net utility in the circumstances but is not morally defensible."[121] Five rules supportable by the principle of nonmaleficence are again cited by Beauchamp and Childress:

1) Do not kill.
2) Do not cause pain or suffering to others.
3) Do not incapacitate others.
4) Do not cause offense to others.
5) Do not deprive others of the goods of life.[122]

To fully act upon the principle of nonmaleficence requires practitioners to exercise their judgment and assessment within given medical situations. Qualities of objectivity and willingness to consult and collaborate with colleagues demand of those in the healing profession an astuteness and sensitivity to all aspects of their patients' "good" on the physical, psychological, and spiritual levels. They require that medical professionals be grounded in their own personhood which will enable them to respect the same quality in the patients with whom they deal.

BENEFICENCE
"Morality requires not only that we treat persons autonomously and refrain from harming them, but also that we contribute to their welfare."[123] Beauchamp and Childress note that the principle of nonmaleficence has no sharp distinction from that of beneficence, but they concede that "principles of beneficence potentially demand more than the principle of

nonmaleficence because agents must take positive steps to help others, not merely refrain from harmful acts."[124] They go on to define beneficence as "an action done for the benefit of others; *benevolence* refers to the character trait or virtue of being disposed to act for the benefit of others; and *principle of beneficence* refers to a moral obligation to act for the benefit of others."[125]

Again, they include five rules which are supportable in the light of beneficence:

1) Protect and defend the right of others.
2) Prevent harm from occurring to others.
3) Remove conditions that will cause harm to others.
4) Help persons with disabilities.
5) Rescue persons in danger.[126]

Within their analysis of beneficence, the authors also mention the idea of paternalism as it might be employed less than ideally in medical situations.[127] I mention this only to reinforce the necessity of discernment and objective assessment in any given situation, requiring a professional to put aside his or her own needs to "help" and implying that a certain circumstance may ask one to refrain from exercising what he or she might feel is correct, in order to respect the patient's decision in his or her own regard. Again, we return to the idea of respect for human persons and their right of self-determination, within reasonable limits, in a medical situation.

JUSTICE

Finally, there are a number of ways to consider the principle of justice as employed in the biomedical ethical field. The first might be that of *distributive justice*, which refers to "what is fair, equitable, and appropriate distribution in society determined by justified norms that structure the terms of social cooperation."[128] For the purposes of biomedical ethics, this includes the fair and equitable allotment of available resources to the greatest number of people. Beauchamp and Childress include six elements supportable by the terms of such justice: 1) to each person an equal share, 2) to each person according to need, 3) to each person according to effort, 4) to each person according to contribution, 5) to each person according to merit, and 6) to each person according to free-market exchanges. This list includes suggestions by various authors "as valid material principles of distributive justice."[129] It is by no means exhaustive, especially in the light of health care considerations.

I believe that the list as the authors have compiled it is open to many varied interpretations. Consider liver-transplant patients who may have brought about their own illness by misuse of alcohol, and who, though they may have a greater immediate need for the transplant, might be looked at by practitioners as "not deserving" of a new liver, or having a case "without merit." Serious political consideration must be given in the area of distributive justice, especially in today's culture of mega-mergers and profit margins. It falls to each professional in his or her own milieu to exert influence which stems from as objective and unbiased a position as possible, given the financial considerations. This is, realistically, extremely difficult, because of outside political and professional constraints on one's actions. (These political and professional constraints could actually determine whether or not a professional keeps his or her position.)

Another view of justice brings in the element of character, which for this study is more applicable. This view considers justice in the more traditional way, as a cardinal virtue, and considers it "a trait of character, empowering and disposing an agent to act in ways constitutive of human flourishing. In other words, it considers the meaning of what it is to be a 'just person.' As a cardinal virtue, justice is an operative habit setting the will in the direction of impartially rendering to each his or her due or desert; but justice requires for its effective realization the power to discern the right means to secure the good toward which justice disposes (prudence), the ability to order the passions for single-minded pursuit of the good (temperance), and steadfastness in the pursuit even in face of threats to the self (fortitude)."[130]

This definition also echoes views of the ancients, Aristotle and Aquinas, as they sought to express their views on the fullness of humanity. They viewed this fullness as inclusive of the proper ordering of the natural human passions under the controlling influence of the intellect and will. Overall, this conception of justice includes "1) a norm for human moral agency that has its source in the being and agency of God, 2) a virtue of the moral agent, 3) a norm for the governing of human relationships that compares and contrasts with a standard of love for neighbor (*agape*), [and] 4) the normative ordering and distribution of social benefits and burdens among citizens of a commonwealth."[131]

For the purposes of this study, then, the consideration of justice includes both the political and the theological aspects, especially as we place emphasis on ourselves as individually acting moral agents within a specific culture. That culture is the culture of the medical world, actually our culture-within-the-culture, within which professionals live out their individual and collective roles. The principle of justice, both as distributive in the social sense and as an element of character, requires personal awareness of one's own deeply held beliefs and attitudes. A full expression of just behavior toward one another in the medical context, both professional-to-professional and professional-to-patient, obliges practitioners to exercise control over themselves both as persons and as professionals. Such control requires, once again, strong discernment and assessment skills and the ability to put one's understanding into practice in a beneficial manner, contributing to the welfare both of the patients and of society.

COVENANT RESPONSIBILITY

Significant in the consideration of biomedical ethics is an approach which calls us to revisit the biblical sources of ethical behavior. That approach is the one which focuses on the elements of "covenant" as it concerns the relationship of those who profess to heal and those who come to them for healing.

Covenant (*berith*) is the linchpin of the Old Testament as it tells the story of the relationship between God (Yahweh) and the Chosen People (Israel). Several forms of covenant are cited in the history of Israel, one of which is noted in the Covenant Code of Exodus 20:23–23:33. Therein the People of Israel receive the Decalogue, or Ten Commandments, which delineate their responsibility to their God. "Covenants in the Old Testament between God and the people are initiated by God, not negotiated, and are expressions of God's power and grace. . . . In some covenants, God's action is self-binding: e.g. those with Noah, Abraham, and David, in each of which God makes a promise to the people but does not lay corresponding obligations upon them. In other cases, God's covenant includes explicit obligations laid upon the people, as in the giving of the law at Sinai and in the covenant at Shechem (Joshua 24)."[132]

William F. May addresses the concept of a *covenant ethic* as one which, "above all else, defines the moral life responsively. . . . Covenantal obligation in its ancient and most influential form—the biblical covenant—arises from the exchange of goods between partners that leads to a fundamental promise, which, in turn, shapes the future of both parties to the agreement."[133] His reference is to the great covenant between God and Israel to which he ascribes four main elements. These are "1) a gift—the deliverance of the people from Egypt, 2) an exchange of promises (at Mt. Sinai), 3) the shaping of all subsequent life in response to the original gift and the promissory event, and 4) the ritual means whereby Israel returns regularly to the foundational events that shape her life."[134] Acknowledging that subsequent applications of the word *covenant* throughout history have not always been admirable, he cites his reason for including it in regard to medical practitioners. He states, "The four-part covenantal story can illuminate the medical covenant and practice in two ways: it can throw light on basic principles that should shape practice, and it can highlight the character and virtues required in the practitioner."[135]

For the purposes of this study, this view is important in the sense that in order to come to a positive alliance in the healing art, practitioner to patient, committed caregivers are called upon not only to *do* something but also to *be* something for their patients. Accepting responsibility for the utmost use of their talents for the benefit of their patients can be framed in covenantal terms. "A covenant, such as the covenants of religious people before God . . . engages and transforms the identity of both parties involved in it. A healer's covenant fully commits the practitioners. . . . The covenanted healer must be attentive to the whole patient."[136]

The biblical covenants required the participants to swear to fulfill certain obligations in return for certain benefits. With the God-initiated covenants formerly mentioned, God granted favor and love to the Chosen People—protection and security if they fulfilled what was asked of them. May states that in the light of such a covenant morality it behooves practitioners to exercise "a disciplined attentiveness to the patient as a whole," and to employ "careful discernment of what distinguishes the patient's case from those of others."[137] To this end is employed the dedicated self-scrutiny which allows professionals to be honest about their own interior motives in regard to the practice of medicine.

May attempts to detach the modern approach to covenant morality from the biblical by stating that in the increasingly pluralistic culture there will be persons who will consciously choose not to be identified with biblical morality, yet who wish to commit to binding relationships with their patients. He refers to Paul Ramsey, who, in his preface to the volume *The Patient as Person*, refers initially to the biblical covenant morality but then expands it in a more general application. "Ramsey spent little time in that volume on the biblical covenant except for a few paragraphs in his preface. He seemed convinced philosophically and theologically that the basic moral commands (the third element in the covenantal story line) are statable as moral principles, relatively detachable from the Commander."[138] May considers Ramsey's action in this regard as an element which freed the Christian ethicist to view moral issues from the standpoint of philosophical terms rather than religious ones. This approach would serve in some ways to eliminate "divisiveness" in ethical discussions. "One tends to expect these standards to be relatively acceptable and independent of the accidents of personal biography, philosophical conviction, and religious disposition."[139]

If professionals operate within a covenant morality their inner character will be changed, with the development of specific qualities of character allowing them to act in honorable and respectful ways toward their fellow human beings. In the light of the covenant morality, May states,

> Covenanted men and women do not simply accept a set of rules and principles guiding their actions; they also bind themselves over in the course of an event that alters and continuingly defines their identity. . . . As covenanted people take up the particulars of their several vocations, their identity will display itself in the character and virtues that properly typify their practice. No ethic that adequately explores the medical covenant can focus simply upon the quandaries that emerge in medical practice and the bearing of moral principles upon those quandaries; it must also explore the identity and nature of those agents who profess medicine.[140]

In light of his view of covenant morality, May himself goes on to explore several of the virtues of a professional as he sees them. He includes *purity of heart*, for which he claims the secular term is *integrity*. To him this encompasses a professional's ability to be upright and whole in relation to his or her patients. He also includes *prudence*, which he characterizes as "attentiveness and discernment."[141] Referring to Thomas Aquinas (*Summa Theologica* I–II, q.57, a 5), May states that in order for a choice to be good, "two things are required. First, that the intention be directed to a due end. . . . Second, that (man) take rightly those things which have reference to the end: and this he cannot do unless his reason counsel, judge, and command aright, which is the function of prudence and the virtues annexed to it."[142]

Other virtues considered by May in the actions of a medical professional are fidelity, courage, gratitude, and hope. Overall, he places these virtues in the realm of covenant morality because he considers covenanted professionals who possess the inner qualities that motivate them to carry out their professional responsibility in a way which can be traced to biblical covenant fidelity.

Paul Ramsey stresses the *faithfulness* of one human being for another as an important element in covenant fidelity, basing it on God's fidelity to humanity in Jesus Christ.[143] He centers this fidelity in the "righteousness" of human beings, one to another. Within this righteousness one discovers "the meaning of *care*, to find the actions and abstentions that come from adherence to *covenant*, to ask the meaning of the *sanctity* of life, to articulate the requirements of steadfast *faithfulness* to a fellow man."[144] To place his thought in the medical context, Ramsey states, "This means that the conscious acceptance of covenant responsibilities is the inner meaning of even the 'natural' or systemic relations into which we are born and of the institutional relations or roles we enter by choice, while this fabric provides the external framework for human fulfillment in explicit covenants among men."[145]

The modern medical environment contains some elements of elitism in the sense that initially the profession admitted only men and until very recently was almost impenetrable to the outside world for analysis of its own behavior. Exercising a covenant mentality within such a profession takes courage on the part of individuals who are not only willing to question their own ethical behavior but also that of their peers. Basing one's professional commitment on something beyond oneself—such as a covenant responsibility to one's fellow human beings—gives individuals the courage to stand alone at times, if they must, to fight for what Ramsey called the sacredness of life. "Superego morality can become a prepotent agent of all the dark powers that draw persons eventually into collective sinfulness, hypocrisy, belligerent group egotism and the slavery of falsehood. . . . Covenant morality opens one to ever new and creative responses to God and neighbor."[146]

A biblically based view of covenant morality refers practitioners back to their own beliefs and religious foundations. It allows for the expansion of their considerations into the realm of the overarching principles and virtues that go into the making up of persons of integrity within professions. As professionals grow both in their medical art and in the art of being decent human beings, a covenant mentality can provide direction as to which virtues are essential in both realms. We will now consider briefly the return of an approach to virtue ethics in today's biomedical ethical decision making.

VIRTUE ETHICS: A RETURN TO THE BEGINNING

For the consideration of the revival of virtue ethics, I will rely primarily on Edmund Pellegrino, who has written a book with David C. Thomasma on the subject, as well as a number of articles framing his view that a reintegration of virtue and principles is an important aspect of biomedical ethics.

For the purposes of this study it is significant to note this approach to ethical practice within the health care field. As Pellegrino states, "In [the clinical setting] it is obvious that the way principles are selected, interpreted, ordered in relation to each other, and applied, is dependent on the character of each participant in a clinical activity."[147] Yet another scholar has named a primary task within the moral life as a process of taming the "fat, relentless ego."[148] Both of these authors focus on the importance of a disciplined practice of selected virtues within the health care field, as practitioners strive to integrate medical expertise with the ability to understand and communicate with their patients. This responsibility falls upon each professionally committed person in the healing professions. To this point in the development of the biomedical ethical field it has been necessary to situate decisions in a common vocabulary. At this point in time the further necessity of an analysis of the character of persons in medical practice is very apparent.

There is "a widespread dissatisfaction with an understanding of the moral life which focuses primarily on duties, obligations, troubling moral dilemmas, and borderline cases."[149] Gilbert Meilander refers to Aristotle, for whom virtues were skills which could be learned and practiced, not teachable "techniques."[150] The ancients' views of virtue, or *arete*, which signified "excellence," described virtues as both the "means to an end and constitutive of the good" (the good being the goal of humanity in its fullness), again stressing the teleological nature of their works.[151] Within this view toward the ultimate end of human striving there was the sense of virtues as specific human dispositions toward one form of behavior or another. The cardinal virtues of prudence, justice, fortitude and temperance contributed to the ethical behavior of humans toward one another.

In the view of Thomas Aquinas, the ultimate goal was union with God, and to this end all decisions pointed, their foundation being a firm grounding in the God-given virtue of charity. For Aquinas, "there is no such thing as natural moral goodness, there is only habitual moral goodness, goodness that is achieved through a resolute history of virtuous choices" (*Summa Theologica* I–II, 49, 4).[152] For Aquinas, the initial capacity of persons to act ethically was strengthened by deliberate, conscious practice over time, in response to grace infused by God.[153] Aquinas's treatise included an important element which can be seen in the dilemmas of today's bioethical practitioners—the complications of "specific situations," where overarching principles are confronted with changing circumstances. To the primary virtues in any context, then, was added the quality of *phronesis*, or practical wisdom, which enabled one to exercise proper judgment in context, to the optimum benefit of all concerned. Pellegrino himself considers *phronesis* "medicine's indispensable virtue," which from ancient times proved to be the "capstone virtue, the link between the intellectual and the moral life."[154] He states that *phronesis* is "the intellectual virtue that disposes us habitually to attain truth for the sake of action, as opposed to truth for its own sake, which is speculative wisdom or *sophia*."[155]

Pellegrino, as a physician, knows the difficulties inherent in any medical context. Not only are patients and families confronted with the specifics of a disease and its prognosis, but they also possess emotional "baggage" which colors their decision-making in times of stress. Within the medical context, then, are the practitioners, who also possess emotional "baggage" which likewise colors their approach to any given situation. Therefore, it is vital for these practitioners to have analyzed their own demeanor for signs of bias, prejudice, fear, or uncertainty. Possession of certain character traits, or "virtues," strengthened by habitual practice, is requisite for operating fully within the often uncertain medical milieu.

"Formally speaking . . . the virtues are conditions of possibility for the implementation of principles and moral rules . . . no amount of rule making will ever change the behavior of individuals."[156] In situations where it is all too easy to fall back upon rote formulae and objective principles and descriptions, the character of a health practitioner does much to uphold personal strength when facing difficult situations. "If the physician is too compassionate and comes too close to the experience of suffering, he or she will lose the objectivity necessary for proper diagnosis and selection of treatment, thus defeating the end of medicine in its healing function. On the other hand, not to have compassion is to treat the patient as an object, as simply a particular instance of a disease process. The patient is divested of the rich particulars of age, occupation, sex, race, situation in life, values—all those particulars that define us as persons and give us identity."[157]

We have already noted the views of the ancients on virtue in the human life. Pellegrino states, "Virtue is the most perdurable concept in the history of ethics. If virtue is to be restored to a normative status, its philosophical underpinnings must be reconstructed."[158] He considers the essential elements of the moral life to be "1) the agent, 2) the act itself, 3) the circumstances of the act, and 4) the consequences of the act."[159] Again this returns to the classical approach of the ancients. After an overview of their approach, he recognizes that "ethicists continued to confront the question of character of the agent. Principles, rules, maxims, intuitions, language analysis, and technical skills in solving moral puzzles did not encompass the full complexity of the moral life."[160] He also acknowledges the fact that in our pluralistic culture it has become exceedingly difficult to come to a general consensus on what the answer to any one dilemma is to be.

Overriding most decisions in today's medical world is the emphasis on the patient's autonomy, which cries out for recognition, and the determination of which is one of the first steps in medical assessment. As well, the choice of which virtues should be emphasized is almost as perplexing as the initial choice of principles was for the first bioethical scholars at the beginning of the growth of the field. "A shared notion of the good gave focus to Aristotle's *Nichomachean Ethics*, to Aquinas's *Summa Theologica*. But it is disagreement on the good that divides modern and contemporary ethical and metaphysical theory."[161]

Virtue ethics as such suffered a decline in the initial years of the development of the field of bioethical studies. Pellegrino attributes this decline to "1) principle-based ethics, which appealed to health professionals as being more definitive than virtue because of its concreteness and applicability to clinical decisions, 2) socio-political change toward participatory democracy, greater public education, distrust of authority, and the character failings of some physicians [which] focused public attention on autonomy-based, contractual relationships rather than trust-based, covenantal ones, [and] 3) the challenge to the religious and philosophical consensus that undergirded professional ethics, at least in the West."[162] He also sees the original Hippocratic Oath as being, for all practical purposes, almost destroyed by the modern bent toward patient autonomy over the exercise of beneficence. The original proscriptions against abortion and euthanasia contained in the Oath have also been challenged in recent years with the advent of "pro-choice" political movements and patient "rights."

Pellegrino focuses on professional ethics as the arena which may be most impacted by revisiting the concept of virtue ethics. What many see as the failings in the principle-based system (overly rationalistic, too abstract, and removed from daily clinical practice), may be able to be applied positively, as rational thinking and solid abstract theory grounding intelligent clinical practice. For this, the system will need to establish itself in a new appreciation of the original *telos* of the medical profession, the "good of the patient."[163]

Pellegrino has a specific framework and reasoning for the new focus on virtue in the medical profession. He states it in this way:

1) that virtue is an irreducible element in medical ethics,
2) that virtue ethics must be redefined to take into account the contributions of analytical, so-called quandary ethics,
3) that the virtues characteristic of the good physician are a fusion of general and special virtue ethics,
4) that, as in other professional and social roles, the virtues of medicine are derivable from the nature of medicine as a human activity,
5) that the derivation of the physician's virtues from the ends of medicine helps us to escape some of the difficulties inherent in a 'free-standing' virtue ethic,
6) that some link must be made between principle-, duty-, and virtue-based ethics, and
7) that some link must be made between moral philosophy and moral psychology, that is, between cognition of the good and motivation to do the good."[164]

Both in his book and in his article, Pellegrino goes on to list the virtues he feels are appropriate in the medical context. All the virtues, if practiced faithfully within that context, lend themselves to the building up of a trusting relationship between physicians and nurses and their patients. This trust is the basis for any healing, either on the physical or spiritual level, which may take place as a result of the medical relationship. The virtues upon which Pellegrino focuses are:

1) Fidelity to Trust and Promise, which stresses the "importance of trust to healing,"
2) Benevolence, which "intends the good of the patient,"
3) Effacement of self-interest, which seeks to avoid "exploitation of the patient" as a means to "advance the physician's power, prestige, profit, or pleasure,"
4) Compassion and Caring, by which the physician seeks to "adjust the treatment to the particularities of *this* patient's life story, time of life," and in which he or she exercises "concern, empathy, and consideration,"
5) Intellectual Honesty, by which a physician will admit the fact that he or she may need outside consultation for full understanding and treatment of a patient's condition,
6) Justice, both commutative, through which all are treated equally, taking into account "the specific needs of the patient, even if those needs do not fit the definition of what is strictly owed," and distributive, "whereby what is owed to others in a more distant relationship to the physician takes a lesser place," and
7) Prudence, through which a physician exercises practical wisdom, attempting always accurately to discern and assess a particular patient's true needs, as well as his or her unique situation.[165]

Again he refers to the four aspects of moral behavior (the agent, the act, the circumstances, and the consequences) illustrating how each intertwines with the others for full consideration of any ethical decision.[166] This reference is important for the linkage between the classical approaches and the modern approach to virtue ethics in medical practice. The focus lies with the moral agent acting within a certain context and directing his or her actions toward a specific goal or "end." The difficulty in attempting to formulate a "list" of virtues stems from the fact that the subject is a bit "untidy."[167] By this is meant that virtues "seem to invite a subjective arbitrariness into moral considerations that it has been the purpose of modern moral philosophy to avoid. Thus, the virtues have largely been treated as morally secondary to an ethics of obligation that emphasizes the centrality of rules and principles. The latter, it is assumed, are more likely candidates to ensure widespread agreement. Yet defenders of the stress on the virtues argue that rules and principles in fact involve the same kind of problems."[168]

Thomas Aquinas, in his recognition of the complexity which particular details bring to the decision-making process, stands close to the modern day ethicists in their attempt to synthesize centuries of ethical thought in a new approach. Today's field also considers the elements of personal narrative and lived experience, as well as the ever-evolving feminist concerns and multicultural applications as it seeks to integrate the principles first settled upon with the deepening approach inherent in spiritual concerns and the ethics of character. "The challenge becomes one of the interrelationships between a variety of theories, each illuminating important facets of moral judgment."[169]

SUMMARY

This study is being done from the standpoint of a faith-based approach to ethical behavior. Its Judaeo-Christian roots reach back into the depths of belief, to the Scriptural values which, from this standpoint, continue to call for a covenantal response within today's medical context. Furthermore, it considers the early ethical writings of Aristotle and Aquinas as the basis for the development and continued broadening of the field of biomedical ethics. Throughout history, the philosophical thought of serious thinkers has also provided a framework on which the modern bioethical field has developed.

Within every element of consideration, however, there has remained the person-in-context, the individual who—through his or her considered, deliberate, focused choices—acts as a moral agent. It comes down to the personal integrity of a given individual and his or her response within that context. Situating oneself in that particular context, then, if one keeps in mind the idea of "covenant fidelity," which in a medical milieu can be considered professional faithfulness, we might echo Bernard Häring's words: "Covenant fidelity is not merely a question of how to protect my individual freedom and my interests; rather, it is to realize how to respond faithfully to that freedom which organized society makes possible, and to bring my freedom home into it as expression of solidarity and justice, for the benefit of others."[170]

Whether or not one operates out of a specifically faith-based point of view, by calling on the ancients as well as the fathers and mothers of faith, modern practitioners can ground their professional behavior in solid values. From these values, experienced in their own deeply personal life histories and sets of circumstances, come the professionals who exhibit integrity, faithfulness, trustworthiness, and wisdom. Likewise, these same individuals, operating in the culture of the medical world, use their powers of discernment, assessment, and analysis to navigate wisely through the general principles of ethical behavior. These general principles go a long way toward establishing the specific standards of ethical medical practice in today's modern technologically expanding world.

A full synthesis of the development of biomedical ethics into the field as it stands today can be found in the myriad of books and articles in print. It is evident, however, that all ethical behavior eventually centers itself in the commitment of individuals within unique cultural, spiritual, political, and personal situations to the carrying out of the basic principles of medical care, one human being for another. Thus a reintegration of the initial focus on the character of those who practice in the medical field, as well as acknowledgment of the diverse points of view so well expressed in *A Matter of Principles: Ferment in U.S. Bioethics* will provide immense depth and breadth to this evolving field.

We will now proceed to yet another possible source of wisdom for health care practitioners—*Dark Night of the Soul* by St. John of the Cross. Spiritually sound individuals, well acquainted with the uncertainties and fears inherent in the practice of the healing arts, may discover in the work of St. John of the Cross a source of personal guidance as they seek to exercise covenant fidelity as moral agents in specifically medical contexts.

CHAPTER THREE

DARK NIGHT OF THE SOUL

This chapter contains an exploration of the person and work of St. John of the Cross, a sixteenth-century Spanish Carmelite friar whose reflections on his own mystical experience and spiritual journey are enjoying a renewal of public interest.[1] Several selected references provide the framework for this exploration, laying the groundwork for the application of John's insights, in a subsequent chapter, to the lives of today's healthcare practitioners. Modern American culture differs greatly from this mystic's sixteenth-century world, yet our spirituality, lived in the midst of modern technology with all its newly available choices, can gain much from a deep appreciation of and commitment to John's spiritual principles. What will be apparent in John's works considered here, *Ascent of Mount Carmel* and *Dark Night of the Soul*, is his deep commitment to a life lived for love of God and expressed outwardly in his care for others. Such an ideal can be a valued element of professional life in today's world. It can provide a personal spiritual grounding and focus for all of one's work. I will begin with a look at the world of St. John of the Cross, sixteenth-century Spain and the world of the Spanish mystics.

MYSTICISM

What is a mystic? A full exploration of this title begins in ancient times. The word itself is not found in the Bible.[2] The earliest accounts include Hellenistic mystery cults and religions existing long before the Christian era. Secret rituals, the essence of these cults, were available only to those initiated into the group.[3] These secrets concerned the material aspects of the rites and rituals, not the spiritual knowledge granted by a God far beyond the group.

The Greek verb *myo* meant "to close the eyes." Neo-Platonic philosophers used the word mystical to explain their own doctrines, "deliberately shutting the eyes to all external reality in order to obtain a secret, or mystical knowledge fostered by introverted contemplation. Withdrawing from everything external to sink within oneself allowed a person to receive inner, divine illuminations."[4] This definition evolved smoothly into its later development by Philo of Alexandria (20BC–AD50), who focused on the inner meaning of God's word. Harvey Egan states that Philo was probably the "bridge between the Jewish and Greek worlds," since his focus on Scripture interpreted allegorically is found in the works of the Fathers of the Church in subsequent centuries.[5]

More in the spirit of this study is a brief look at the contribution of Pseudo-Dionysius, a sixth-century Syrian monk who spoke of "knowing God through Divine Darkness."[6] To this scholar, the "unknowing"—consideration of what God was not—was the primary means of understanding the Being of God. Stated another way, "many Christians have been nourished by his beautiful cosmic sense and by his insights into the dark, silent, nondiscursive knowledge of God born in the darkness of the mind beyond all thoughts and concepts."[7]

For the Roman Church, the word *contemplation* was often chosen over *mysticism*. The use of the term *mystical theology* was understood as "the knowledge of God attained by direct, immediate, and ineffable contemplation," and "was distinguished from other types of theology (natural—knowledge of God obtained from creatures, and dogmatic—knowledge of God obtained from revelation) . . . the best of Christian tradition never reduced mysticism to the psychological level nor dissociated it from its biblical, liturgical, and sacramental basis."[8]

St. Bonaventure (1217–74) wrote that mystical theology was "the raising of the mind to God through the desire of love."[9] St. Teresa of Avila, a contemporary of St. John of the Cross, emphasized God's desire that the soul understand its complete inability to understand the things of God, a thought which blended with John's mention of the "secret wisdom" only available to the soul by God's infused love.[10]

Teresa's primary form of prayer was *kataphatic*, also known as *via affirmativa*, which "emphasizes the similarity that exists between God and creatures. Because God can be found in all things, the affirmative way recommends the use of concepts, images, and symbols as a way of contemplating God."[11] On the other side was *apophatic* prayer, also known as *via negativa*, which "emphasized the radical difference between God and creatures. God is best reached, therefore, by negation, forgetting, and unknowing, in a darkness of mind without the support of concepts, images, and symbols."[12] This sort of prayer more clearly applies to St. John of the Cross, as we will subsequently see, although elements of the *kataphatic* may certainly be detected in John's expression of his spiritual life in his care and concern for others.

As Egan illustrates, St. Teresa presents herself as "an impulsive person of expansive nature, enormous vitality, courage, humility, and a lively and nimble imagination . . . compared to an experienced mountain climber who never loses sight of the top, but who wants to show the person she is guiding the beautiful view from all levels of the ascent."[13] John, however, "may be compared to an experienced, yet uncompromising mountain climber who has been so impressed with the extraordinarily beautiful view from the top that he refuses to allow the ones he is guiding to look around or to rest until they reach that summit. For various reasons, John rejects systematically and unhesitatingly all secondary mystical phenomena."[14] As we will subsequently see, St. John did accept that at times the secondary phenomena were an important step in spiritual growth, though as a final focus or as goals to be sought in themselves they were to be rejected.

These authors focused on their own experience of union with God. They were fully aware of their human inadequacies, realizing that any knowledge came from outside themselves, lovingly infused by God. To them, grace and knowledge of God were "wholly God's gift." Though many of the mystics experienced outward manifestations (visions, locutions, levitations), Egan stresses, "Genuine mysticism is rarely showy and spectacular, as is too often assumed today."[15]

Any modern study of the mystics with a view to application in today's world must include the awareness of the difference between cultures. Because of the different societal influences, inventions, and knowledge not available to the people of that time, any application of spiritual disciplines and focus on the growth of the spiritual life needs to consider the heart and soul of the mystical life rather than the outer trappings. As William Johnston notes, "Mysticism is the core of authentic religious experience, and all are called to it."[16] For us today, then, it is possible to seek "the self-surrender required for authentic love in hectic, secular activity."[17] Noting the milieu in which John of the Cross lived, modern spiritual seekers may borrow elements of his thought and experience and seek a harmonious application in their own lives. Each spiritual seeker is as unique as John. Thus, each application will find its deepest roots in personal discernment and prayer.

Another mystic noted by Harvey Egan is Evelyn Underhill. She will perhaps resonate well with those of us in today's modern world as we consider John's teachings in our everyday lives, especially as we attempt to make ethical decisions. She stated, "Mysticism is no isolated vision, no fugitive glimpse of reality, but a complete system of life carrying its own guarantees and obligation."[18] She enumerated five aspects of authentic mysticism. For our purposes here, I will include them as an important basis for our application of the thought of St. John of the Cross. First, Underhill noted the "active and practical" features of the mystical life, which removes it from a merely theoretical aspect and places it squarely in the realm of changing who we are as praying people, not merely what we know. Second, she described mysticism as "a totally spiritual and transcendental activity," meaning by this that such a person relinquishes all desire to "control" the outside world. Rather, the goal is "giving, surrendering, and letting go." Third, she stated that love is the element which distinguishes mysticism "from all other transcendental theory and practice." This removes it from "transcendental social work, spiritual aesthetics, occult practices, philosophy, and magic." Fourth, she noted that a focus on the relationship of one's soul with God "redirects or kills all lesser relationships." For our purposes here, and in light of what we will see in John's work, her emphasis on "the divine Beloved as one to be loved, and not explored as some impersonal Absolute" is very important. Finally, she observed that the "authentic mystic is never selfish."[19] This is a quality very much evident in the life of St. John of the Cross.

Underhill's five elements of authentic mysticism speak to today's health care practitioners, because their field of practice has grown exceedingly complex. Within that field there is a vital need to choose a pattern of life which will keep one's priorities less ego-centered and focused on professional accomplishment than on the pattern of life grounding the soul in sound ethical choices. In a subsequent section, I will address some expressed concerns about the application of such an "ego-less" approach in today's health care setting, since competent professional behavior stems from appropriate use of all one's intellectual faculties and not a rejection of their validity in one's practice.

Egan's volume goes on to analyze the modern misconceptions about mysticism. Spiritual movements in recent decades have confused people with an array of practices taken from Eastern mysticism; unfortunately, many of them have served to make one's own ego the center of attention rather than God. Especially after the Enlightenment, proof of one's position on a scientific level took on major importance. Sadly, in the spiritual realm, this led to judgmentalism and inappropriate appraisal of others, leading not to a deep spirituality, but rather to a clinging to externals and condemnation of those not following the same practices. None of this was evident in St. John of the Cross, even under the strongest persecution from his contemporaries. We will now turn to a look at John's life.

JOHN OF THE CROSS: SIXTEENTH-CENTURY SPANISH MYSTIC

The character and works of St. John of the Cross came into new prominence with the fourth centenary year of his death in 1991. For this occasion a commemorative volume was compiled, including photographs, reflections, and extensive historical tracings of John's life journey. *God Speaks in the Night: The Life, Times, and Teaching of St. John of the Cross* provides thorough coverage and analysis of this newly rediscovered saint.

For the purposes of this study, I focus on the highlights of John's life, which began in poverty in 1542, John being the youngest of the three sons of Gonzalo de Yepes III and Catalina Alvarez. Gonzalo was the "administrator or accountant of a good silk business . . . in Toledo."[20] He had met Catalina, an orphan working as a silk weaver, on one of his trips to Fontiveros. He chose to marry her over the objections of his family, who saw her social status as less than complementary to Gonzalo's. The couple began their own weaving business and did well until Gonzalo died, leaving Catalina with three young children and in poverty. After a series of moves, to Toledo, Arévalo (Avila), and Medina del Campo—made in order to provide for her children—the little family finally settled in Medina, where they would remain. There, under the influence of the Jesuits, John received his education. Moreover, his experiences with his own family provided an important study of life itself, especially strengthening his facility for caring for the sick. This work was done at the Hospital of the Conception, or of *las bubas*.

This hospital, which had been founded as a medical haven for the treatment of those with contagious venereal diseases, grounded his innate compassion in the reality of day-to-day caring for the very ill, mostly terminal patients. Their disease, "so feared and widespread at the time, so in need of discreet attention,"[21] held much the same terror for people as the AIDS epidemic does for us today. The training John received there prepared his heart and soul for great hardship, and was one of the strongest elements in the development of his character.[22] John's gift of compassion for the sick carried through his own life, especially his religious life, where he became infirmarian and cared for his fellow friars. His education continued and his vocation grew during these early years. In the school run by the Jesuits, the well-rounded curriculum prepared the young man well for his future studies at the University.

John's Carmelite vocation began when he received the habit in 1563 in Medina. His novitiate year showed him to be a willing participant in community life.[23] Taking the name of Fray Juan de Santo Matía, he was professed in 1564 and went soon afterward to study in Salamanca. There, he "pursued his studies on a very different level. By reason of the subject matter, in Medina they consisted more of grammar and literature, and in Salamanca they centered on philosophical and theological thought."[24] Always, though, John considered his Carmelite vocation the center of his life. "In the midst of the community life, in itself elevated, the piety and penance of Fray John always stood out."[25] It was this total dedication to a life of prayer that was to lead John to consider joining a much stricter Order— the Carthusians.

His desire to live a life of contemplation suffered in the contemporary milieu of the Carmelites, since a certain laxity had developed in the living out of the Rule. Only his confiding of this thought to St. Teresa of Avila, whom he met in October 1567, turned that desire in a new direction. As she herself was planning the Reform of the Nuns, she enlisted John's help and asked him to join the movement as chaplain. For several years after this meeting, as he worked with St. Teresa, jealousies arose in certain of the Carmelite authorities toward John, and officials sought to have him removed, leading to his capture and imprisonment in a cell in Toledo from December 1577 until August of 1578.

His imprisonment was a time of total physical and mental deprivation. (A fully detailed account continues in Ruiz's commemorative volume.) Important to note is John's strong spirit and continuation of his ideals, even in the midst of the cruelty. "He experienced the greatest desolation imaginable: total solitude, both spiritual and human; fears of being poisoned, thinking that with every mouthful he might be swallowing death; undefined anxieties; insistent reproaches for hypocrisy and stubbornness of a kind that gradually do their damage."[26] All of these experiences gave John unutterable sorrow, but solidified in him a strong experience of the presence of God, which was later to be captured in his poetry and prose writings. Likewise, as one who knew John during this period of trial, Juan de Santa Maria, his second jailer, with whom John had forged a relationship, recalled the character of the saint in this way: "By observing him, I formed my idea of him. He was a very virtuous man, a person of great sanctity. He showed in the midst of the restraints placed on him great humility, fortitude, and magnanimity. Nothing that he had to endure caused him to show disquiet, distress, or affliction; rather, he manifested a great spirit of tolerance."[27]

One night, after completing a long-planned escape from his prison, John took refuge in the monastery of the discalced Carmelite nuns in Toledo, where he recovered. He regained enough strength to live out the final years of his life, until December 1591, in various settings where he not only participated in the Reform, but was able to enjoy time in beautiful natural settings as well as live the life of dedication and prayer he had so strongly sought.

SIXTEENTH-CENTURY SPAIN: LITERATURE AND MILIEU

A brief note about the cultural milieu in which John lived includes the observation that "St. John of the Cross lived the 49 years of his earthly existence in a particularly brilliant moment of Spanish history, the sixteenth century. . . . This period is commonly called 'the golden age,' on account of its exuberant vitality and valuable creations in those fields most representative of life: socio-political, cultural, and religious."[28] It was the high point for Castilian literature, but "what was most universally felt and cultivated throughout the century was the world of faith and spirituality. . . . There were longings for spiritual renewal; initiatives were taken on all levels, among the simple people, within organized and established groups, and as a necessity for any general Church reform. The preferred themes were recollection, evangelization, rites and ceremonies, asceticism, and mysticism."[29] Specific groups included the *alumbrados* (the illumined), comprising such groups as the *recogidos* (the recollected), who were often members of specific religious orders, and the *dejados* (the self-abandoned), who were often laity gathered around a "charismatic" individual.[30] Problems existed in these groups, most especially the belief that they had the "vision of the divine essence," which unfortunately led to a sense of presumptuousness on the part of those embracing such groups, and a proclaimed certainty about the possession of God's grace. These movements were soundly condemned by the Spanish Inquisition.[31]

THE SPANISH INQUISITION

The scope of this study will not allow for in-depth analysis of the men and methods of the Spanish Inquisition. An awareness of the parameters within which John of the Cross wrote provides insight into the structure and emphasis of his writings. The spirituality of the early sixteenth century had been greatly influenced by the work of Cardinal Francisco Ximénez de Cisneros (1436–1517).[32] A man who wielded great power as confessor to Queen Isabella, archbishop of Toledo, vice-regent of Spain, and inquisitor general, Cisneros opened the way for a fruitful expression of mystical gifts, especially within the Franciscan order. But he not only influenced the religious order; he commissioned Castilian translations of many of the ancient spiritual texts, thus giving the laity access to them.[33]

The movements previously mentioned (*alumbrados, recogidos*) were given support by Cisneros's work, as the laity was encouraged to pursue a disciplined spiritual life. Accusations began to flow against such groups, however, especially those claiming extraordinary visionary experiences. By speaking out against clerical privilege and the "trappings of the institutional church," the lay groups drew the ire of institutional authorities. Because spirituality had grown within the lay ranks, institutional officials established boundaries beyond which these laity were not to stray, especially the women whose own mystical experiences were not necessarily grounded in typical Scholastic philosophy.

Between 1519 and 1525 the Inquisition grilled members of these movements—spurred on also by the spirit of the Counter Reformation's fight against the rise of Protestantism—issuing their first edict in 1525. Within the ranks of the Inquisitioners were those known as *letrados*, persons who "understood religious faith as a matter of doctrine rather than of personal experience."[34] These men focused on any expression of unorthodox spirituality, attempting to stamp out all such questionable movements. Alongside the *letrados* were the *espirituales*, who relied more on their ideal of mystical prayer than on specific doctrines. These men "discouraged speculation on theological issues among the laity and suggested that the pursuit of virtue ought to be the main focus of their devotion."[35]

The Valdés Index of Prohibited Books, published in 1559 and revised in 1583–84, further illustrated the Inquisitional control over what was to be available to lay persons seeking development of their spirituality. Each addition to the publications of this group further removed the laity from official access to "suspicious" and "unorthodox" writings. "The encounter between the Inquisition and this group of dedicated Christians [*alumbrados*] was extremely important in the evolution of sixteenth-century spirituality, for it fed the authorities' growing suspicion of nearly *any* form of religious experience, particularly one that involved direct access to God."[36] Understanding the effect of the Inquisition on the mid-to-late sixteenth century enables today's reader to see John of the Cross as truly a man of his time, fully aware of the attitude of Church authorities toward mystical experiences and yet operating at the request of his own superiors to set down for his directees his own manner of prayer.

His highly poetic and mystical nature, in order to be acceptable to those in authority, had in some ways to be restrained, a necessity which could easily have thwarted his own creativity and insight. "The Valdés Index of 1559 interrupted this flourishing by making it difficult for both authors and publishers to produce books that put advanced spiritual techniques in the hands of the masses (though John specifically states he was not initially writing for the masses but rather for his own spiritual directees). According to Melquiades Andrés, the Valdés Index 'tried to banish affective spirituality in its various manifestations, encouraging the traditional spirituality of the practice of virtues and the destruction of vices over other ways of spirituality considered mystical.'"[37]

THE SPANISH MYSTICS: JOHN'S PLACE

Into this milieu came John of the Cross. His character itself was noteworthy. His demeanor was holy; his entire being spoke of him as a "free and energetic man." He was "kindhearted and understanding with others, sober and austere with himself," profoundly intelligent, well-educated, and ever joyful.[38] He also had the "soul of an artist," painting and carving many works, and loving both architecture and music as art forms, as well as creating dramas illustrating liturgical themes. But above all, in his own writings, he expressed his experience of God with warm, intense terms, especially in his *Spiritual Canticle*, which illustrated the experience of the imprisonment, surprisingly not written afterward, but during his months of isolation. His *Dark Night* was not composed until later.[39]

John was not the first of the Spanish mystics. One previous to John was Francisco de Osuna (1492–1540), who was, like John, a professed religious. He was among the early Spanish mystics whose writing was more concerned with "morality, rigorous practices, and maceration of the flesh than it was with speculative mystical thought aided by psychological observation and theological reflection."[40] He had no access to the translations of the German mystics such as Eckhart, Tauler, and Ruysbroeck, which were not completed until John's time. Their influence on John, who did have access to these masters, led to a mysticism whose "writings offer a peculiarity which is rather unusual in the history of mysticism. He did not simply write mystical treatises but first wrote poetical work of high quality which were then followed by treatises."[41]

John's commentaries were an extension and elaboration of his own mystical experiences. Because of his role as spiritual director, they were designed to provide "a systematic exploration of his mystical experiences regardless of the correspondence to the original mystical experiences . . . the distinction between mystical experience and mystical thought."[42] A core element of John's experience is his dedication to Christ. Though many interpreters have questioned the "Christ-motif" through the centuries, attributing more general interpretations to John's works, a close look at the writing itself illustrates plainly his awareness of the Christ-event and his realization that imitation of Christ's suffering and death were the path of the spiritual life.[43] John's own personal experience of condemnation by his fellow friars began with his belief that to "be condemned unjustly was the highest imitation of Christ which he could achieve on earth."[44]

John's poetry echoed the poetry of the Renaissance, but did not have as its basis the mythological images. Rather it was based in Scripture and in the Tradition of the Fathers of the Church, a fact which is clearly seen throughout his commentaries.[45] This devotion to the Church and John's faithfulness to tradition are what led one author to speak of John's work with the Reform as "submissive rebellion." At all times he remained dedicated to the Church and respectful of its authorities. It would seem that John's desire to share his own mystical experience, as well as his commitment to a return to the primitive observance of the Carmelite Rule, portrayed a man who wished not to bolt from his roots, but rather to serve as a humble guide on a path back to those roots, with special focus on his relationship with God.[46]

Thus, a view of John as a passive spiritual milquetoast who sank into a solitary oblivion in order to be with God, alone, devoid of all outer expressions of devotion is highly inadequate. John was far from passive. He worked diligently throughout his life to bring about his vision of true spirituality in the lives of the Carmelite friars and nuns. As teacher, he brought to his students reflections on his own profound spirituality. To this we will now turn.

ASCENT OF MOUNT CARMEL AND DARK NIGHT OF THE SOUL

As previously noted, the sixteenth century in Spain was a period of resurgence of interest in matters of spirituality. For John, his role as spiritual director was central. It was for this reason he composed his commentaries, *Ascent of Mount Carmel* and *Dark Night of the Soul*. His education had steeped him in studies of Aristotle, Augustine, and the Scholastic masters.[47] This is seen throughout his commentaries in myriad references to their works. Likewise, his grounding in Scripture is evident throughout his work, and in the works considered here, especially the poem *The Dark Night*, the imagery of the *Song of Songs* is quite evident, e.g. references to the "Beloved."

DARK NIGHT: THE POEM AND THE PURPOSE OF JOHN'S COMMENTARIES

Here, then, is the poem *Noche Oscura* ("The Dark Night"), included here in both Spanish and in translation, from *The Collected Works of St. John of the Cross*, translated by Kieran Kavanaugh, O.C.D., and Otilio Rodriguez, O.C.D. The poem itself is thought to have been written in 1578, the year after John's imprisonment. The commentaries were written in the years between 1582 and 1585.[48]

Canciones de el alma que se goza de haber llegado al alto
estado de la
perfección, que es la unión con Dios, por el camino de la
negación espiritual.

Songs of the soul that rejoices in having reached the high
state of
perfection, which is union with God, by the path of spiritual negation.

En una noche oscura,
con ansias, en amores inflamada,
¡oh dichosa ventura!
salí sin ser notada
estando ya mi casa sosegada.

One dark night,
fired with love's urgent longings
—ah, the sheer grace!—
I went out unseen,
my house being now all stilled.

A oscuras y segura,
por la secreta escala disfrazada,

¡oh dichosa ventura!
a oscuras ya mi casa sosegada.

In darkness, and secure,
by the secret ladder, disguised,
—ah, the sheer grace!—
in darkness and concealment,
my house being now all stilled.

En la noche dichosa,
en secreto, que nadie me veía,
ni yo miraba cosa,
sin otra luz y quía
sino la que en el corazón ardía.

On that glad night,
in secret, for no one saw me,
nor did I look at anything
with no other light or guide
than the one that burned in my heart.

Aquésta me guiaba
más cierto que la luz del mediodía,
adónde me esperaba
quien yo bien me sabía,
en parte donde nadie parecía.

This guided me
more surely than the light of noon
to where he was awaiting me
—him I knew so well—
there in a place where no one appeared.

¡Oh noche que guiaste!
¡Oh noche amable más que el alborada!
¡Oh noche que juntaste
Amado con amada,
amada en el Amado transformada!

O guiding night!
O night more lovely than the dawn!
O night that has united
the Lover with his beloved,
transforming the beloved in her Lover.

En mí pecho florido,
que entero para él solo se guardaba,
allí quedó dormido,
y yo le regalaba,
y el ventalle de cedros aire daba.

Upon my flowering breast,
which I kept wholly for him alone,
there he lay sleeping,
and I caressing him
there in a breeze from the fanning cedars.

El aire de la almena,
cuando yo sus cabellos esparcía,
con su mano serena
en mi cuello hería
y todos mis sentidos suspendía.

When the breeze blew from the turret,
as I parted his hair,
it wounded my neck
with its gentle hand,
suspending all my senses.

Quedéme y olvidéme,
el rostro recliné sobre el Amado,
cesó todo y dejéme,
dejando me cuidado
entre las azucenas olvidado.

I abandoned and forgot myself,
laying my face on my Beloved;

all things ceased; I went out from myself,
leaving my cares
forgotten among the lilies.[49]

John's poetic ability was nurtured in his earliest years at Medina del Campo. Although there are no extant records of the work he did during those years, observation of the poem *"The Dark Night"* shows that his works were grounded in Holy Scripture.[50] Not only John, but also St. Teresa of Avila, considered poetry an important way of celebrating the liturgical seasons, as well as other special occasions.[51] For John, then, the poetry became the expression of his inmost experience of God. "The commentaries on his three outstanding poems help us discern the theological and spiritual riches in the other poems that received no commentary. . . . The particular introductions to the commentaries on *The Spiritual Canticle*, *The Dark Night*, and *The Living Flame of Love* will deal with those three, the most resplendent of John's poems."[52]

Most of all, a study of *"The Dark Night"* reveals the symbolism inherent in the biblical *Song of Songs*. His education led to the self-analysis of the commentaries which contained several constant themes. There was, primarily, the soul's union with God; this union was grounded in the Trinity, with Jesus Christ, the "Word and the Beloved," as the focal point.[53] John's works were fully grounded in Scripture, in the works of Thomas Aquinas, and in elements of Augustine's works and the Neo-Platonic scholars. Calling upon Aristotle as well, it was apparent that John's scholarly background came into good use as he attempted to "explain" his poetry for his directees.[54]

Three levels of language are evident in John's work. First is his discourse, which was designed to convey systematic information to those for whom he was asked to write his commentaries. Second, there is the highly symbolic poetry. Third, there are what have been called the "primordial words," such as "Ah" and "Oh."[55] Being a product of the Scholastic school, John saw "the need for using a technical, reflective, critical knowledge obtained through reason."[56] In explaining the poetic expression of his mystical experience, John, being wary of a too-subjective interpretation and misuse of the images, knew that his commentaries were "complete in the sense that they preserve the poems from being misconstrued to mean anything else than they are meant to be in the mystical poems."[57]

What did this mean as people began to read the commentaries? For

John, the "poetry opens up the depth of his being to the very source where the symbol, the image, and the bubbling of the spring running underground are diffused together in the dark night of faith and in his own unconscious. Poetry makes use of emotive feelings expressed in a-rational terms. The Commentaries are meant to be a clarification of the obscure, a rationalization of the super-rational and a de-symbolizing of the symbolic."[58]

Here we are dealing with the intense mysticism of a man immersed in the historical milieu of the sixteenth century, steeped in the spirit of the poetry of the era. John's wariness for total trust in extraordinary experiences led him to compose the commentaries for those who might read his poetry and fly off into their own personal interpretations, totally missing what he was trying to convey. However, John's trust was not only in his own commentaries, but in the guidance of the Holy Spirit (*Ascent* II, 29:1; II, 29:6).[59] Within each human person there was the *capax Dei*, which was the capacity to receive all that God offered to the soul.[60] Again, this was a return to the studies of the Scholastics. Employing the terms of the Scholastic school, John spoke of the action of God taking place in the "substance of the soul," a description of the innermost regions of the human person. Into this "substance" the knowledge of contemplation was infused, and it was there that the deepest cleansing of human imperfection was to occur.[61]

John dealt with three types of contemplation. The first was called "philosophical" or "natural." This type of contemplation was familiar to both Christian and non-Christian philosophies and dealt with the rational or intellectual illumination—knowledge gained through human effort. The second was "acquired" or "active" contemplation, which was included in the religious realm, but not yet reaching the heights of mysticism. It was achievable by religious exercises, practices, and asceticism. Finally, there was "infused" or "passive" contemplation, which was the highest degree of contemplation, totally given by God and not dependent on human striving. It was God's gratuitous gift.[62]

As we continue into a more specific look at John's poem "The Dark Night" and the commentaries, *Ascent of Mount Carmel* and *Dark Night of the Soul*, more will be seen of John's use of the spiritual and philosophical elements in his attempt to translate the depth of his own spirituality for others. Like the Scholastics, at times it will be noted that he digresses into lengthy explanations and divisions of themes. In the end, his commentaries were incomplete. It is not known for certain why they are incomplete. Some theorize that John actually did complete them, but on the heels of his imprisonment he may have destroyed some of them, for fear of how they would be used against the Reform movement. Others have said that he did not have enough time to finish them because of his work and heavy schedule, and finally, others surmised that John did not feel that it was necessary, that what he had done was enough, and the rest was to be left to those who would read them.[63]

THE STRUCTURE OF *ASCENT* AND *DARK NIGHT*: MAJOR EMPHASES

"The *Ascent* provides a systematic presentation of both the theory and the practical norms governing the development of the spiritual life; it is a work of spiritual theology."[64] St. John of the Cross was thoroughly schooled in the thought of Aristotle, Augustine, and the Scholastics. His two commentaries on the poem "*The Dark Night*" were also filled with references to Scripture as well as to the scholars with whom he was so familiar.

> The *Ascent* comments only to the second stanza, and the *Dark Night* comments only to the third stanza. Two such commentaries based on the same stanzas would seem to be repetitious or similar; however, they are not so. This is because John's commentaries are not tied down to the letter but to the spirit of the poem: the spirit which originally created the poem. The mystical experience which John conveys in these two commentaries of the same poem stretches materially beyond the actual doctrinal content of the stanzas. This is because John's commentaries go beyond the limits of the stanzas themselves. John feels free from the limitations imposed by the letter of the poem.[65]

This explains why the incompleteness of the commentaries is perhaps a benefit. Nieto states, "The commentaries are arrows pointing the way, but the way has to be travelled alone by the mystic reader through his own experience. In this sense, a complete commentary to all the stanzas of all the poems would be a burden rather than a help, lead weights rather than wings."[66]

As Kavanaugh and Rodriguez have noted, the structure of *Ascent of Mount Carmel*, with all its divisions, categories, and delineations, was a demonstration of John's Scholastic training, and thus was the way he knew best to attempt to capsulize what was for him a most personal spiritual experience. His focus on the necessity for spiritual purification echoed Aristotle's thought that "two contraries cannot coexist in the same subject," as well as St. Paul's statement in the Letter to the Corinthians: "Quae conventio lucis ad tenebras?" (What conformity is there between light and darkness?).[67] In other words, John's goal was to provide for his directees a framework of spiritual growth that was solidly based in Scripture and the Tradition of the Church.

The images used in John's poetry and in the commentaries served much the same purpose as did parables for Jesus' disciples—they provided the learners with totally familiar images, thus bringing to life the reality behind the symbol. For example, John used the image of the contemplative as "a wet, green, dirty log thrown into a cleansing fire," saying that "as the log takes in the heat, it gives off noise, smoke, and odor. The more heated the log becomes, the less violent and more interior the purification. One's deepest, most subtle, spiritual imperfections require an intimate, subtle, spiritual suffering to produce complete transformation."[68]

It was this sort of inner transformation John was trying to convey through his elaborate commentaries. The poem itself was only eight stanzas. The overriding symbol was "night," which illustrated "John's natural experiences of night; the biblical and patristic tradition that notes the darkness in which God communicates with mortals; and the poet's own experience of darkness and abandonment in Toledo, representative of sensory and spiritual purification."[69] Further, the stanzas themselves show the spiritual journey. Stanzas one and two recall his nighttime escape from prison, stanzas three to five his memory of nighttime as a guide, and stanzas six through eight offer a reflection on the ultimate communion with God.[70]

For John, this ultimate communion was the final goal of the human spirit. The entire *Ascent of Mount Carmel* and *Dark Night of the Soul* combined to become themselves a light to John's students. One particularly apt image was that of a bird bound by a cord, which was to John a symbol of all the earthly attachments from which souls were to be detached (*Ascent* I, 2:4). "It makes no difference whether a bird is tied by a thin thread or by a cord. Even if it is tied by a thread, the bird will be held bound just as surely as if it were tied by a cord; that is, it will be impeded from flying as long as it does not break the thread."[71] The purpose of John's commentaries was to give a spiritual roadmap of the steps necessary for progress in the spiritual life. The bird and its binding cord, symbols of the souls of aspiring contemplatives, illustrated the dangers of allowing one's heart to be too attached to things, persons, and even to spiritual phenomena. The ultimate goal being total communion with God, such a "cord" could be a hindrance to complete union. John's reflections gave detailed instructions on how to proceed.

There were four specific divisions of the spiritual journey: 1) The Active Night of Sense, 2) The Active Night of Spirit, 3) The Passive Night of Sense, and 4) The Passive Night of Spirit.[72] The soul was divided, as with the ancients, into the superior, or spiritual, part (*Dark Night* II, 13:4) and the inferior, or sensitive, part (*Ascent* I, 1:2). In the superior part of the soul dwelt the faculties of will, memory, and understanding (*Dark Night* II, 21:11).[73] Here, both Aristotle and Plato came into play, in their "psychological anthropological" approach, wherein a human person on the journey toward God is purified in his or her very essence.

Since the most readily available is the sensitive part of the soul, John also divided it in the manner made prevalent by the Scholastics. The interior bodily senses were the imagination and the fantasy, through which humans formed thoughts, images, and forms. In these two faculties lay one's potential to use the intellective ability and to engage in "sensory meditation."[74] The five exterior bodily senses of sight, hearing, touch, taste, and smell had the potential to be the sources of many disordered appetites if followed indiscriminately.[75] John had the poetic ability to describe both beauty and "ugliness" in his work, employing the sensual imagery that distinguished sixteenth-century literature. Thus, in describing a soul in the throes of inordinate appetites, he said, "There is as much difference between the soul and other corporeal creatures as there is between a transparent liquid and the filthiest mire. . . . Strokes of soot would ruin a perfect and extraordinarily beautiful portrait, so too inordinate appetites defile and dirty the soul, in itself a perfect and extremely beautiful image of God (*Ascent* I, 9:1).[76]

John employed the Scholastic method of analysis, with numerous divisions and definitions. Kavanaugh lists these divisions, those of *Ascent* on pages 107 and 108 of his text, and those of *Dark Night* on page 357. It is obvious that in John's effort to explain for his directees the continuing journey inward toward God, he made use of many specific details and divisions. In the light of the close inspection given to writings of this period by the members of the Spanish Inquisition, perhaps he sought to make absolutely clear the points of spirituality he considered most vital. In this, he may have sought to avoid condemnation of his teachings by writing within the acceptable framework of his Church.[77]

John's own private communion with God could not adequately be contained even in such a massive use of words. But he believed in God's initiative as the starting point. "God moves each thing according to its mode" (*Ascent* II, 17:2).[78] Quoting Aquinas, he said, "As the Philosopher says: 'Whatever is received, is received according to the mode of the receiver'" (*Summa Theologica* I, 79, 6).[79] Finally, he again employed the homey image most readily held in the minds of his listeners in this way: "Rather, he gives according to each one's mode, as we have said. He is like a fountain from which people draw as much water as the jug they carry will hold. Sometimes he lets them draw water through these extraordinary spouts, but it does not follow that the desire to draw water in this way is lawful, for it belongs only to God to bestow water in this manner, when, how, and to whomever he wills, and for whatever reason he desires, and without any right on the part of the soul" (*Ascent* II, 21:2).[80]

Although it has been claimed that St. John wrote only for an "elite" audience, that is, the "some" who were already "somewhat detached from the world,"[81] he believed deeply that all had the potential for union with God, due to God's initiative in the matter. He stated that "every person has the potential for contemplation, because the 'pure light' that makes contemplation possible is always present. However, various obstacles and barriers prevent this simple light from being 'infused.'"[82] Personal imperfections could hinder the receptivity of souls. God's constant offer of grace remained to these imperfect, searching souls, however, whose hearts continued to experience the drawing of the Beloved even in the midst of their imperfections. This he attributed to this fact: "If a person is seeking God, his Beloved is seeking him much more" (*Living Flame of Love* III, 28).[83]

The four divisions of the journey, for John, were complementary. Much as the modern approach to death and dying of Elisabeth Kübler-Ross, which includes five stages of emotional involvement in the dying process.[84] John's four divisions are signposts for the progressive journey, and the active and passive elements "progress simultaneously."[85] That is, there are elements of each stage in the other stages, human beings progressing in their own way, as they are able, in response to God's initiative. The journey is not a straight line, but rather it takes twists and turns as each person internalizes the growth process in his or her own way. Like the stages of death and dying, we can learn much from a closer look at each of the four stages.

THE ACTIVE NIGHT OF SENSE

Addressed in Book I of *Ascent of Mount Carmel*, the Active Night of Sense is compared by John to the twilight hours, when "sensible objects begin to fade from sight."[86] This stage is appropriate for the "beginners" in the spiritual life, the first division of the three used by John to describe the spiritual journey. These traditional divisions are those of beginner, proficient, and perfect. Likewise, John also refers to the purgative, illuminative, and unitive ways of spiritual progress, as did Thomas Aquinas.[87] During the period of the Active Night of Sense, the aspiring contemplative may initiate practices designed to curb the appetites, both natural and voluntary, with the goal of eliminating all that stands between the soul and God.

We have previously noted that the same attitude is necessary for hospice and palliative care professionals as they seek to interact with their patients. Anything that stands in the way of openness and straightforward communication must be eliminated as much as possible from one's personal attitudes and outward demeanor. In the spiritual life, this comes by way of personal choice, the individual placing his or her relationship with God above all earthly emotional attachment.[88] John views one's growth toward relationship with God as "progressive interiorization,"[89] beginning with the recognition of one's own passions and attachments, an "active programme of ascesis [in which] there is a virtuous discipline of life of which the vigour of self-commitment to God is necessary for a deeper communion of prayer."[90]

Following Thomas Aquinas's division of the sensory appetite into two faculties, "the concupiscible and the irascible, John assigns three pairs of passions to the concupiscible power: love and hate, desire and aversion, joy and sadness. Similarly, there are three groups in the irascible faculty: hope and despair, fear and courage, and anger which has no opposite passion (*Summa Theologica* I–IIae, 23, 4)."[91] For John, the progression from love, through desire, and on to joy, and the progression from hatred, through aversion, and on to sadness, illustrate the common pathways of souls drawn to God. All the passions are similarly to be ultimately controlled by one's will under the guidance of love.

Ascent of Mount Carmel, in its entirety, addresses primarily this active aspect of the soul's journey to God. During the initial period of personal choice and deliberately elected disciplines, the soul, always in response to God-given grace, seeks to detach itself from all that prevents a total union with the Creator. During this time, mortification of the five external senses (sight, hearing, touch, taste, and smell) and of the four major passions in life (joy, hope, fear, and grief) cleanses the heart and soul of even the good things, since "over-attachment (even to conversation and friendship under the color of good) can prevent spiritual growth" (*Ascent* I, 11:5).[92] Basing this thought in his reverence for Christ's total submission to the will of the Father, John likens the effects of unbridled passions to "storms on the calm sea of the soul, depriving it of the peace of the Holy Spirit."[93] Discursive meditation is a primary method during this initial phase. Images derived from one's sense experience provide the substance of this meditation, although John consistently reminds the beginner not to become attached to any of the images themselves, but rather to concentrate on the life of Jesus. "Have a habitual desire to imitate Christ in all your deeds by bringing your life into conformity with His. You must then study His life in order to know how to imitate Him and behave in all events as He would" (*Ascent* I, 13:3).[94]

It should be noted that John does not counsel the complete disregard of the God-given passions. Rather, he appreciates the gift they are. "Many blessings flow when the four natural passions (joy, hope, fear, and sorrow) are in harmony and at peace."[95] His counsel is to leave the senses "as though in darkness, mortified and empty of that satisfaction."[96] Since the ultimate goal is complete union of the soul with God, a fruitless clinging to the satisfactions gained through sensual pleasures stands as a barrier to that union. John states, "Renounce and remain empty of any sensory satisfaction that is not purely for the honor and glory of God. Do this out of love for Jesus Christ" (*Ascent* I, 13:4).[97]

To John, the primary root of sin is the inordinate love of one's self, disordered passions being the sign of such inordinate love. The type of love of which John speaks in the first stanza of the poem "*The Dark Night*" is the love which is able to transform disordered passions and inordinate love into the love of God. "A more intense kindling of another, better love (love of the soul's Bridegroom) is necessary for the vanquishing of the appetites and the denial of this pleasure" (*Ascent* I, 14:2).[98]

John's awareness of the inner weakness of human souls comes from not only his own experience but from reference to the work of Thomas Aquinas (*Summa Theologica* I–IIae, 77) in which Thomas spoke of the three-fold concupiscence of humanity. Scriptural reference to the Letter of John (I John 2:16) also grounds this reference. The three-fold concupiscence, to be brought into order by dedication to God, was "inordinate love of the world, of the flesh, and pride of life."[99] It is to this end that John's thought turns as he advises the beginners to release everything, desiring nothing in itself, neither satisfactions, knowledge, possessions, or "being," in order to reach the ultimate satisfaction of union with God (*Ascent* I, 13:11–12).[100]

Out of the reflection on the first stanza of the poem, John begins the long commentary on his own experience, with the purpose of helping his directees take the first steps in their spiritual lives. Assuming that these souls were already committed to discovering their relationship with God, John also knows that the faithful practice of these outward mortifications of the senses, both interior and exterior, will draw his students toward the next step on the spiritual ladder, that of the Active Night of Spirit. He is not unaware of the emotional perils in this first stage, however, reminding these souls of the dangers of a "secret pride," which includes "spiritual greed and complacency, a desire to appear holy before others, to be the favorite of the confessor, and easy disturbance in seeing others praised.[101]

John's goal for the first stage of the ascent is the voluntary curbing of the senses and the passions. He distinguishes between the natural passions and the voluntary passions, comparing the desire for God with the desire for food. A hungry person has no choice but to be attracted to food, yet the choice belongs to him or her whether or not to overindulge in that food.[102] Likewise, persons possessing natural senses and passions, good in themselves, have the choice to follow them deliberately toward a voluntarily chosen goal, in this case the growth in their spirituality. The next stage of growth will call forth an ever-deepening commitment on their part.

THE ACTIVE NIGHT OF SPIRIT

The next phase of the spiritual journey begins with a cleansing of the intellect, requiring faith, of the memory, requiring hope, and of the will, moved by charity.[103] John's treatment of this stage includes the second and third books of *Ascent of Mount Carmel* and covers myriad divisions of the categories of knowledge, both natural and supernatural, in both corporeal and spiritual manifestations, as well as the sorts of goods which cause the passion of joy to be aroused. In this latter category, John continues his many divisions by focusing on the sorts of goods which fill a human heart with joy and gives his counsel on how best to disengage one's attachment from them for the glory of God alone. The goods John names are temporal, including riches, dignities, children, and relatives; natural, including beauty, intelligence, and talent; sensory, including the objects of the five senses and the imagination; moral, including the virtues, mercy, and the observance of law; and supernatural, including miracles, prophecy, and the gifts which benefit others, such as the gift of tongues, and healing.[104] To this category belong the aspects of spirit which include awareness of visions, revelations, locutions, and spiritual feelings of both corporeal and spiritual nature.[105]

Here it is that John launches an analysis of all that he deems worthy of both appreciation and release, all in the spirit of Christ's own emptying, but in which he "sets aside the procedure followed with the five preceding kinds of goods in which he dedicated three chapters to each. He now so multiplies subdivisions that he allows himself to enter a forest without exit."[106]

"The active night of the spirit consists in the willing and perfect rejection of all understanding, experience, feeling, imaginings, fantasizing, and even supernatural communications" (*Ascent* II, 1–5).[107] This again falls under the voluntary quality of self-discipline in the light of an ultimate goal. It engages the virtue of faith, which he calls the "secret ladder," indicating that all the steps of the spiritual life are hidden from both "the senses and the intellect."[108] John also considers faith to be the "only proximate and proportionate means to union with God."[109] For the spiritual aspirant, faith, completely stripped of all the natural and supernatural manifestations, "is a divine light, and it is rooted more firmly in the soul by means of darkness and spiritual poverty."[110]

Because of the active nature of this part of the journey, it lies within the capability of the soul to place itself willingly in this state. Having once employed discursive meditation in its spiritual quest, it may "learn to remain in God's presence with a loving attention and a tranquil intellect. . . . For little by little and very soon the divine calm and peace with a wondrous, sublime knowledge of God, enveloped in divine love, will be infused into their souls. . . . This is indeed what our Lord asks of us through David: *Vacate et videte quoniam ego sum Deus* [Ps. 46:11]" (*Ascent* II, 16:5)[111] To sit still and become aware of the presence of God, willingly and deliberately, is for John the primary step in understanding the road to union with God.

Not only in the intellect, but in the memory and will, the active night of spirit undergoes a profound cleansing. John calls this phase "midnight," where all is dark save for the occasional light of faith's belief in God's presence, even though it for the moment remains hidden. The cleansing of one's memory requires the virtue of hope, for to let go of one's past experiences necessitates a moving forward in hope toward yet another goal.

"The exercise of hope is itself the discovery and the expression of this new liberty, and John uses strong language to convey the vigour of the active night of spiritual hope."[112] To John this means placing the memory in a state of "forgetting," because the human soul in seeking to cling to prior graces prevents itself from moving forward to God. John stresses this point by saying that "union with God who is of his nature incomprehensible cannot be reached unless the memory 'rise above itself—that is, above all distinct knowledge and apprehensible possessions'" (*Ascent* III, 2:3)[113] John considers clinging to such apprehensible possessions a form of bondage which must be broken in order to climb higher in one's ascent to God.

Memory, to John, includes all remembrances, "the soul's capacity to store and recall a person's knowledge and life-experience."[114] John, not being one to disparage the blessings in God-given gifts, recognizes the benefit of certain memories. However, *Ascent* III provides, in fifteen chapters, continuous redirection of the positive recollection of one's life experiences to the active process of relinquishment of these very memories. The virtue of hope, then, willingly received from God by the soul having deliberately chosen this way of spirituality, provides the ability in this active night for that soul to let go of all "that is not God."[115]

John's path also includes voluntary remembrance, however. He states, "This knowledge may be remembered when it produces a good effect, not in order to retain it but to awaken the knowledge and love of God" (*Ascent* III, 14:2).[116] Again, this highlights John's foremost teaching that the ultimate goal is an unencumbered relationship with God.

The virtue of charity provides for John the motivation of the will itself. John addresses this aspect in the final chapters of *Ascent* III, where he teaches that the full consecration of one's will to God results in the "release of its full potential."[117] Chapters 16–45 illustrate the complexity of the divisions John employs in this task. Although he originally had mentioned four primary passions of the human spirit (joy, hope, fear, and grief), he covers fully only the first—joy.[118] He succeeds in making his point, however, that the control of this, as well as the other passions he does not consider in his analysis, must be set in order by the will, motivated by the charity originally bestowed by God, but ultimately returning toward God through the response of the aspiring soul. John states, "The strength of the soul comprises the faculties, passions, and appetites. All this strength is ruled by the will. When the will directs these faculties, passions, and appetites toward God, turning them away from all that is not God, the soul preserves its strength for God, and comes to love Him with all its might. . . . When these feelings are unbridled, they are the source of all the vices and imperfections, and when they are in order and composed they give rise to all the virtues" (*Ascent* III, 16:5).[119]

The multiple divisions of goods, dispositions, and God-given gifts, — in themselves worthy of human appreciation — continue through the many chapters devoted to teaching John's directees what they may experience, but what ultimately they must release from emotional attachment and move away from toward God. He remarks that the aspiring spirit experiences "liberty of spirit" is a sign that this stage of the journey has had a positive result.[120] A full appreciation of the goodness of the various experiences is possible, but that is subsequently to be released in favor of a "joyful, pleasant, chaste, pure, spiritual, glad, and loving knowledge of God" (*Ascent* III, 26:6).[121]

Having placed oneself willingly on the journey toward union with God, with the passions and appetites ordered under the command of one's reason,[122] the soul of the aspiring contemplative is free to continue its journey toward God. The next phase of John's commentary is the Passive Night of Sense, in which God takes over the initiative, cleansing the soul of further attachments and drawing it closer to ultimate union.

THE PASSIVE NIGHT OF SENSE

The soul, having engaged all its own capabilities to this point, now is asked to surrender its power totally to God for further transformation. John's analysis and the many chapters to this point have covered only the first two stanzas of his poem, those stanzas which end with the words "my house being now all stilled." He has taken the aspirant through the categories of passions and appetites which, if left unbridled, prevent ultimate union with God. Now, in the next sections of the commentary, he further instructs the searching soul in what he calls the "passive" night, of both sense and spirit.[123] The original work by John actually contained no formal divisions. In 1618, Diego de Salablanca introduced the edition which is still used today, in order to provide a more "manageable" work, since John had gone astray in his explanation from his original purpose of describing the poem.[124] He has at this time, however, reached the point of explaining what he himself believed to be the central aspect of inner transformation and direction toward God—the "dark night of purgative contemplation."[125]

For the passive purgation, the soul has disposed itself through the willing submission of its natural and voluntary passions and appetites to the power of God through a program of discipline freely chosen. Now John describes the continuation of the process of purification by the analogy of a mother who wishes to wean her child. "It should be known, then, that God nurtures and caresses the soul, after it has been resolutely converted to his service, like a loving mother who warms her child with the heat of her bosom, nurses it with good milk and tender food, and carries and caresses it in her arms. But as the child grows older, the mother withholds her caresses and hides her tender love; she rubs bitter aloes on her sweet breast and sets the child down from her arms, letting it walk on its own feet so that it may put aside the habits of childhood and grow accustomed to greater and more important things. The grace of God acts just as a loving mother by re-engendering in the soul new enthusiasm and fervor in the service of God" (*Dark Night* I, 1:2).[126] Note that the awareness of God's presence has not left the soul; rather, the willing release of transformative power to God has come from the soul's dependence on the grace always present to it throughout this purification process. But now the soul has reached the limits of its own ability and may even have followed certain disciplines in error, so now in surrendering to God it is enabled in its journey by a strength beyond itself.[127]

It is during this passive night of sense that the imperfections of the beginner are cleansed. These include pride, spiritual avarice, spiritual lust, anger, spiritual gluttony, envy, and sloth.[128] In the earlier stages of this journey toward contemplation, the soul was well aware of its own choice to surrender its intellectual gifts to something quite beyond them. "As in any kind of prayer, the ultimate initiative always belongs to God, but this grace is largely hidden below the threshold of consciousness. However, in this further grace of contemplation, the 'one act, general and pure,' is now *experienced as given* passively. The divine movement, which was previously a subliminal ontological reality, now wells up to become part of the person's conscious awareness in prayer."[129] In this way, the soul realizes that the process which began by the voluntary submission of the intellect, memory, and will to the transforming power of God's love is continuing without any effort of its own, and that it "originates quite perceptibly from the more interior realms of the spirit, the still hidden regions of divine indwelling, its effects spreading outwards to the senses."[130]

John gives three signs that indicate an aspiring contemplative is following a true path during this passive night of sense. In Chapter 9, John elaborates by saying that, first, the soul does not "get satisfaction from the things of God, nor from creatures either."[131] John describes this state as one of aridity and dryness. The first seven chapters having described the imperfections of beginning contemplatives in great detail, he demonstrates that all prior satisfactions are now at the stage where they give no joy to the soul, and thus there is the necessity of moving on in the spiritual quest, though not by the soul's own efforts. This state gives way to the second sign, which is the turning of the memory to God with the thought that somehow it has failed to serve God. It feels this because it now has a distaste for the things of God.

Finally, the soul experiences the third sign, when it finds it impossible to continue in its former method of prayer, through the interior senses of imagination and fantasy. These final two signs indicate that all previous sensible consolations are now useless to the spirit, and that God has stripped it of all satisfaction grounded in the interior and exterior senses. In this God steadily draws the soul closer to ultimate union.[132] The aridity itself is not, according to John, the cause of the deep afflictions of this stage; rather, it is the thought that somehow the soul has "gone astray" from its Beloved, and has been abandoned.[133]

John continues his commentary by encouraging the soul to stand firm at this stage and trust in God completely. He says, "All that is required of them here is freedom of soul, that they liberate themselves from the impediment and fatigue of ideas and thoughts, and care not about thinking and meditating. They must be content simply with a loving and peaceful attentiveness to God, and live without the concern, without the effort, and without the desire to taste or feel (God)" (*Dark Night* I, 10:4).[134]

Having entered into this stage of expectancy, the soul does then experience several benefits. In Chapters 12 and 13 John explains. First, he states that the soul comes to a greater knowledge of itself and its own misery, recognizing its own true status before God. This brings about an increased humility and submission to God, which leads the soul to a deeper love of its neighbor with a corresponding lack of judgment about that neighbor. Likewise, the soul becomes more obedient to the desires of God, more able to remain in a gentle remembrance of God, more faithful in the practice of the virtues, and a deep, holy fear of God as the Creator who is the source of all that is good.[135] It has achieved this state by the constant inflow of God's grace, and will remain in this state for as long as is necessary to purify it from all that will prevent its complete union with God in love and faithfulness. "In the measure of the degree of love to which God wishes to raise a soul, (he) humbles it with greater or less intensity, or for a longer or shorter period of time."[136]

Finally, it is important to note that John does not teach that the soul "becomes God" to the extent that it loses its own identity. Rather, "John insists . . . that the soul remains distinct from God in its natural being. In short, John's mysticism is one of differentiated unity in which two become one, yet remain two. This is an echo of what he says in *Ascent* II, 5, 7—the soul "becomes God by participation." However, to John, "Love has no meaning when either the lover or the beloved merges into the other."[137]

Going into the final division of the Dark Night, we see that the souls who have the perseverance at this point to continue (and for John these are very few), are now prepared to experience the depths of the love of God by a freely given offering of Self by the Creator. John notes that "there are very few who will endure the night and persevere in entering through this narrow gate and treading this constricted road that leads to life, as our Savior says [Mt. 7:14]" (*Dark Night* I, 11:4).[138] At this point we may now consider the Passive Night of Spirit.

THE PASSIVE NIGHT OF SPIRIT

During the passive night of the senses, there is a cleansing of vice from the soul of the aspirant, and the first steps are taken, leading from the meditative state to the contemplative state.[139] Now, as the soul enters the passive night of the spirit, it becomes what John calls a "proficient," and the final "radical" purgation may begin, under the complete control of God, the soul having willingly relinquished all effort of its own.[140]

There are twenty-five chapters in the second book of the *Dark Night* commentary, three of which deal with the afflictions in this part of the journey, and twenty-two of which deal with "the benefits of light and love that come to the soul."[141] Again, the commentary has covered only part of the original poem, and John's insights and divisions have become a tool of instruction for the aspiring contemplatives.

The afflictions of which John speaks concern the three faculties of intellect, will, and memory, much like *Ascent* and the first book of *Dark Night*. However, in this final division, John, in Chapter 10, brings out the image of the log of wood engulfed by fire. Here, he says, "Fire, when applied to wood, first dehumidifies it, dispelling all moisture and making it give off any water it contains. Then it gradually turns the wood black, makes it dark and ugly, and even causes it to emit a bad odor. By drying out the wood, the fire brings to light and expels all those ugly and dark accidents that are contrary to fire. Finally, by heating and enkindling it from without, the fire transforms the wood into itself and makes it as beautiful as itself. Once transformed, the wood no longer has any activity or passivity of its own. . . . It possesses the properties and performs the actions of fire: It is dry and it dries; it is hot and it gives off heat; it is brilliant and it illumines; it is also much lighter in weight than before. It is the fire that produces all these properties in the soul" (*Dark Night* II, 10:1).[142] Having undergone this transformation, the soul then finds itself "much more solitary than before, withdrawn more from externals and much more engulfed by the presence of God within itself" (*Dark Night* II, 17:6).[143]

This phase of the night "takes place in the inmost depths of the soul," and roots out the source of all the disordered passions and appetites in the "very substance of the soul."[144] John calls this a "secret wisdom," and likens it to a ladder of ten steps. It is secret, because it is totally given by God to the soul which has come this far in its spiritual quest, and it is a ladder in the sense that John uses an image common in his time—the ladder employed as a means of gaining entrance to a fortress "in order to plunder, know, and possess the goods and treasures, as . . . the soul ascends in order to plunder, know, and possess the goods and treasures of heaven" (*Dark Night* II, 18:1).[145]

John gives his ladder ten specific steps, traversing the terrain of the spiritual journey of increasing closeness to God (*Dark Night* II, 19–20).[146] These ten steps describe the effect on the soul of the drawing power of God's love. From initial stirrings of love felt deep within itself, the soul pushes forward unceasingly, even amid discouragements and fears that it has somehow failed, toward a union with its Beloved. This particular section of the *Dark Night* is filled with Scriptural references from the Psalms, Isaiah, the Song of Songs, describing the soul's determination and the power which draws it. John states, at the end of Chapter 20, "For love is like a fire that always rises upward as though longing to be engulfed in its center."[147]

John ties in his focus on faith, hope, and love with a further symbol—color. His soul in going out is "disguised," and wears a certain "livery," to disguise it from the power of "the devil."[148] The garments John describes are of three primary colors, signifying the theological virtues of faith, hope, and love. For faith, John employs the color white, which is for John the symbol of the blinding light of the intellect. It also serves to hide the soul from the wiles of the devil. The second color, green, symbolizes hope, which gives to the soul "courage and valor" and removes it from all desire for the earthly hopes in which it formerly placed its trust. This virtue protects the soul from "the world," and John likens it also to a helmet, which will protect the soul from the onslaught of the worldly pleasures. Finally, John uses the color red to signify the virtue of love, which he describes as "a precious red toga," covering all other garments and bringing the soul close to God. For John, love "makes the other virtues genuine, strengthens and invigorates them in order to fortify the soul, and bestows on them loveliness and charm so as to please the Beloved thereby. For without charity no virtue is pleasing to God" (*Dark Night* II, 21:1–10).[149]

Finally, John capsulizes the entire garment in a description which encompasses all that he has taught in the previous chapters:

> The colors are a most suitable preparation for union of the three faculties (intellect, memory, and will) with God. Faith darkens and empties the intellect of all its natural understanding and thereby prepares it for union with the divine wisdom. Hope empties and withdraws the memory from all creature possessions, for as St. Paul says, hope is for that which is not possessed [Rom. 8:24]. It withdraws the memory from what can be possessed and fixes it on what it hopes for . . . Charity also empties and annihilates the affections and appetites of the will of whatever is not God and centers them on (him) alone. . . . Because these virtues have the function of withdrawing the soul from all that is less than God, they consequently have the mission of joining it with God (*Dark Night* II, 21:11).[150]

John attributes this entire journey to the "sheer grace" of God. Now that the soul has experienced the intense love of God, it feels the desire to act virtuously for the sake of God, rather than for the earthly satisfactions and honors which may have motivated it before it embarked on this spiritual journey. We will subsequently consider the virtues which flow from one who has undergone such a purgation of "self."

Natural Human Passions—Acceptable or To Be Negated?

The modern world may not feel comfortable with the idea of negating all the natural human passions which flow from an appreciation of ourselves as embodied spirits. Natural passions, emotions, the body as God-given gift, expression of pleasure and the union of one sex with another—all these play a vital part in our understanding of ourselves as "whole" persons. But does St. John of the Cross demand that we relinquish our appreciation of these human factors? He has been accused of being a "neo-platonic dualist."[151] But John's divisions are not dualistic in a negative sense. Rather, he is fully aware of the giftedness of the human senses, the internal and external senses as he calls them, as part of the soul, the *alma*, in the Hebrew sense of the wholeness of the person, with both spiritual and sensory aspects.[152] John believes in the fundamental unity of the human person, all aspects of which are to be brought into harmony as the soul strives toward God. Nevertheless, scholars have sometimes interpreted John's writings "in a rather ethereal, disembodied fashion."[153]

To be realistic, modern health care practitioners may very well not be patient with a theory which suggests that they must deny significant portions of their human nature, particularly with regard to natural human pleasures and enjoyments. A full understanding of the work of John of the Cross will show that "the fear many in the Christian churches have of body, passion, and love has, in fact, led them to misinterpret St. John's view of love. They have made it 'something ethereal,' 'purely spiritual,' and therefore disembodied or disincarnated."[154] An initial reading of *Ascent of Mount Carmel* and *Dark Night of the Soul* may convey such a view—in that John appears to withdraw from all sensual pleasures. But a closer study will show that John in no way negates the natural human passions and pleasures. Rather, and this can be seen more vividly in his works *The Spiritual Canticle* and *The Living Flame of Love*, he employs imagery such as is used in the Bible's *Song of Songs*. The transformation of human passions in the fire of the love of God is John's goal. Richard Hardy writes,

> This transformation, John tells us, is accomplished ". . . through love in *this* life." The source of any life is love. To love makes one live in a fully human way. Furthermore, human beings live where they love, says John, and once transformed, they love God radically and most naturally (*Canticle*, 8, 3).
> . . . The *whole* person is involved. According to St. John of the Cross, this is so totally an incarnated love—and hence life—in God that all the elements of human nature are brought into harmony, body and soul, sense and spirit.[155]

Again we see that John emphasizes the difference between "what *is* and what *is desired.*"[156] His focus is on the inordinate passions, the disorder which ensues as a human being replaces desire for God with desire for what is not God. Acceptance of what is naturally beautiful, God-given, and to be enjoyed also entails an acceptance that these gifts, treasured as they are, are not our ultimate goal. This is the point where John calls for total surrender. "To truly accomplish such a surrender requires incredible strength, and an integration of the whole human person and personality. . . . No one can produce this total integration by his or her own unaided efforts. John clearly informs us that *God* causes this personal wholeness, so that persons can indeed give all they are unreservedly to God. Such a surrender is a graced human act."[157]

St. John's later works, *The Spiritual Canticle* and *The Living Flame of Love* demonstrate the flowery image of the sixteenth-century Spanish literary world. John describes a God who delights in creation. "John portrays God and the human person as lovers who delight in each other and interact with real joy."[158]

> God relishes this relationship with human beings, even if John cannot adequately describe or define how we experience it. Perhaps a certain fear or hesitation of ascribing passion and delight to God has kept us from understanding and expressing the intimacy of the relationship God desires and in fact establishes with human beings. John is not afraid to celebrate it in prose and poetry, even though he lived in a time when it was sometimes dangerous to state such things under the suspicious eye of the Inquisition. Such courage is one more reason to take seriously what he says about the presence of joy, delight and pleasure in God.[159]

For modern practitioners seeking a realistic spirituality for themselves in today's medical milieu, an appreciation of the body as gift, and of human emotions and passions as expressions of that gift, is significant. An awareness of the effect on one's own psyche of an inappropriate emotional investment in these gifts (known to John as the disordered passions) will be the product of a sincere process of spiritual discernment. Within such a framework, it will be possible for modern practitioners to integrate John's spiritual counsels in a realistic professional practice, remaining psychologically healthy in the process. That being said, we may address John's treatment of our intellectual capacity in the light of our modern medical milieu.

DOES JOHN NEGATE OUR NATURAL INTELLECT?

A brief digression from consideration of the virtues as expressions of a contemplative soul seems appropriate at this point, as we consider the realistic application of the principles of St. John in today's health care settings.

The modern medical milieu may be one of the most difficult arenas in which to apply the teachings of St. John of the Cross. Some of the most critical objections to John's work throughout the centuries since it was written have centered on the "negativity" toward human faculties seemingly emphasized in his works. This would appear to be innately opposed to the highly detailed, technically complex situations in which practitioners apply their intellectual gifts. Why would anyone wish to lay aside innate mental gifts, to negate them, in order to "float" in an atmosphere totally devoid of the scientific certainty on which medical progress and treatment thrive? And does John himself totally negate our intellectual gifts, our "ego," as we understand it?

Especially in the Western spiritualities, there was a higher incidence of "proofs" of God's existence in the past.[160] Recently, though, a greater emphasis on "experience" has resurfaced, bringing about the thought that somehow the former emphasis on "rational" proofs had somehow failed.[161] But it may also indicate a general awareness that those former "proofs" were not enough, and that a combination of abstract proofs and human experience will provide a fuller understanding of what we are able to express of our human relationship to God.

Early reactions to John's work included statements that he was "unnatural and quietistic," a "nihilist," "a-cosmic," a "horrible ascetic," and exhibited a "complete subservience to Church tradition and authority."[162] On first glance, all these attributes might seem to be true. We have already noted the historical atmosphere within which John wrote. Caution was essential with the eyes of the Inquisition constantly searching for the "unorthodox." As well, John was not just an emotionally driven man completely without theological and philosophical training. His educational background included in-depth Scholastic training, and he was known by his contemporaries as "a first rate scholar."[163] Within the strict boundaries of what was allowed by the Spanish Inquisition, John sought to teach his students how to live a spiritual life, based on the sound spiritual teachings of those who had come before him.

One of the main arguments against the work of John was that he had fallen into a "neo-platonic dualism," soundly condemning the body as evil. Further analysis of this accusation reveals that John did not condemn the body as evil. Rather, he extolled it as God's gift to us, but was very aware that inordinate attachment to it was a hindrance to ultimate union with God. Following along with this was John's view of the "soul" of a person in its wholeness, with both sensory and spiritual parts. The body and its senses were the sensory; the intellect, memory, and will the spiritual.[164] John believed in the fundamental unity of the "person," but his spirituality grew out of an understanding of the fallenness of our human nature since the original sin.[165] What concerns John is not human intellect in itself, but rather humanity's relation to all of creation in light of its "perverted" will. Herein lies "John's fundamental pessimism."[166]

So where does John fit into a modern medical milieu, if all intellect and ego is to be "rejected?" To understand the possibility, it is necessary to see beyond what initially appears to be rejection but on further exploration is John's putting all created things in their proper perspective in relation to God.

John considers the intellect a spiritual faculty, deeply intertwined with the memory and will of human beings.[167] These faculties are dependent on one another, each being unable to receive information from the sensory part of the soul without its companion faculties (See *Ascent* I, 8:2; III, 1:1). John's four-stage growth in the spiritual life culminates in the Passive Night of the Spirit, where all natural human capacities are totally released to the power of God's Spirit working within the soul. The active intellect and passive intellect are vital elements of human understanding. Following St. Thomas's statement (*Summa Theologica* I, 79, 3 ad 1) where he states that the "intellectual part is something both active and passive," John goes on to say that as necessary as the active intellect is in forming specific concepts for us, somewhat clarifying what our original sense perceptions convey to it, the passive intellect is our "capacity" to grow in knowledge.

He qualifies this, however, by stating that the "intellect cannot profit from natural knowledge, which is always disproportionate to God" in an ultimate sense.[168] Here Payne refers to *Ascent* II, 8, 2–6; II, 3, 2–4; II, 4, 4; II, 12, 4–5; II, 16, 3–9; and III, 12, 1. In *Ascent* II, 8, 4, John reminds his students that "nothing here can be a proximate means to union with

God," and urges that the intellect be divested of all "particular knowl-edge."[169] This is not to say that one discounts this knowledge as not valid:

> The emphasis on emptying the intellect of "clear and distinct concepts" is based on the assumption that, in mystical union, God takes on the role played by the active intellect in ordi-nary knowledge, and "informs" the possible intellect directly, producing an obscure apprehension or "knowledge of the Di-vine." And just as a piece of clay cannot be molded into a new shape (e.g. that of a statue) until the old shape (e.g. that of a bowl) is destroyed, so too the possible intellect cannot receive the divine "form" conveyed in mystical experience until the "forms and intelligible species" of creatures are ex-pelled.[170]

The "possible intellect" here indicates the potential of all human beings to grow in further knowledge of God through the infusion of the God-given grace of understanding. In *Ascent* II, 3, 1 there is a reference to John's view that "while the intellect by its own power extends itself only to natural knowledge, it has a potency for the supernatural whenever Our Lord wishes to raise it to a supernatural act."[171]

Some scholars today have referred to John's methods as "anti-tech-nique."[172] We have seen previously how John encourages even proficients to return at times, if need be, to previously practiced techniques in order to get themselves back on track in their spiritual lives. What John employs is "the rejection of (man's) reliance on (his) own mental or emotional abilities to reach mystical union—to rely on the divine darkness, the divine force of love, the divine intelligence, in the practice of dark faith."[173] John's belief was in God's ultimate desire to communicate with humanity in the depths of the human soul. "The point which John of the Cross seems to want to make is that the final goal is beyond any technique, and to attain such a goal one has to go a way which leaves all technique behind in the end. The technique itself should never become that goal" (See *Ascent* I, 1:14).[174]

John's emphasis on the stripping away of all inordinate ego-attach-ments lay in his belief that "while the intellect is single-mindedly preoccu-pied with creatures it is unreceptive to the 'obscure knowledge' of God, and that while God is active all other thoughts are banished" (See *Ascent* II, 14:11–12; II, 15:3; II, 16:11).[175] Thus, when John states:

Those united with God in contemplation are divested of all "particular concepts" and "distinct knowledge" he does not mean that they lose their understanding of mathematics, for example, or their ability to swim, to distinguish colors, or to do philosophy. John does not advocate an inhuman suppression of our natural cognitive powers, nor the pursuit of ignorance or amnesia. His point is rather that during the period of intense mystical union itself, mystics "cannot actually advert to any other thing (*Spiritual Canticle* 26, 17)" because their intellects are being informed by God and are therefore not receptive to being actually informed by the species of creatures. Put in more contemporary terms, this means that during such moments mystics are unable to exercise their ordinary concepts of material objects. But they retain their "acquired knowledge" and are free to use it again once the effect of this union passes (*Spiritual Canticle* 26, 16).[176]

These considerations address the fact that "John does not require the annihilation of reason, but only the recognition that what the mystic receives in contemplation cannot be attained by our unaided rational powers."[177]

I have included this section specifically to address the difficulty that some in the modern health care field may have with the idea of releasing all intellectual knowledge, or even the expression of their own egos within a professional situation. There is an important element here which must be addressed. This is the realization within today's scientific milieu that intellectual knowledge *is* important, is a vital element in the administration of proper health care procedures, and is to be respected and employed. To provide adequate health care we cannot ignore the scientific reality, much less forego a professional application of it. Nevertheless, especially in a hospice situation, where often the major application of medical techniques has finally been suspended in the face of certain death, it becomes apparent to physicians and nurses that a reliance on "techniques" does not ultimately cure, or even physically heal a patient. It would seem that many futile medical situations have been made that much more emotionally exhausting and painful by continued use, perhaps in university hospital situations, of "state-of-the-art" treatments, which may hold no true benefit for some patients. To cling futilely to such methods of treatment brings about the sorts of emotional traumas already noted in our overview of John's work. Where externals and "consolations" are inordinately grasped, there ultimately occurs tremendous emotional stress and sadness, especially with a terminal illness.

Health care practitioners are often caught in the middle of such emotional trauma. They may also have a need to be perceived as "successful," in the sense that techniques have "saved" their patients. Only by competently using their skills, God-given talents, or natural abilities, yet accepting the limitations of those very skills, will practitioners allow themselves to suspend futile techniques and practices. These by their nature as human activity cannot be the ultimate answer for the spiritual part of a person. St. John, had he access to such techniques, would most likely have used them in his care for others, but his spiritual nature may well have recognized the limits of their application in specific situations. His focus was on the ultimate spiritual union of the spiritual substance of the soul with its source and Creator. For practitioners, the essence of their discernment process may be a fine-tuned sense of balance between a professionally executed technical task—bolstered by mental application of learned skills— and a sense of when ultimate reliance on such tasks needs to be released.

What then may health care practitioners see in themselves as they attempt to modify their total ego-dependence on externals and proceed on the spiritual path of "release?" We have already seen that, according to John, steeped as he was in the demanding era of the Inquisition, a fruitful spiritual life not only contained elements of personal discipline (also necessary in today's modern health care settings) but also the practice of the virtues of the Christian life. These elements remain important to practitioners in today's medical settings, and as each person develops his or her own spiritual practices, certain virtues will be seen to develop naturally. To these we may now turn.

VIRTUE AS AN EXPRESSION OF THE CONTEMPLATIVE SOUL

The soul's journey has been described as "a trial, a way, and a result."[178] This description occurs in the second book of *Dark Night*. As a trial, it is described in Chapters 4–8, as a way, in Chapter 16, and as a result, in Chapters 9–13.[179] The result of this ultimate purification—of the intellect, the memory, and the will—is the total reliance of the soul on the power it has now discovered in its very "substance." It is here in this depth that our "faculties," our "various capacities for personal action and initiative" lie, and it is here, in the "ground of our personal being," that the strength for our "reflective knowledge and deliberate action" lie.[180] It follows that, after this purification, the soul will not only live out the infused theological virtues of faith, hope, and love, but will also express outwardly the other virtues which are grounded in these three basic virtues.

But the stance which the soul takes now is not one that is full of its own powers. Rather, the soul now holds itself "in emptiness and attentive receptivity to God's dark presence."[181] Initially, the soul's faculties of intellect, memory, and will might have been based in the thought that, of itself, these faculties were possessed. After the realization that all is "gift," however, the soul's faculties are seen to be their own opposites. "These three virtues all cause emptiness in the faculties: faith in the intellect causes an emptiness and darkness with respect to understanding; hope in the memory causes emptiness of all possessions; and charity causes emptiness in the will and detachment from all affection and from rejoicing in all that is not God" (*Ascent* II, 6:2).[182]

Likewise, the soul having realized that the virtues of faith, hope, and love are "infused," totally God-given, it also realizes the difference between these virtues and those which are naturally acquired, perfected through faithful practice.[183] Because of its intense period of purification, the soul's focus has now changed. Rather than performing virtuous acts for the personal satisfaction gained, it will "practice the virtues, do works of mercy, obey the commandments, and exercise good manners for the love of God and not for the joy these moral goods contain in themselves."[184] John does not totally dismiss the appreciation of these moral goods, but he encourages moving beyond them to the appreciation of the ultimate source of all human moral action. He calls for the soul's detachment from human satisfaction. He states: "But even for the first reason (for what they are in themselves), moral goods merit some rejoicing by their possessor. For they bring along with them peace, tranquility, a right and ordered use of reason, and actions resulting from mature deliberation. Humanly speaking, a person cannot have any nobler possession in this life" (*Ascent* III, 27:2).[185]

Thus, though John does emphasize the spiritual detachment which ultimately flows from the experience of the dark night, there is within his work, especially the works following *Ascent* and *Dark Night*, "a genuine incarnational, sacramental spirituality and mysticism [which] demand both an acceptance of the symbol of God's presence and passing beyond it to the ever-greater God. . . . To cling to the symbol too long is to idolize what should be a means to the ever-greater God."[186]

John, throughout his commentaries, mentions the effect of the "devil" upon the aspiring soul. Mainly, this effect is one of disorder and distraction, "presumption and pride." To the true contemplative, as the soul passes out of the influence of the devil, comes what John calls a "holy fear," which to John is the "key to and guardian of all the virtues."[187] Experiencing the passive darkness, and having been made willing by the passage through the active darkness and the disposition of itself to God's influence, the soul now "advances rapidly, because it thus gains the virtues."[188] The quality of humility becomes deeply imbedded in this soul through the grace of God. "Even a genuine contemplative will at times cling to the gifts instead of to God."[189]

To pass beyond this human quality, humbled by the realization that one's own powers have been totally surrendered to the power of God, the soul is enabled by this grace to release those God-given gifts humbly and peacefully. Virtues spring naturally from such a soul, and the practice of virtues becomes not a burden, but a cherished goal. Within a community, such a soul undergoes "not an *un*conditioning or *de*conditioning of consciousness, but rather . . . a *re*conditioning of consciousness . . . "[190] In other words, the soul experiences a new awareness and a return to qualities within itself which might previously have remained hidden under the veneer of socially acquired preconceptions of what is good. John states this thought in this way: "Souls are misled by understanding God's locutions and revelations according to the letter, according to the outer rind. As has been explained, God's chief objective in conferring these revelations is to express and impart the spirit that is enclosed within the outer rind. This spirit is difficult to understand, much richer and more plentiful, very extraordinary and far beyond the boundaries of the letter" (*Ascent* II, 19:5).[191] The soul's "outer rind," when intellect, memory, and will are transformed in the experience of night, will be peeled away, unmasking its innermost depths. It is there that the soul discovers the virtues, along with the strength to carry them out. But after the transformation in the dark night, the soul is aware that such strength comes not from itself, but from God.

MODERN AUTHORS

The application of the teachings of St. John of the Cross in recent generations has occurred because of the work of spiritual teachers and guides who incorporated his insights into their own lives. The scope of this study does not include the full array of these scholars, although Evelyn Underhill's work on mysticism has been previously mentioned, as several others will be in subsequent chapters. Here, special mention of Thomas Merton (Father Louis), a twentieth-century Trappist monk who wrote extensively on the spiritual life with special emphasis on the dark night of the soul, should be made.

Merton, who lived from 1915 to 1968, speaks to contemporary people in a most practical way. He brings the idea of contemplative prayer, too long relegated to those entirely dedicated to a formal, vowed religious life, into the realm of modern individuals in the midst of their daily lives. Through the centuries, there have been a multitude of approaches to the spiritual life which attempted an appeal to the masses. "Unfortunately, the popular, contemporary misunderstandings of mysticism are greatly at odds with (many) of the definitions, descriptions, and characteristics of authentic Christian mysticism. For example, many today identify mysticism with ir-rationalism, vague speculation, otherworldliness, dreaminess, or a lack of practicality in dealing with daily living. Others incorrectly associate it with parapsychological phenomena, theosophy, the occult, magic, witchcraft, and demonology."[192] Likewise, other approaches to mysticism include a view of it as "moments of ecstatic rapture, or 'peak experiences' triggered by music, poetic inspiration, nature, lovemaking, psychedelic drugs, prayer, giving birth . . . repressed eroticism, deviant behavior, madness, psycho-logical regression, biological and psychological pathology, or a variety of 'altered states of consciousness.'"[193]

Because of these recent emphases, the Christian element of mys-ticism is far too often lost for those seeking deeper spiritual lives. Impor-tantly, a view of the writings of the Christian mystics shows that "the Christian mystic claims to experience an immediate contact with God as Beloved that eventually dominates his entire life and being. Christian mys-ticism is the palpable loving union of the mystic with the God of truth and love. The felt presence of a loving union with this God purifies, illuminates, and eventually transforms the mystic into truth and love themselves."[194]

Merton wrote in the spirit of St. John of the Cross's apophatic tra-dition. Not only did he include his life experiences, especially the process of his own conversion, in his work, but he spoke of "darkness, radical emptiness, and the desert experience."[195] Important for the modern reader, steeped in the pluralism of today's society, Merton's writings include con-siderations of "the scriptures, the Fathers of the Church, the Desert Fathers, the great Christian mystics, the Russian Orthodox mystics, contemporary Catholic and Protestant theology, modern psychology, art, poetry, literature, existentialism, Taoism, and Buddhism with an incredible sensitivity for how all this bears on civil rights, racial discrimination, the peace movement, nuclear disarmament, social justice, urban violence, poverty, ecumenism, and the East-West dialogue."[196]

A study of the spirituality of modern individuals finds in the works of Thomas Merton an approachable synthesis of the basic elements of the works of St. John of the Cross. Because of Merton's immense writing talent, he conveys the principles of the search for God in a way that is accessible to the minds and hearts of modern men and women in various walks of life. For those who might find the writings of St. John a bit too distant from their own experience, the work of Thomas Merton provides a bridge to understanding the ideals and practices of which St. John so strongly spoke. Not only does Merton believe that each soul has within it a natural inclination toward God, but he teaches that each soul must undergo a complete recentering of itself around God.[197]

This process, says Merton, is neither easy nor quick. To enter into this process, it is necessary to experience "radical silence, detachment, and humility."[198] Merton's methods of reordering the human spirit toward God include the inner aspects of "attitude and outlook, faith, hope, love, trust, joy, openness, attentiveness, expectation, reverence, and supplication."[199] Like St. John, Merton recognizes that the deepest part of the soul undergoes this transformation, far from the surface elements or various religious engagements. But above all, he "emphasizes the arid and dark side of the purifying, illuminating, and transforming contemplative experience of the God of truth and love. Firmly rooted in the apophatic tradition, Merton focuses upon mystical contemplation as essentially a self-emptying activity that fills one with God."[200]

Today's spiritual searcher may consult the works of Thomas Merton for further insight into his integration of the spirituality of the dark night into the modern milieu. His inclusion of the reality of each person's transformation in a dark night of the soul experience illumines what St. John taught in his own commentaries. Merton has a deep appreciation of the purifying elements of spiritual darkness, and urges aspiring contemplatives to trust in the transformative power of God in the deepest part of their being. Like John, Merton teaches that the soul, in its search, remains distinct in its loving relationship with God, completely itself, completely "identified with God in love and freedom, but . . . metaphysically distinct from God."[201] For today's searchers, who often strive to "find themselves," retaining their own identities while still being able to be connected in the ultimate spiritual union with God is an important element in their quest for

an authentic spiritual life. This is especially true with the scientific emphasis so prevalent today, and will have a strong bearing on how health care
practitioners integrate such a spiritual search in their own professions.

WOMEN, SPIRITUALITY, AND HEALTH CARE

One final consideration remains before we conclude our overview
of St. John of the Cross and move into how his work may be applied in
today's medical milieu. This is the view of women's spirituality prevalent
throughout history. Again, a full analysis is not possible within the scope
of this study, but there remain traces of early attitudes toward the ability of
women truly to serve as examples of valid spirituality. Some of these traces
extend into today's professional world. Some are subtle; some are not so
subtle. But there will be questions posed which may need to be addressed.

The twentieth century has shown a tremendous awakening toward
the situation of women in the professions. But these concerns have not been
new, in the sense that women throughout history have struggled to have
their strengths acknowledged as definitively as men's exploits have been.
As far as theological and spiritual concerns go, there has been the long battle to overcome the story of Adam and Eve, where the woman is seen by
some as the one to blame for the downfall of her partner and thus the entire
human race. Anne Carr, in *Transforming Grace: Christian Tradition and
Women's Experience*, reminds us,

> Feminist thinkers have shown the androcentric character of
> traditional understandings and have suggested new readings
> of the Genesis story that underscore the subjection of women
> as the consequence of sin, from which Christian salvation is
> meant to liberate. They have shown how male theological
> perspectives have dominated understandings of sin as pride
> and rebellion against God and have failed to attend to the sin
> of those who are powerless, who lack agency, selfhood, and
> responsibility, who have suffered violence and abuse. While
> women can sin in the ways of "masculine" culture, especially
> in the new roles they have assumed in that culture, their own
> "feminine" formation suggests sins of passive failure to de-
> velop a sense of self, a sense of agency and responsibility.
> Sin is understood, in a feminist perspective, as the breaking
> of relationship with both God and with human beings that
> can take the form of weakness as well as pride in its denial

of the importance of human responsibility in both the personal and the political realms.[202]

Anne Carr was, in this reference, consulting earlier feminist authors' articles written as reflections on women's situations with specifically theological concerns. Gerda Lerner, in *The Creation of Patriarchy*, explores the development of institutions whose operating methods exhibited exactly the attitude expressed by Anne Carr, in a historical overview of early men's socialization amid certain tribes. Stating that "in civilized society it is girls who have the greatest difficulty in ego formation," she goes on to relate that boys in earlier societies were often intimidated by the strong female figures in their upbringing, thus leading to a situation where "[t]he ego formation of the individual male, which must have taken place within a context of fear, awe, and possibly dread of the female, must have led men to create social institutions to bolster their egos, strengthen their self-confidence, and validate their sense of worth."[203]

Earlier scholars had referred to the work of Margaret Mead as she studied the cultural patterning of male and female children in primitive societies. They move from her initial findings into their own theories which pointed out the physical basis for the development of men's aggressiveness and determination. Emphasizing the visible rites of passage of womanhood (such as the onset of menses, childbirth, and menopause), these studies point out that without such obvious landmarks, males somehow find the need to "prove" their manhood.[204] This article, originally published in 1960, focuses on the need of the male to exhibit extraordinary performance and achievement to prove his manhood. Such desire brings about anxiety, uncertainty, and the need to prove himself over and over again. Women, in that they give birth, thus fulfilling the physical element of procreation, have thus had to seek recognition not by the completion of such natural physical tasks, but through education. The "divine discontent" shown by men in their efforts to become self-differentiated through challenges and adventures has then been shown in women's struggles to go beyond a mere physical manifestation of their maturity to an expression of their inner selves.

Many of these women, who were brought up to believe in the fundamental equality of the sexes and who were given the same kind of education and the same encouragement to self-realization as their male contemporaries, do not really discover until they marry and bear children—or, perhaps, have been forced to admit to themselves that they never will marry—that there are real differences between the masculine and feminine situations which cannot be blamed on a cultural lag in the definitions of femininity or upon the "selfishness" and "stupidity" of men. It is only at this point, when the ultimate actualization of their specific sexuality must be either accepted or given up for good, that they become aware of the deep need of almost every woman, regardless of her personal history and achievements or her belief in her own individual value, to surrender her self-identity and be included in another's "power of being."[205]

Maturity brings about such realization. At the same time, each woman in her spiritual search comes to the awareness of her own need to seek solitude:

She learns not only that it is impossible to sustain a perpetual I-Thou relationship but that the attempt to do so can be deadly. The moments, hours, and days of self-giving must be balanced by moments, hours, and days of withdrawal into, and enrichment of, her individual selfhood if she is to remain a whole person. She learns, too, that a woman can give too much of herself, so that nothing remains of her own uniqueness; she can become merely an emptiness, almost a zero, without value to herself, to her fellow men, or, perhaps, even to God.[206]

If women's identity has thus been so interwoven with the physical manifestations of her womanhood, as well as how she interrelates with all those around her, it is easy to understand how self-differentiation of the sort required in the release of the ego could be non-existent. Women's role has often been defined as "living for another," which basically means one is expected to "submerge [themselves] in the other's identity, needs, interests."[207]

One's identity was defined as who one was in relation to others. This fact has led to a problematic vision of goodness and virtue.

Recent studies show that women's behavior that is praised as virtuous (i.e., loving) and mature (i.e., other-directed) is actually often behavior symptomatic of severe immaturity. Women spending themselves on their family, their students, patients, or members of their religious community often have low self-esteem, and thus their emotional dependency makes them subtly very demanding on others for appreciation and adulation. Their inability to be assertive and their lack of self-worth can result in covert manipulation, pretended helplessness, evasion of conflict situations.[208]

The spiritual journey of women thus takes a turn which is difficult to negotiate. "Because spiritual growth demands movement from an orientation toward heteronomy through autonomy in order to reach an ultimately mature, free relationship to God, women's conditioning toward conformity to a passive 'merger self' rather than a 'seeker self' is an especially cruel seduction. Women are led to believe they are virtuous when actually they have not yet taken the necessary possession of their lives to have an authentic 'self' to give in self-donating love. They are often praised as holy when they are still spiritually dwarfed!"[209]

St. John of the Cross was thoroughly schooled in the works of Aristotle and St. Thomas Aquinas. His own work did not appear to demean the ability of women to experience profound contemplation. This fact most likely stemmed from his relationship with St. Teresa of Avila and his knowledge of her spiritual experiences. But Aristotle's view has colored history in ways women throughout the centuries have struggled to overcome. For example, referring to Aristotle's volume *De Generatione Animalium*, Lerner revisits his view that even the matter out of which women were created was inferior to that of males.[210] Women were therefore inferior beings, and quite passive, referred to by Aristotle as "mutilated males."[211] Such a view was entrenched in those officially responsible for theological concerns in the early Church.

Throughout the centuries, however, there has been some recourse available. As Lerner goes on to state,

Yet there have always existed a tiny minority of privileged women, usually from the ruling elite, who had some access to the same kind of education as did their brothers. From the ranks of such women have come the intellectuals, the thinkers, the writers, the artists. It is such women, throughout history, who have been able to give us a female perspective,

an alternative to androcentric thought. They have done so at
a tremendous cost and with great difficulty. Those women,
who have been admitted to the center of intellectual activity
of their day and especially in the past hundred years, academ-
ically trained women, have first had to learn "how to think
like a man." In the process, many of them have so internal-
ized that learning that they have lost the ability to conceive
of alternatives. The way to think abstractly is to define precisely, to create models in the mind and generalize from them.
Such thought, men have taught us, must be based on the ex-
clusion of feelings. . . . Thus (women) have learned to mis-
trust their own experience and devalue it.[212]

The era of St. John was steeped in such attitudes toward women.
Writings "about 'womanhood,' an ideal created by men which many
women found difficult or even undesirable to achieve [categorized them]
as *mujercitas*, 'little women," a term that signaled women's political, social,
and spiritual powerlessness."[213] Even St. Teresa herself was referred to as
"a manly soul, enduring all conflicts with manly courage."[214]

It is not surprising, then, that such attitudes have prevailed throughout the centuries, causing great frustration among women who wish to express their spirituality and be taken seriously. Within the institutional
churches, "officially nurturing" topics may be taught by women, but all too
often for the more "academic" topics the first choices have been men, although in recent decades that has begun to change.

Within health care settings, too, women have progressed from
being the "handmaidens" to physicians to being professionals in their own
right, something we will address in the following chapter. The struggles of
historical women have not been in vain, and the restrictive attitudes formerly taken for granted in many circles are now being transformed, albeit
slowly, as women have researched, written, taught, and generally moved
the discussion forward. Authors such as Ingrid Trobisch, Miriam Therese
Winter, Marianne Williamson, Lisa Sowle Cahill, Marie Augusta Neal,
Joan Chittister, O.S.B., Kathleen Fischer, Carol Lee Flinders, Judith
Plaskow and Carol Christ, and many more, have pushed the growing respect for women's spiritualities, enhancing public understanding for mar-
ginalized groups, Native American spiritualities, and others not in the
mainstream churches. There is much work to be done in this arena, but
there has been progress.

This section may have seemed to digress from the specific application of St. John of the Cross in health care settings. However, the "letting go" of ego considerations, "identity," intellectual gifts and aptitudes which John advises would be impossible for women if, as early authorities taught, they had not the ability to develop ego or intellect in the first place. Within John's spirituality, there appears to be more of a "human" application, not discriminating on the basis of gender. This, with the awareness that there are still those who feel women are inferior, will give female practitioners the courage to believe in their own spiritualities in the light of their relationship with a God who will sustain them in the darkness of uncertainty.

As we will also see in the following chapter, men within the nursing profession have experienced their own sense of "powerlessness" as a formerly "female" profession has opened its ranks to highly competent, sensitive individuals.

SUMMARY

The overall focus of this chapter has been on the work of St. John of the Cross as a model for the spiritual journey. Placed within the context of the mystical movement, the emphasis employed by John serves an important role in the life of modern spiritual searchers. Because of the emphasis on scientific knowledge in the past century, much of the element of "blind faith" has been subsumed, looked at as impractical and unscientific. This, in the midst of the tremendous scientific and technological achievements of this past century, has confused those engaged in the pursuit of an authentic spiritual life. The element of "control" of facts and information overshadowed the ability of the human soul to release itself into a power that is strongly felt, but largely unseen.

In the work of health care professionals, scientific and technological facts are important, but the human element of all medical interactions never disappears. It is this element which causes so many questions for any health care practitioner, and it is this element which the development of a strong spiritual life will address in depth. In the two subsequent chapters, the practical application of the work of St. John of the Cross will be considered, especially as it concerns end-of-life issues, which are today made even more complex by the possibilities now existing in the world of science and medicine.

CHAPTER FOUR

PRACTITIONERS AND THE DARK NIGHT

MEDICINE AND THE LAW—INFLUENCE OVER
HEALTH CARE PRACTITIONERS' DECISION-MAKING

Within any society there exists a framework of laws governing human actions. This fact is increasingly applicable to the field of health care, judging from the number of lawsuits brought against both institutions and individuals in recent decades. These lawsuits grow out of specific instances of dissatisfaction with either the practitioners themselves or the medical interventions employed. This framework of laws, however, is an external means of control, unfortunately necessary for the regulation of activity within the profession and within society as a whole. Human foibles, mistakes, misjudgments, and misinformation all contribute to less-than-satisfactory results in given medical cases. Sometimes the only recourse available is appeal to the external means of control—the law.

The American medical profession developed in the mid-nineteenth century with the advent of "healers" who competed for the "public's respect and a share of its pocketbook: midwives, abortionists, eclectics, homeopaths, herbalists, faith healers, and even 'patent medicine' or 'snake oil salesmen.'"[1] Most of the public, however, still received its medical care at home, from family members.

As the formal medical education of physicians and nurses began, more complex external means of control were needed, specifically for the licensing of practitioners. There was still much skepticism regarding the new science. As well, means of financing the new health care offerings were being organized to provide opportunity for the majority of the populace to have access to needed medical care. These efforts continue today, with varied levels of success.

Moreover, there has been an increasing need to regulate what can be done for patients, especially those with terminal diseases. Means of extending life sometimes "take on a life of their own," and consist mainly of efforts by the health care providers to do all they can to extend life, "even if it does not benefit the whole person."[2] Recent developments have highlighted the efforts of various groups either to allow humans to end their own lives with the assistance of a physician, or, on the other end of the spectrum, to continue life by all possible technological means. Technology has truly "proven uncontrollable"[3] in these instances.

Within medical institutions, the hospitals and clinics where physicians practice, the function of the law has been "to protect [physicians] against liability and oversight imposed by lay juries, or by government agencies, hospitals, and insurance companies."[4] The ranks of physicians, which at one time had grown strong and almost impermeable to outside critique, continued to exercise almost complete control over what went on in the profession. As new technologies developed, deliberate focus on the quality of care given to patients increased. Here, the categories of consideration were "technical error, judgmental error, normative error, and quasi-normative error (this final category is not explained in the referenced volume)." These categories were, respectively, a physician's "competent or incompetent use of skills, incorrect use of medical strategy in a given case, and the failure to exercise professional skills in a conscientious manner, leading to breaches in the relationship between physicians, staff members, patients, and families."[5]

The appearance of increasing levels of legal consideration stemming from the exponential increase in levels of technology in recent years thus indicates a serious concern for the proper regulation of health care. Above all, the development of malpractice law has attempted to protect the public from illegal, unethical, or incompetent medical practices. But "the entire design of malpractice law seems ill-suited to serve as the major means for achieving quality of care."[6] Merely external means of control fail to reach into the actual character of the practitioners in question.

American Health Law, edited by George Annas, contains case studies of legal actions brought for a large number of cases. Each one addresses specific concerns about quality of life, quality of care, financial mismanagement, miscommunication, and perceived failure of the medical profession's efforts to reach satisfactory ends. Such cases will only increase as technology develops and as the professions increasingly self-regulate. It falls to the many individual health care practitioners to be the source of their own regulation. Some legal regulation must continue, but there is a far greater dimension of control which we may, as practitioners, enter into freely, having chosen the way of internal commitment and transformation. It is at this point that we may begin to move beyond the external means of control within which we operate and commit ourselves to exploring the internal impetus fostered by true spiritual surrender.

PERSONAL PRACTICE: PRACTITIONERS AND THE DARK NIGHT

We have now reached the point of departure for the central focus of this chapter on practitioners and *Dark Night of the Soul*. John of the Cross was well aware of the failure of external means alone to succeed in transforming one's character. As noted in Chapter Three, John's analysis of the levels of personal transformation began with the external manifestations of inner character. He began with the human senses, through which each person receives manifestation of his or her place in creation, and by which an appreciation of the gifts of that creation is possible.

Where do we begin our search? Without centering on one specific denomination, yet always aware that John's context was Roman Catholicism, an approach for today's practitioners will do well to appreciate the varied cultures in today's society. "Universal mysticism transcends confessional, denominational, and cultural barriers. Its objectives are the same even when expressed differently. Its expression is a language or verbal form which takes the confessional and cultural shape of the individual mystic. Still the nature of the mystical experience is to transcend completely the world of fragmentation, shapes, and forms."[7]

Such a realization will give today's practitioners access to the interplay of various cultures' contributions to the practice of spirituality. Though John claimed Roman Catholicism as his own, each human being of whatever denomination possesses the *capax Dei*, as the deepest human dignity,[8] and has the potential to discover the very best mode of relationship with God. Nevertheless, since the Enlightenment, with its emphasis on scientific knowledge and technical progress, the need for "proof" of theories has subsumed true contemplative practice under a heavy coating of over-analysis, even of forms of prayer.

"How-to" books abound. Study of various prayer forms leads a searcher to trial after trial of new methods, at times preventing the very "sitting still" necessary for deep, interior prayer. Today's culture has a "strong bias against humble submission,"[9] which, of itself, is the very attitude necessary for the "letting go of attachment to distinct forms"[10] advocated by St. John in the entirety of his treatise. As was noted in Chapter Three, this ego-abandonment becomes especially difficult in the medical milieu. Practitioners have to walk the fine line between the professional application of intellectual, scientific processes and the release of futile adherence to the scientific method. In the face of its occasional failure to be the ultimate solution, they must seek to balance the intellectual and spiritual elements of their own souls.

"*Vacate et videte quoniam ego sum Deus* [Ps. 46:11]."[11] This phrase, which means "Be still and see that I am God," is the crux of the approach of St. John of the Cross. Today's medical milieu is riddled with the atmosphere of competition—advancement, recognition, appreciation of one's competence in one's field. Placing emphasis on one's own accomplishments stands directly in the way of allowing God to work within the soul. "If spiritual persons, then, were to desire to make use of their own efforts, they would necessarily impede by their activity the passive communication of God, which is the spirit" (*Ascent* III, 13:3).[12] The realization that "All natural ability is insufficient to produce the supernatural goods that God alone infuses in the soul passively, secretly, and in silence" (*Dark Night* II, 14:1)[13] may open the door to modern health care practitioners' understanding of spiritual surrender in the face of unknown or uncertain outcomes.

What seems to be an appropriate spiritual first step is a removal of the focus on personal accomplishments and spiritual "progress." True character transformation and spiritual deepening will only occur when one focuses "on God, not on transformation."[14] Such a focus takes the burden off ourselves as the source of growth.

One of the most difficult realizations for us "in our age, so hopeful of finding efficient spiritual techniques, is that it is fundamentally sheer grace of God rather than a matter of a person's own spiritual contriving."[15] Though modern medical technology seeks always the next higher level of efficiency and performance, all thoughts of self-mastery (as an ultimate goal in itself), for the spirit of the contemplative person, must be released. In other words, one comes to "a highly differentiated condition of personal awareness, of an equanimity which is achieved through deliberate rational detachment from one's immediate flow of experience."[16] Each person, after a peaceful self-analysis in the light of one's God-given talents, may embark on his or her own unique spiritual journey. Unique, because talents differ, and natural intellectual and intuitive strengths appear in varying degrees, but all may be transformed by reflecting on the fact that God (by whatever name God is known) is the only ultimate source of our natural human gifts.

The deliberate release of all ego-based, self-satisfying attachment to external forms causes tremendous uncertainty in the hearts of modern, scientifically taught practitioners. In some ways, we may have lost confidence in the voices of our own intuition and innate knowing. Both St. John and St. Thomas Aquinas believed in the natural ability of human beings to discern, to know, and to understand both their own relationship to their Creator and to other human beings. The natural law, at least in the tradition of St. John and St. Thomas, is understood to be the claim that "moral knowledge is accessible not just to believers but to anyone who is willing to reflect critically on human experience."[17]

Richard Gula lists three "convictions" yielded by the natural law in the Catholic moral tradition. First, he states that natural law "claims the existence of an objective moral order," indicating that morality is "grounded in reality," and is therefore discoverable.[18] In essence, this conviction removes the natural law from dependence on the whims of any one group or individual, and grounds it in a reality which must be discerned. Granted, situations are unique in themselves, but that reality remains constant, part of the eternal truth, and the foundation for moral decision-making.

The second conviction is that natural law morality "is accessible to anyone independently of one's religious commitment."[19] This is especially important in a pluralistic society where many cultures and religions blend. Such a view broadens the scope of understanding for those truly interested in discerning the truth of a given situation.

The third conviction is that the "knowledge of moral value can be universalized."[20] For modern practitioners this is also important, again reaching beyond the boundaries of any one faith system, and proclaiming that moral values are actually objective values which "render some actions right and some wrong."[21]

If, as Gula goes on to state, such a view of natural law theory places it, as grounded in reality, "in opposition to legal positivism which makes something right merely because it is commanded . . . [and] against a morality based on personal whim whereby one can arbitrarily decide what is right and wrong,"[22] then it also places high responsibility on each individual practitioner to exercise honesty and discernment. Likewise, unique situations call for a synthesis of one's experiences into a larger picture of the relationship between oneself, one's patients, the community as a whole, and a God who leads us to truth.

The influence of natural law theory for modern practitioners includes consideration of the personal, the historical, and the consequential elements of any decision, based in consultation with one's community.[23] In the Catholic Church, for instance, the importance of consultation of one's community of faith echoes St. John of the Cross's exhortation that the truth is never found in isolation from others, but rather in consultation with others (*Ascent* II, 22:11–12).[24] (Again, we remember the open dialogue necessary between hospice and palliative care team members in order to foster clearer perspectives on particular cases.) Even such a discerning community recognizes that there is "great complexity and ambiguity of human, personal reality."[25] For modern-day searchers, then, in the atmosphere of constant technological change and scientific progress, each moral value as personally interpreted and validated in consultation with others is subject to greater scrutiny and possible revision. We are not speaking of the basic moral value as grounded in the eternal truth, but in its application to a particular, unique situation.

As Gula states, "Legalism stifles creativity, initiative, and conversion. Where legalism abounds, moral minimalism and spiritual laziness are not far behind. Asking 'How far can I go?' for example reflects such a posture. It looks for a rule to define the scope of personal responsibility, rather than exercising moral muscle to engage in moral discernment."[26] A blind clinging to "rules and regulations" will also stifle, in these unique instances, one's ability to sort out the personal realities of patient, family, and practitioner, thus discovering the truth of a particular situation. Hindered in this way from an accurate assessment of each person's truth, the practitioner will stumble blindly forward, possibly causing harm to all by an incomplete moral perspective.

For those of us who may attempt an understanding of St. John of the Cross's spirituality in relation to our practice, the first step will be to come to know our own capacity for discernment. We will need a confidence in our own abilities, as human persons, truly to discern the truth not only of our own hearts, but of the hearts of our patients and their families. At times this will be extremely painful, and the process will only be deepened for us by consistent, faithful practice. Gula states that "the morally mature person must be able to perceive, choose, and identify the self with what one does."[27] That "self" as a God-given reality, in the view of the natural law theory, has the capacity to be a fully functioning moral agent, employing an understanding of the processes of nature itself as well as a competent use of reason, which, when enlightened by in-depth reflection, places the self in direct contact with the eternal law.[28] This takes seriously a prayerful relationship with the Creator, and greatly extends our considerations to the ultimate good for each human person, rather than becoming mired in endless overanalysis of particular situations.

With its immense technological progress, modern medicine at times has seemed to lose focus on the dignity of the human person undergoing treatment. What sensitive practitioners may do, in refocusing on the ultimate goal of human life, is to slow down the tremendous pace of the modern medical milieu and enable both practitioners and patients to enter into a "safe space," where true moral discernment will take place.

At this point we may look at the experience of one practitioner, who is both a physician and a professed religious brother. His insights may enrich our understanding of the conflict between the modern health system and the spirituality of practitioners. In light of *Dark Night of the Soul*, it becomes clear that the conscious stripping away of all that hinders the well-being of human persons, be they patients or practitioners, is a vital element in a spiritual approach to the health care ministry.

ONE MAN'S PERSONAL EXPERIENCE—SPIRITUALITY AND THE HEALTH CARE SYSTEM

Daniel Sulmasy, M.D., a Franciscan friar, who at the time of the writing of his volume, *The Healer's Calling,* was the director of the Center for Biomedical Ethics at Georgetown University Medical Center in Washington, D.C., offers the insights of one who is both medical practitioner and professed religious. Well aware of the technological advances made in recent decades in the medical field, he is also aware that our very technological success has imprisoned us, in a way, and that "there are no technological solutions to the problems that technology has engendered."[29] Commenting on the walls of physicians' offices laden with degrees and plaques, he states that even such recognition fails to satisfy the deepest longings of the human heart.[30] He reminds all practitioners that even the most conscientious development of one's professional skills will not lead to spiritual fullness. "This is why even the doctor who diligently works on the perfection of his or her craft will never ultimately be satisfied by technical excellence alone. Technical competence is necessary, but it is insufficient for healing."[31]

Both men and women experience this sense of spiritual searching. As we saw in Chapter Three, the specifics for each gender may be different because of varied cultural patterning. But having gone through the rigors of medical training, and having performed professionally and skillfully, both men and women experience the need for a further grounding in something beyond superb technical skill and professional competence.

The path to true healing is discovered in the relationship of trust between practitioner and patient, acceptance of the ultimate uncertainty of medical science, and acceptance on the part of the practitioner that he or she does not know all the answers. "Consistent, trusting, faithful action in the face of uncertainty and doubt demands other virtues, such as practical wisdom, patience, and courage."[32] Such a view places high demands on health care practitioners—for self-discipline, self-effacement in the face of such uncertainties, and a deep sense of humility. This is difficult in the medical milieu, for as Sulmasy observes, "Perhaps this is why contemporary culture, fanatically oriented towards results, has such a difficult time with spirituality. And all of this is made much harder by the tremendous emphasis on outcomes in medicine today."[33] Modern medical settings offer little opportunity for the withdrawal necessary for reflection. In a return to the vision of Jesus as teacher, healer, and man of prayer, Sulmasy notes that "Jesus invites all who call themselves Christian and doctor [or nurse] to this rhythm of prayer and work. . . . It is not easy for physicians or other health care professionals in the late twentieth century to find time for prayer."[34] But in the face of the often deeply disturbing decisions needing to be made in both acute and long-term situations, this time of drawing-away and spiritual reflection becomes even more necessary. In a poetic turn of thought, Sulmasy comments, "Each physician or nurse is called to write the symphony for which God has commissioned him or her."[35] Like an artist finding expression in the well-ordered sounds of a composition, the health care professional, as artist in the field of medical practice, must allow some time for silent, unpressured reflection so as to be able to reach insightful decisions for and with his or her patients and their families. The emotional intensity of hospice and palliative care work calls for exceptional sensitivity which can be fostered in such silent, unpressured time for reflection.

Like St. John of the Cross, a deep awareness of the senses of human beings pervades the practice of health care today, despite the often rushed atmosphere of areas of practice. And as with St. John of the Cross and St. Thomas Aquinas, there is also an awareness of the need for "proper balance discovered only in prayer, [using] the tools of silence, memory, and imagination."[36] As previously noted, John of the Cross, throughout his *Ascent of Mount Carmel*, advocated the appreciation of the gifts obtained through one's senses. His strong exhortation, however, was that appreciable as these gifts were, they were yet not the ultimate goal. Rather, they were to be moved beyond, not grasped out of fear, and were to push us toward the union with God which would truly satisfy the soul (*Ascent* III, 2:2).[37]

Likewise, for health care practitioners, the awareness of the human senses is acute, for proper diagnoses are made by understanding functions which are impaired and thus indicate illness. "Doctors and nurses, by virtue of their occupations, are keenly interested in the senses. They make use of all five of them in their daily work. Much of their work involves helping patients who have developed problems with the function of one or more of the senses."[38] And yet even with this acute awareness, practitioners attuned to the wholistic approach to medical treatment are mindful of the signs of spiritual distress also involved in physical illnesses. There are many stresses in the medical field. Health care practitioners must make a conscious effort to block out the many influences which may impair their ability to apply their own inner processes of discernment.

"Health care professionals, especially, can get so caught up in the routine of work, so bored by the hypertensives and the diabetics and the somatizers, so angry about the government and the insurers, so cynical about their patients' inability to change, that they fail to recognize those moments in which power goes out of them."[39] The power of which he speaks here may be that very power of discernment. Relying on the mere external performance of duties and procedures, when that power fades, a practitioner loses the innate ability to see past appearances and understand his or her patient's real distress. Then, health care practice becomes merely rote repetition of learned skills, with each practitioner hidden behind a facade of duty and withdrawing from healing contact with patients.

Sulmasy reflects on the "waiting" necessary for true insight. St. John of the Cross spoke repeatedly in his *Ascent of Mount Carmel* and *Dark Night of the Soul* of the necessity of letting go of all external consolations, a painful and frightening process. Likewise, the deepening of spiritual insight and discernment in any medical situation calls for such waiting. "There will be moments of sudden illumination for everyone, eventually, if one keeps at it. But these moments come on God's time, not human time."[40] He notes that during these painful times of waiting, there will be "painful silences [which] are necessary in order for us to recognize the demons that possess us and to ask God to expel them."[41] This is a vital element in any spiritually sound approach to the practice of health care.

There is much to be said for the healing arts as practiced by persons who are humble in the true sense of the word, completely aware that even with all their skills, practiced to perfection, a true healing may only be obtained when the idea of "cure" has been abandoned. As for pain, Sulmasy notes, "Most, but not all pain can be controlled. But even if it could, not all suffering is caused by pain. Feelings of fear, loneliness, embarrassment, helplessness, hopelessness, and abandonment are all aspects of suffering that morphine does not touch."[42]

On the subject of practitioners, Sulmasy also notes the propensity of some practitioners to place themselves above those they attempt to serve. "Health care professionals are often far too convinced of their own perfection and of their own invulnerability. Doubtless, the system of training that physicians undergo helps to foster thoughts of invulnerability. But these thoughts are delusional. And delusional health care professionals are dangers to patients and dangers to themselves. Unless health care professionals are convinced of their own fallibility and vulnerability, they will either make serious mistakes or begin to take out their angers and frustrations upon patients, or both."[43]

Professional "delusions" such as those Sulmasy describes lead practitioners to an extreme need to "control outcomes." Convinced that they possess all necessary insights into a given situation, they often exhibit rigidity in their interactions with others. The flexibility needed for revision of one's initial approach is absent in such people. While intellectual knowledge, professional training, and consistent practice of one's profession are all important elements in the medical field, they stop short of giving practitioners such flexibility. In fact, these elements may often give professionals a harmful pride in their accomplishments, which if exercised indiscriminately can alienate them from true encounters with patients and families.

Sulmasy explains one view of suffering in this way. "All suffering may be understood, in its root form, as the experience of finitude. Human beings are fundamentally oriented toward the infinite term of transcendence, yet aware that everything about them is radically limited. Human beings are oriented toward the truth, yet plagued by their nature as fallible, ignorant, and prone to make choices that are opposed to the truth—lying, cheating, deceiving, and exaggerating their greatness."[44] This is much the same experience described by St. John in his *Dark Night* where he notes that a soul in the throes of this stage of the spiritual journey has a tremendous "knowledge of self and of (its) own misery" (*Dark Night* I, 12:2).[45]

For practitioners in today's health care settings, the humility brought about by the realization that they have no control over suffering, but rather may only be able to walk through a painful situation with their patients and not solve it for them, will enable them to gain strength from a source outside themselves. In this way, they will transcend the need to depend on scientific, exact answers, and exhibit an equanimity of soul which will actually strengthen their patients. John states it in this way: "Spiritual persons enjoy tranquility and peace of soul due to the absence of the disturbance and change arising from thoughts and ideas in the memory, and consequently they possess purity of conscience and soul, which is a greater benefit. As a result they are disposed excellently for human and divine wisdom and virtues" (*Ascent* III, 6:1).[46]

Finally, there is a tendency in the medical world at this time to be impatient with unsolvable problems. "The practice of making medicine into a science of engineering is the most thoroughly dehumanizing stance one can take toward a patient. Conceiving of the patient merely as an object to be scientifically manipulated, essentially no different from a tadpole in a dish, undermines the meaning of healing by denying the mystery of the clinician-patient relationship."[47]

In the spirit of St. John of the Cross, then, in order to transcend the tenor of today's medical milieu, each practitioner will need the courage to enter into the mystery each patient presents. Certainly a competent grasp of the essentials of one's practice is needed, but the ability to enter into the many uncertain aspects of each medical outcome will require an ability to stand firm in the face of what may seem unsolvable. Knowledge of oneself and one's own spirit comes from a time of withdrawal from immediate facts and a synthesis of the elements of each situation. Our mystery as professionals is contained in those very uncertainties. St. John states, in quoting the prophet Isaiah, "Vexation makes one understand" [Isaiah 28:19]; and St. Augustine says, "Let me know myself, Lord, and I will know you" [*Soliloquia*, 2.1.1, in Migne, *Patrologia Latina*, 32.885].[48]

The person who undergoes the experience of "the dark and dry night" will come to understand what it means to find one's true place in the scheme of things, neither disparaging things understood through sense awareness, nor clinging to them out of uncertainty and fear. In the realm of patient care, such a self-understanding will allow practitioners to recognize that they are not above their patients, removed from the imperfection of their own humanity, but rather that they, too, are "wounded and in need of healing."[49] The entry into the mystery not only of their own spirits but also into those of their patients will be the basis for honest appraisal and discernment of the best course of action, and true healing.

The spiritual journey of practitioners takes many forms. The next consideration will be a look at the life of a nurse-turned-priest, as he came to realize his own need to commit to a spiritual life.

DELVING INTO ESSENTIALS:
FROM NURSING TO PRIESTHOOD—ONE MAN'S JOURNEY

This section will explore the journey of Reverend James P. Holland, who at the time of our interview had just celebrated his forty-first birthday, and was parochial vicar of St. Anne's Parish in Castle Shannon, Pennsylvania. Father Holland was ordained to the priesthood in the Roman Catholic Church in 1998, after spending twenty years as a critical-care nurse. During those years he also worked as a flight nurse, and did research toward advanced degrees. Embarking on a long delayed entry into seminary studies in his mid-thirties, this young man, the eldest of three children, experienced in depth both the demands of critical-care nursing and the aspects of personal spiritual conversion. Having asked his permission to use his personal journey as part of a doctoral study, I sat down with him in his office and listened as he related experiences which of themselves are indicative of the sort of spiritual "stripping away" advocated by St. John of the Cross.

The nursing profession today is no longer a group of "handmaidens to physicians." In its early years, nursing drew candidates from social classes that might otherwise not have had opportunities for advancement, and in many ways was a "maid service" to patients in hospitals. Thus, the development of the profession through this century has emphasized the vital role nurses play in patient care.[50] Specialized certifications now exist for many types of nursing practice—certified nurse anesthetists, certified hospice nurses, certified operating room nurses, and others. Within each branch of nursing, recognition of skills highly developed through specialized training is an important factor in nursing practice. As a male practitioner in this field, Father Holland also experienced what in corporate settings has been called the "glass ceiling," though in nursing it was felt more strongly by the male nurses than by female, somewhat the reverse of what women in the corporate world have experienced. For whatever gender, though, such experience is difficult, and is one of the elements of the profession a spiritually centered person will address.

With all these concerns, Father Holland endured the discipline of highly specialized training, and it was this that he practiced until his ordination. He loved his work, and relished the aspects of research and development of new techniques and equipment which he discovered at the University of Pittsburgh and the Center for Emergency Medicine. Advancement was encouraged, with the ever-improved nursing skills and techniques, which kept practicing nurses attending workshops and conferences in order to keep pace with all new developments in the field.

Though Father Holland was committed to nursing, there had been a point early on when he had made a choice—either go to seminary or go to nursing school. At that time, being young, and with family members in the field, he chose to follow the path of nursing. After several years, however, he reached a stage in his life journey where he felt that he had hit bottom both emotionally and professionally. The spirit of his practice had become deadened, and he felt his soul being drawn in a new direction. Though he had sought grants for his work and had entered into personal relationships, there was something missing in his life. Seeing the stresses of the nursing profession taking their toll on his friends as well as on himself, he realized that daily exposure to the traumas and tragedies of critical-care nursing often led people into pursuit of self-medicating practices such as alcohol. Seeking to deaden the pain of dealing with death and severe injury on a daily basis accomplished nothing for any of them. Likewise, spiritual debilitation had all but overpowered him, and he sank deeper into a sense of futility about his spiritual life.

St. John of the Cross, fully aware that the pursuit of external satisfaction for internal spiritual distress would lead only to despair and hopelessness, stated in the first stanza of the *Dark Night* that his soul "went out unseen, my house being now all stilled."[51] The stillness had taken place in all his natural, earthly passions, and his senses were quieted. John went on to speak of the fact that "those who value their knowledge and ability as a means of reaching union with the wisdom of God are highly ignorant in God's sight and will be left behind, far away from this wisdom" (*Ascent* I, 4:5).[52] It would appear that Father Holland had reached a personal realization that all his natural intellectual knowledge was not satisfying the deepest part of his soul. Neither was his pursuit of the relief of deeply emotional pain by any external means. It was at this time that his spiritual aloneness was most profound. He was about to enter into his own experience of the Dark Night.

St. John taught that there are two means of experiencing this stage of spiritual growth—active and passive (*Ascent* I, 13:1).[53] At this time in his life, Father Holland began searching for means to bring life to his own spirit. He chose to return to the tradition of the Roman Catholic Church, of which he says that he was then a nominal member. Surprisingly, at a most unexpected moment, when he was alone and quiet, watching a movie about one of the miracles of the Catholic faith, he experienced a profound sadness and personal grief over what he saw his past life to be. His conscious seeking of a new direction, which St. John called the "active" aspect, gave way to the "passive" aspect, brought about by what John called "the sheer grace" of personal understanding and profound tears. This comprehension of his soul's alienation from the God-given grace he so earnestly sought completely overpowered him.

No one pointed a finger of judgment at him; no one harshly accosted him about his personal practices. In all probability such encounters would have hardened his heart and soul, making him resistant to further growth and alienating him from the peace of soul he desired. But in the quiet of reflection, through the instrument of a miracle of his own faith, he found the strength to make his soul vulnerable to whatever change was going to be asked of him. It was this deeply personal encounter with a God who had taken second place to his nursing practice that was now calling Father Holland to a deeper commitment.

As St. John stated, the passage of a ray of sunlight through a window is not dependent on the ray of sunlight itself, but rather on the state of the window through which it is to pass (*Ascent* II, 5:6).[54] Father Holland, at this point in his search, became aware that he needed a great deal of change in his spiritual life, and began to place himself in situations where he might reawaken what he felt was a very dead spiritual life. Again, his active participation in a pattern of choice for a solid spiritual life opened the way for the passive aspect, through which a soul receives the grace of God actively at work within it.

An unexpected illness, one which demanded twice-weekly treatments and caused misunderstanding between himself and his supervisor, cast a pall over Father Holland's professional life, and his personal relationships underwent a change as well. It was this darkness of spirit that led him to understand that there was a final choice to be made. Though his newfound spiritual strength had enabled him to deal with his patients in a different way, addressing at times their spiritual distress as well as their physical injuries, the spiritual stripping away was to continue until he at last made the choice to follow completely his vocation to the priesthood.

St. John spoke of the spiritual "nakedness" through which the spirit finds "its quietude and rest" (*Ascent* I, 13:13).[55] Father Holland's final decision to leave the active practice of nursing and to follow the vocation to the priesthood brought him an incredible sense of spiritual peace. Nevertheless, he openly states that he did not handle the initial process of "detachment" well. The life offered to him through the practice of nursing was a good one. Even giving away a little pet, his small parrot, caused him pain. But again, in the spirit of John of the Cross, it followed "a more intense enkindling of another, better love (love of the soul's Bridegroom) which (is) necessary for the vanquishing of the appetites and the denial of this pleasure" (*Ascent* 1, 14:2).[56]

Throughout *Ascent of Mount Carmel* and the *Dark Night of the Soul*, John exhorted his readers to take delight in the aspects of creation which are given by the Creator. In order to come to complete spiritual union with that Creator, however, the soul cannot cling to them as ends in themselves.

The nursing profession today offers many tempting inducements, such as professional recognition, pride of accomplishment, a sense of technical mastery, and the means of helping others reach their optimal level of health. As St. John stated, however, no intellectual knowledge will satisfy the longing for spiritual union. In fact, the very inducements of a professional life, if clung to indiscriminately, can cause what John called "wearisome and tiring appetites," which "agitate and disturb one just as wind disturbs water," and the intensity of which "does not diminish when the appetite is satisfied, even though the object is gone" (*Ascent* I, 6:6,7).[57] Unfortunately the pursuit of prestige and recognition in the nursing profession does sometimes cause a person to feel agitated, highly competitive when comparing oneself to others, and always seeking the next level of recognition. Such an atmosphere is hardly conducive to the development of a spiritual outlook, and unfortunately is often instrumental in the emotional and professional burnout experienced in the medical milieu.

My interview with Father Holland gave me an insight into the spiritual journey of a health care professional who struggled to come to a clear view of his own identity not only as a medical professional, but also as a spiritual person. Though his journey led him away from the immediate clinical setting and into the priesthood, the insights of nursing have not left him. He speaks openly about the strength and the confidence that he is given in his ministry to hospitalized patients, attributing it to his years as a professional nurse. His memory of the spiritual "night" also remains with him, along with the recognition that the spiritual life is never a finished product. He is aware that the path will not only call forth from him the willingness to enter into the mystery of his own spiritual development and relationship to God, but also the willingness to stand with others as they face their own.[58]

PRACTITIONERS: DISCERNMENT, HONESTY, AND VIRTUE-CENTERED PRACTICE

The previous reflections by practitioners from two different areas of health care practice illustrate individual points of view, shaped by each one's unique situation in life. Each man dealt with his own spirituality and professional life in a most personal way, solitary as is every spiritual quest, yet involved with others as he traveled the path leading him to new insight and determination. Though neither dealt solely with terminally ill patients, each one encountered the reality of death in one way or another. For Father Holland, one memorable instance occurred in an intensive care unit where a man, severely injured in an accident as well as suffering from HIV, came to a personal decision to amend his life and reconcile himself to God. It is this sort of experience which those who deal exclusively with terminally ill patients face frequently. Not all patients are able to make life-changing decisions, but each practitioner discovers that great courage is called forth from health care personnel in the face of patients who face their own mortality.

WOMEN'S ISSUES: A PERSONAL NOTE

As a female practitioner in hospice work, and as a woman studying theology, I reflect momentarily here on several aspects of what we have been examining in this study. At one time, while assisting a male physician with a procedure, I heard the doctor tell the patient, "We can wait a minute while the nurse cleans up, and then we'll talk over the results of your test." Fortunately such comments have been rare in my own experience, but they illustrate what we studied in the previous chapter—the attitude of males toward females striving for professional competence. The development of nurses from the handmaidens-to-physicians status to one of skilled professionals has been a long struggle. The special certifications previously mentioned are hallmarks of that development. Women's ego-development has basically been an uphill battle for the nursing profession.

Father Holland experienced the reverse of this battle, sensing an almost reverse discrimination toward men in what had been known as a female profession. Having struggled to "prove" themselves much in the same way professional men do in their executive roles, nurses dealing with terminally ill patients have a task that is thus made more difficult. The somewhat defensive posture which has in the past been necessary in hospital settings precludes a comfortable "letting go" of the very ego concerns they put in place to succeed in their professional lives. Thus, for females in the medical world, and this applies to physicians as well, the release of the external consolations is quite a different issue than that experienced by men. While both, in seeking a spiritual surrender, need to accept the ultimate lack of control of the scientific method, the added element of the subtle shadow of doubt about one's competence may make the woman's role slightly more complex.

HOSPICE, HUMILITY, AND A VIRTUOUS PROFESSIONAL LIFE

Early in the hospice movement, Dame Cicely Saunders reflected on the sorts of people who entered into hospice work. She said at that time, "But we in this work, I think, are always somehow missing one layer of outer skin, and we must take care to renew ourselves. It must be done from within, by means of prayer above all, but celebration as well. The work of a hospice must be done right, and its spiritual dimension cannot be grafted on."[59]

The essence of hospice, to one of the first practicing nurses in a United States hospice, was this: "It is a spiritual thing . . . because it is a way of life, really. It isn't just a job."[60] Speaking of the rapport among hospice personnel, this nurse commented on the deep bonds between coworkers, almost family-like, which not only demonstrated the dedication involved, but also served to cement it between practitioners. Healing, to hospice workers, does not necessarily mean curing. Rather, in the eyes of many, "To heal is to enable the patient to achieve integration, to realize himself, whatever his physical condition, as a whole person. When the physical component cannot be restored, then the spiritual and psychological elements begin to assume greater importance."[61]

What does this demand of practitioners who deal frequently with terminally ill patients? In the face of death, one finds it necessary to release all grasp on earthly, physical life. How may health care personnel come to a place in their own psyche which will free them to interact confidently with their patients?

Demetrius Dumm, O.S.B., speaks of the virtue of humility in a way easily applied to such health care workers. He states, "Humility is a simple recognition of the reality of one's limitations, especially in relation to God. To be humble is to be realistic about what one can or cannot achieve by personal effort. It is opposed, not to self-esteem, but to the illusion of personal autonomy."[62] As was noted previously, today's medical milieu lends itself to the pursuit of recognition, advancement, and pride of accomplishment. For those involved in the care of terminally ill patients, there is a tremendous need for the practice of the virtue of humility.

As Demetrius Dumm states, "[It] is so much easier to live in the illusion of the importance of one's own projects."[63] But in the face of a terminal illness, the reality sinks in that all human projects and all human accomplishments will fade completely at one's death. Thus, for all who deal with those facing their own deaths, an acceptance of one's own vulnerability is vital. It entails a complete stripping away of all illusions, and realization that while sitting beside a dying person, nothing one has accomplished or achieved matters in an ultimate way. Rather, one's presence becomes all one can give to that person. The responsibility, then, lies with each individual practitioner to make that presence, offered simply in the course of caring for that patient, something that does not detract from their dying process, but which by its very essence fills that patient with hope. Again, Demetrius Dumm reflects on what at first is a threat—for dying patients it is often the threat of the unknown—but which translated by the loving presence of one human being to another, converts that threat into a promise of something much greater.[64]

Bernard Häring, in his volume *The Virtues of an Authentic Life*, reflects on the idea of the formation of our character as "our greatest task in life."[65] Like St. John of the Cross, Häring observes that sincere persons have a "transparency" in all their relationships, and encourages all to be "transparent windows." For him, as for St. John, "sincerity forbids all forms of deception, including self-deception."[66] Like the transparent window in St. John's *Ascent* II, 5:6, in order to be free of the smudges which would prevent the ray of sunshine from shining through, each sincere person must make a decision to follow the path of honesty and sincerity in his or her own spiritual life.

In the health care field, the pursuit of what Häring calls "dominating knowledge"[67] often overrides all other forms of knowledge. By dominating knowledge he means that information which "is the kind of knowledge and skill through which I gain my own advantage over other people, the community, my subordinates, or those entrusted to me for education or pastoral care," and which may be dangerous, in that it "is the art of working one's way to the top, whatever the cost to pursue their 'careers' in an all-too-hierarchical religious institution, or in the way those devoted to success clamber to the top reaches of corporate power."[68] This knowledge is the tempting knowledge of which we spoke earlier, which drives people to seek recognition in their work, often blinding them to the immediate needs of their own patients. It is this knowledge, too, that may cause health care practitioners to exercise informational power over others, retreating behind diagnoses and tasks rather than interacting on the much more demanding personal level in the face of serious, perhaps terminal illness. The formation of a strong moral character necessitates a deliberate choice against using this "dominating knowledge" as a weapon against others.

Häring also speaks of two virtues which will enable persons to reach honest appraisals of specific situations. Each practitioner will, of necessity, have to discover his or her own most authentic response. Again, in the spirit of St. John of the Cross, the awareness comes that "God moves each thing according to its mode (*Ascent* II, 17:2)."[69] The virtues which will enable each person to discern the proper action in a given situation are *epikeia* and *oikonomia*, that is, "just kindness," and "spiritual housekeeping," as Häring names them.[70]

First, *epikeia* allows a discerning individual to use the powers of one's rationality to come to a just observance of specific laws and regulations. For difficult situations, it allows a certain flexibility in the following of these laws which will not destroy higher values in order to follow the letter of the law rather than its spirit.

For *oikonomia*, especially as it is applied in particular situations, the overarching concern for the welfare of individual persons in their own unique situations prevents a totally legalistic, rigid application of the general guidelines. As Häring states, these two virtues are closely akin to one another, and to embrace them is to grow in spiritual maturity, seeing and accepting one's own responsibility in a given situation.

Likewise, the virtue of humility—as cultivated by spiritually mature persons working with the grace of God—will allow persons to "plumb the abyss that reminds us how we emerged out of nothing."[71] Especially in dealing with terminal illness, this perceived abyss has the potential for instilling horror in our hearts, if in fact we see the abyss as annihilation rather than simply as an emptiness. Most important in one's ability to let go of perceived accomplishments and achievements is the faith that there is something beyond these things.

St. John advocates a focus on Jesus Christ, for as he says, "I have already told you all things in my Word, my Son, and if I have no other word, what answer or revelation can I now make that would surpass this? Fasten your eyes on him alone, because in him I have spoken and revealed all and in him you will discover even more than you ask for and desire. . . . For he is my entire locution and response, vision and revelation, which I have already spoken, answered, manifested, and revealed to you by giving him to you as a brother, companion, master, ransom, and reward" (*Ascent* II, 22:5).[72] (This quotation followed in the spirit of Thomas Aquinas's liturgical hymn *Verbum supernum*, as noted in John's footnote.)

To follow in the steps of Christ we may also strive for the spirit of *kenosis*, or emptying out of our "self" for the express purpose of being filled with God's wisdom. For Christ, it meant releasing his hold on his identity as God,[73] while for us, such a spirit may entail the releasing of all of our ego's hold on the recognition of our professional abilities, skills, and knowledge in order to travel with the patient who experiences the vivid reality of mortality. The sometimes painful "ego-surgery" does not deny our abilities, skills, and knowledge; it merely places them in proper perspective in relation to their "givenness" by God.

Kenosis, at first glance a frightening prospect, may be entered into with a spirit of trust and confidence, thus cleansing all the rubbish from our ego-filled pursuit of reward. "Letting go of tense egoism, self-conceit, and the rage of ownership can be momentarily painful and strenuous, but only as long as thankfulness for the grace of *kenosis* does not completely fill our hearts."[74] Unless one has sat beside the bed of a dying person, it is difficult to understand what emotional depth such a release entails. St. John, again in his first stanza, speaks of his "house" being all stilled. As seen by Häring, this virtue of *kenosis* "sweeps away useless refuse in the house of our soul, to make room for the wealth of God's love."[75] Some of this refuse has been deposited through years of training, vital to the competent practice of nursing, but useless as the ultimate answer when facing death. The "garbage dump" of our memories, then, must experience the cleansing fire of "letting go," perhaps the most difficult aspect of one's practice.

Discernment is our most precious task in such situations. Gula states it in this manner: "Discernment is not for determining right and wrong in the abstract. It is for determining which of the possible courses of action available would be most consistent with who I am and want to become in response to God's offer of love and call to be loving. Discernment is primarily a matter of the heart. . . . The strict logic of a scientific nature is necessary in morality in order to defend publicly what we have decided. But we do not actually make our decisions in the same logical way that we try to justify them. Ordinarily, in the moral life, we lead with the heart."[76] This concept derives from the *prudence* spoken of by Thomas Aquinas (*Summa Theologica* II–IIae, q.51) that enables one to "sift through all [the difficulties and consequences] to come to a decision which fits the particular configuration of circumstances at hand."[77]

Aware that all unique situations were not easily solved by the application of overarching rules, St. Thomas's work included a particular "respect for subjective sensing and grasping the invitation of God in a particular instance when material norms do not adequately take into account the complexity of the particular situation. His interpretation of prudence goes beyond the application of the objective criteria of moral norms and aligns the virtue of prudence more closely with discernment's attending to the internal stirrings of the heart."[78]

For the stirrings of our hearts to be transparent to the inflow of God's grace in a given situation, we as practitioners must be conscious of this virtue of prudence in ourselves. In the medical world, facts and regulations hold vital importance, but these facts and regulations must at times take second place to our respect for individual persons. "Neither virtue alone nor norms alone satisfy as an adequate expression of the moral life."[79] Relying neither solely on one's "heart stirrings" nor on the scientific facts of a given situation, we might aim for a balance—thoughtfully considered actions within the framework of the medical milieu, but permeated with the wisdom of discernment. Gula states, "Through the process of discernment, then, we try to cut through all the 'shoulds' and 'have-tos' which belong to someone else, and to cut through all the fantasies and passing fancies which are not of our whole-hearted wanting so that we might follow our heart's deepest desires. Whole-hearted wanting is the only sound basis for an authentic moral choice which is a response to the word of God at some particular moment."[80]

THE PROCESS OF DISCERNMENT

For all of us who are practitioners in an ever-evolving, scientifi-

cally based milieu, there is a method by which we may begin on our journey of discernment in the many "dark nights" we will inevitably encounter.
Gula capsulizes this method by mentioning three components of a spiritual
search. These he lists as "prayer, gathering information, and seeking confirmation both internal and external."

Becoming a person who within such a scientific atmosphere is able
to withdraw for a brief time and apply these principles takes great courage
and strength. First, as a prayerful person, a practitioner gives his or her relationship with God first priority. Knowing that God is the source of guidance and wisdom will lead health care personnel to step back consciously
from the rat-race, believing firmly that such a withdrawal of personal energy and focus from the frenetic pace of medical institutions will enable
them to reach a clearer perspective. Second, personal detachment from an
emotional investment in such situations will allow practitioners time to
gather the necessary facts. These facts are not just the medical diagnoses,
prognoses, treatments, or solutions, but rather the personal facts and awareness of individual patients experiencing their own illnesses in their own
ways. Sensitivity to these unique experiences will come for practitioners
who take the time to use the wholistic approach, conscious of the physical,
spiritual, social, and psychological elements of each unique human person.
Finally, the confirmation of one's internal responses to the situation, proper
discernment of one's own emotional baggage and points of view, as well
as consultation with other members of the health care team, will enable
each practitioner to strive for a balanced approach and a sensitive engagement with the patient, the family, and other professionals.

Such a process is a deliberate choice. We are each unique personalities pledged to serve the patients and families we meet. Within a very
complex medical atmosphere, we too often become almost robotic in our
efforts to complete myriad tasks. However, as John Wright has taught[81] in
A Theology of Christian Prayer, "Doing God's will . . . gives a general orientation for our lives, but the specifics are left to us. They depend on our
own talents, temperaments, upbringing, social constraints, opportunities,
and attractions."[82]

The responsibility of self-knowledge is a great one. Most impor-
tantly, the process outlined above will draw out of discerning professionals
an increased awareness of the obstacles lying within ourselves which hinder
us from responding in a "transparent" and sincere way to others. These
awarenesses are often very painful, as our hidden motives and desires for

recognition come blatantly to the surface, leaving us not only face-to-face with a patient in distress, but with our own inner turmoil, which we must release in order to face others openly and honestly.

This discernment requires "a continuous rhythm of prayer, leisure, silence, exercise to nurture physical and emotional health, and other spiritual exercises, such as spiritual direction, dream work, fasting, and whatever else enables us to unlock our imaginations and to let go of those paralyzing attachments which prevent us from being aware of God's presence in our lives and from bringing our lives into the drift of our deepest desires. The judgment to which the process of discernment leads will be as true for us as the freedom with which we make it."[83]

Ascent of Mount Carmel and *Dark Night of the Soul* contain St. John's analysis of this very phenomenon. Grounded as he was in the teachings of Aristotle and St. Thomas Aquinas, he brought his own deeply emotional temperament into the picture. A man of his times, he nevertheless received the gift of an awareness of the presence of God as source of all moral action for struggling human nature. But he was deeply conscious as well of his own powerlessness in the face of God's love, which was the source of the darkness so vividly described in both the poem and in his two extraordinarily detailed analytical works. He stated, "The road leading to God does not entail a multiplicity of considerations, methods, manners, and experiences—though in their own way these may be a requirement for beginners—but demands only the one thing necessary: true self-denial, exterior and interior, through surrender of self both to suffering for Christ and to annihilation in all things" (*Ascent* II, 7:8).[84]

Like St. Thomas before him, John encouraged the "habit" of acting in a manner responsive to God's grace (*Ascent* I, 5:6).[85] It was out of such habitual, conscious behavior that a new character was formed. He stated, "Moral good consists in bridling the passions and curbing the inordinate appetites. The result for the soul is tranquility, peace, repose, and moral virtue, which is the moral good" (*Ascent* III, 5:1), and "Spiritual persons enjoy tranquility and peace of soul due to the absence of the disturbance and change arising from thoughts and ideas in the memory, and consequently they possess purity of conscience and soul, which is a greater benefit" (*Ascent* III, 6:1).[86]

Many of today's spiritual methods contain the specific lessons taught by John of the Cross. In his *Ascent of Mount Carmel* and *Dark Night of the Soul* John employed the systematic divisions prevalent in the university world of his day. For many practitioners, his many points of analysis might be a deterrent, but on further consideration, even the finest divisions of emotions, passions, tendencies, and human propensities contain subtle directives applicable even in the modern world. Because of the pressures of the medical milieu, the main focus is quite often on intricate details of procedures, tasks, and techniques. Likewise, there are divisions within our own psychological selves which at times pervade our practice. By this I mean to consider the subtle ego strokes which are given in the competitive world of job advancement and prestige. It is here that we may consider our own unique background, upbringing, and religious and cultural heritage, and know that it is within our power to be sensitive to how each of these elements affects our interaction, especially on a spiritual level, with our patients.

PERSONAL BACKGROUND AND POINT OF VIEW: OUR RESPONSIBILITY

As we begin any process of change, particularly in our spiritual outlook on our work, we will realize that many around us will look askance, wondering what has happened to us. Especially in a medical atmosphere, often brimming with competition, taking time to reflect may seem out of the ordinary, if previously we have been caught up in the frenetic pace of hospital or clinic. Today, as in the beginning of the hospice movement, spiritual quests are grounding elements in our practice. But Sandol Stoddard observed that a spiritual quest would bring about immense transformation:

> Fed on this part of our journey by our five senses and by all the beauties and gratifications of this world, we are aware still of being imprisoned by the limitations of ego, and we hunger for something beyond. . . . Mystics are unpopular, however, in a world full of technological marvels and material riches. As consumers of such goods they are strangely lax and disinterested; the signs and symbols of worldly power habitually fail to impress them; and so "mystical" has gradually come to mean foggy and foolish, unrealistic, a little daft, maybe; and we have turned to the engineers, the technicians, and the scientists when we wanted firm truth.[87]

At the risk of seeming "foggy and foolish," the beginning of our attempt to grow spiritually in our approach to our work may feel awkward—we may feel left behind as others strive to climb ladders of accomplishment. We may also find ourselves accused of having no ambition, should we decline positions of authority which by their essence actually distance us from the patients we intended to serve.

Practices such as those advocated by St. John are seen by many in today's world as morbid, as he described the struggles of a soul moving from the darkness of uncertainty to the fullness of God's light[88] Whereas some may view such spiritual darkness as an aberration and attempt to "fix" it with medications, the darkness experienced when one releases all preconceived notions of what "I ought to do," and sits still long enough to listen to deeper insights considered God-given, is a prelude to a powerful use of one's God-given gifts and talents.

The focus of St. John's work was on the relationship between the soul and God, with full appreciation of the gifts granted, both natural and supernatural. As we have noted, however, John exhorted souls not to cling excessively to those gifts. "It is when the Christian loves the gifts of God, including the spiritual gifts, more than he loves God, that darkness engulfs the soul."[89] Too strong an attachment to the certainty of medical facts, to the detriment of a practitioner's engagement with his or her patient, darkens the ability to see clearly the root cause of spiritual distress. As Georgia Harkness states in her work *The Dark Night of the Soul*, "In almost every instance the individual caught in a bad situation can (himself) do something to better it. In order to avoid the supineness of self-pity, it is important to recognize this fact. To be a victim of circumstances does not mean to be a helpless victim. Whatever one can do, one ought to do. What one cannot change, one ought to accept with as much patience and fortitude as (he) can, looking to God for grace to endure it without bitterness. It is the function of religion to enable (men) in evil situations to do what they can and endure what they must."[90]

Illness, particularly terminal illness, is often not "curable" by medical means. An outlook such as the one Harkness mentions is hard won. Surface concern will not suffice. Rather, the spirituality of practitioners as they relate to their patients must allow them to "enter into their world, share their darkness, (and) feel their pain. . . . Is it, or is it not, asking too much of doctors and nurses that they should lower their defences so as to have empathy with those they treat? It is important here to be clear on the difference between sympathy and empathy. Sympathy is being sorry for and is a cheap grace. Empathy is feeling with and is a very costly grace indeed. Carl Rogers, the American psychotherapist, defined empathy as 'entering into the world of another as if it was one's own, but without losing the as-if quality.'"[91]

For professionals in the field of hospice practice, self-knowledge is vital. There is no retreating behind machines and procedures. Understanding one's motivation for helping others in this field goes far beyond wanting to "take care of patients." Books, such as Dale G. Larson's *The Helper's Journey*, address the psychological questions one must ask when working in this field. But the spiritual aspect, unique as it is to each person involved, is not easily contained in a "how-to" volume. Our personal backgrounds, cultural histories and religious experiences vary greatly even within the same faith traditions.

Likewise, we are products of Enlightenment thinking, schooled in the importance of the provability of facts. One author observes this by saying: "The reduction of reality to sense experience, the erosion of the sense of mystery in its positive sense as an indication of humanity's openness to an Unlimited and Divine Horizon—these notions meet with their critique in the dark night of unknowing, which reminds us experientially of our unlimited aspiration."[92]

The process of disengaging ourselves from the need to cling to facts as ultimates is a painful one. As William Thompson states in his volume *Fire and Light: The Saints and Theology*: "Human growth is a struggle against the urge not to grow, but to fixate."[93] Thus, in our struggle to be spiritually in tune with our patients in their final struggles, we enter into a place that is far from a "safe place," where we can point to specific facts and say, "This is your answer." It demands an ability to leap into the chasm of unknowing with our patients. It is an experience of complete powerlessness in the face of that unknown, for which medical training most often does not prepare us.

When all the "props" are taken away and we are left face-to-face with only the person suffering the illness, if we have not recognized our own finitude in practice, the reality of it will strike us fully, perhaps knocking us down in the process. What happens at such times is that our uneasiness shifts us back into "performance mode," where we busy ourselves "doing" things for a patient. "Nothing seems to be able to provide support, and if this condition continues for a long time anxiety intensifies greatly. Frantic efforts are made to fill up the emptiness—distraction or work but these do not meet the real issue which is taking place primarily in the *substance of the soul*. . . . Put simply, there is the experience of being undone, and the more God's mercy and love are active, the experience will be that of being utterly and completely undone."[94] For anyone in the health care field, this experience is traumatic; stripped of our usual "tools of the trade," we are left with whatever personal resources remain. Again, the professional talents we possess are vital in some ways, but as St. John calls for the relinquishment of our dependence on outward signs and consolations, so too our spiritual journey here will consist of "the abandonment of self-mastery and the taking on of a radical dependence on God (necessarily) accompanied by a sense of being undone or being annihilated."[95]

I believe that those who practice their profession in the field of hospice work have an unparalleled opportunity to learn the teachings of St. John of the Cross firsthand. In many medical circles, for those who stress "cure" over "healing," in the deeper sense, placing themselves without "props" before a patient—whose very illness may seem to threaten all they have held dear—is an intolerable thought. Throughout his *Ascent* and *Dark Night*, John sets as a goal the "reordering of our loves," placing all one's gifts, consolations, and talents as a thanksgiving to the One from whom all are received. "John urges an ascetical freeing of the heart. . . . [He] learned that only God's love could entice him from his idols. Right where his desires were exhausting themselves trying to find fulfillment, in the dark of his apparent failure, John experienced a kindling of a deeper love."[96]

Although work with the terminally ill seems to some a depressing, sad endeavor, and those who work in it are sometimes mysteries to those in other fields, in actuality the work brings with it an immense respect for what lies beyond this immediate life. By embracing the spiritual principles of the "Dark Night," hospice workers can, as Peter Slattery notes, "be passionately related to this world, be committed to it, without the heart being fragmented or enslaved, and without distorting the world. . . . [He or she can] love with freedom of spirit, without clutching."[97]

The experience just described comes after a person has recognized the limitations of medical practice, be it as a physician, nurse, or allied professional. This recognition brings about a new sort of "knowing," far beyond the analytical sort necessary for competent practice. Sandra Cronk calls this an awareness that "to the analytical mind there is only emptiness," in the sense that no fact of itself is able to describe the experience of God in relationship with humanity. For us as practitioners, the desire to conquer our own vulnerability by hiding behind skills and roles gives way to a deeper knowledge. Facing our own wounds allows us to face those of others. "Those deep hurts we had walled off for protection can finally be healed. The angers, fears, and lusts we had rationalized away are revealed for what they are. We can be transformed and healed by God's love. This can happen because we no longer must prove our essential worth to ourselves, hiding that which does not meet our approved self-image."[98]

We as health care practitioners are all too used to "proving" ourselves, through performance reviews, skills reviews, continuing education, and plaques on our walls. Stripped of these outer trappings, however, we again come close to understanding what St. John speaks of in his work. Releasing all outer images, we "confront those sinful and broken places in ourselves which block us from loving God and others."[99] John's many pages of examples—of virtues gone awry, faults brought to the forefront, and the dangers of a certain sort of pride—teach us the necessity of searching for our soul's freedom in areas other than our consolations. "When we symbolically fill ourselves with our own meaning, our own doings, and our own thoughts, there is hardly any place in our lives where God can encounter us."[100] As we sit beside the bed of a terminally ill patient, we enter a place where God will most certainly encounter us. Each practitioner will experience this in his or her own singular way. Women will experience it differently than men, though no less painful is their journey, as traditional "roles" dissolve and we meet one another in stark humanity.

Constance FitzGerald, in the volume *Women's Spirituality: Resources for Christian Development*, reflects on the experience of "Impasse and Dark Night," where the knowledge of the essential "opaqueness" of our humanness calls us "beyond ourselves and into transcendence." We thus "are being challenged to make the passage from loving, serving, 'being with,' because of the pleasure and joy it gives us, to loving and serving regardless of the cost."[101] Calling to mind both the *Ascent* and the *Dark Night*, she reminds us, "Even if we view an experience as one of death, the powerlessness we experience is our opportunity for growth into God—that when all our learned skills and usual pattern of communication seem to fail us, it is there that we discover a totally new way of relating to one another (and) a new kind of love and deeper level of communication."[102] This journey, as described by the above authors, takes us beyond the limits of our professional training. It challenges us to be courageous in our relationship with our own inadequacies. It is not an easy journey, and each of us must make it alone, surrounded as we may be by others on their own paths.

In today's medical milieu, especially in university hospital settings, where a strong element of professional competition is present, becoming a spiritually oriented professional will mean for each person a balancing of his or her professional skills with the desire to draw back from the hurried atmosphere and spend time in reflection. John of the Cross experienced something like this in his own life. Not only was he well educated in theology, but he had a strong desire to answer his own calling as a contemplative person. The tension between these elements of his personhood caused him a great deal of pain as he strove to balance them:

> Perhaps he suffered a severe conflict between the task of theological speculation, for which he had a talent, and the mystical tendency that was inwardly pressing him to respond with total commitment to his contemplative vocation. . . . In his surroundings, there was the usual competitiveness, and many students set titles, promotions, offices, and professorships as their primary goal in life. Doctorates, contention over university chairs and promotion to them—everything had a public feature about it, celebrated with ornate parades, regional folklore, and bull runs on the main square. This competition for titles and professorships revealed the misguided priorities of many of his contemporaries. . . . John was later to write that when we give first place to such values as titles and positions, our relationship with God becomes darkened and our intellects clouded. This in turn leads to pride and a scornful attitude toward others; to flattery and vain praise, which conceal deception and vanity; to rivalries and quarrels (see *Ascent* III, 19:3; III, 22:2–3).[103]

This state of affairs is closely akin to our modern academic/professional world, where status is signified by awards, promotions, titles, and various other forms of recognition. It is all too easy to succumb to such enticements, believing that titles and awards speak to the essence of our professional lives. But as John of the Cross taught throughout the whole of both his *Ascent* and his *Dark Night*, reliance on these external consolations is ultimately unsatisfying, and leads to frustration, anxiety, and irritability in our dealings with others.

To discern our true state of mind, then, for all of us who practice in the health care field, and who wish to develop a deeper spiritual approach to our practice, the collaboration with a spiritual guide is vital. Qualities which indicate a good spiritual guide are "genuineness, caring, and under-standing." These qualities lend themselves to an honest relationship be-tween searcher and guide—genuineness, meaning that the guide is totally attuned to his or her own spiritual workings, thus allowing an honest and free interchange between persons; caring, meaning that the guide looks with "unconditional positive regard" on the searcher, seeing his or her unique personhood with all its strengths and weaknesses; and understand-ing, through which the guide is able to enter into the spiritual quest of the searcher with respect and insight.[104] Finding such a guide, the searching professional will then be able to relate his or her experience honestly, re-ceiving insight and guidance from a competent, caring spiritual teacher. Doing so, practitioners will grow spiritually and professionally. The com-petent use of their natural talents and skills will be deepened by the spiritual dimension which will ground their practice.

In the spirit of St. John of the Cross, "Faith tells us of things we have never seen, and cannot come to know by our natural senses. It is like the light of the sun which blinds our eyes, because its light is stronger than our powers of sight. So the light of faith (with hope and love) transcends our comprehension (see *Ascent* II, 3:1–4)."[105] For those in the field of hos-pice work, having been stripped of many of the technical "tools of the trade," and left facing their patients in a heart-to-heart situation, the light of faith sometimes becomes the only strength remaining after the patient's physical illness has taken its toll. It falls to each practitioner to take his or her responsibility seriously to discern the proper role they will fill for each unique patient.

SUMMARY

The first three chapters of this study examined the historical de-velopment of the hospice concept, selected philosophical and ethical the-ories, and a view of the life and work of St. John of the Cross. This chapter has focused on the discipline necessary for practitioners attempting to un-derstand his spiritual teachings. We began with a look at the external dis-ciplines necessary for a well-ordered society—the state of health care law. As cases become more complex and families question outcomes, a frame-work of external control provides structure and a method of accountability. Beyond mere civil law, the law as it applies to health care encompasses a moral dimension as well as a legal one. Combining the standards of practice with a view of a broader, moral framework gives an external means of regulation to all practitioners. Yet this dimension does not automatically spring from internal sources. It is in this area that we, as practitioners in a highly technical and ever-evolving field, come to the realization that our motivation must come from within. The increased focus on a spiritually based practice has taken a solid turn in recent decades, with more people reaching within themselves and into their personal religious traditions for guidance in their professional practice.

A brief consideration of the natural law as a fertile resource for moral insight gave strength to the thought that each person has within himself or herself the ability to discern in a given situation the right moral outlook. This approach moves beyond mere legal obedience to the respect for a moral vision in regard to one's patients. Validated in one's community of belief, it expands to application in the lives of patients and families, respectful of the dialogue necessary for proper discernment.

The personal experiences of two men, both health care practitioners, provided unique points of view from within their unique situations. Each one's experience resonates with the precepts of St. John of the Cross, who advocated spiritual detachment from particular forms, consolations, and attitudes, and counseled freedom of spirit and deepened relationship to God. The spiritual pain involved in this process was transcended by the grace of God working in each man's situation.

A brief mention was made of the experience of women in the medical professions as well, noting (in the light of the previous chapter) the differing emphasis in a woman's outlook as she seeks professional standing in today's medical milieu.

Hospice work, as a spiritual practice itself, was then considered as it demands in-depth honesty and self-knowledge in relationship to one's patients. The various forms of knowledge so important in health care practice at times detract from following a spiritual journey, and it takes self-aware practitioners to peel away the trappings of the modern medical atmosphere and return to reflection and deep consideration of their patients as unique, suffering individuals. Certain virtues arise in the character of professionals who enter into this spiritual quest, the fruits of which are compassionate care and open communication.

Finally, we noted that the process of discernment leads to a greater understanding of the principles taught by St. John. As each person becomes aware of the need for a more focused spiritual approach, an awareness of one's own spiritual vulnerability arises. Releasing the fearful hold on all external consolations, each practitioner accepts his or her own unique background, cultural and religious traditions, foibles, strengths, and attitudes, melding them into an integral whole with which they encounter their patients. Realizing that a "mystical" outlook may strike some as odd, nevertheless they act faithfully in their newfound confidence. Having experienced the darkness in the natural faculties, they move beyond them and attempt to reach an understanding of the light of true, honest spirituality. Likewise, they realize they are never finished products and will at times be faced with seemingly unsolvable problems. But if they have managed to incorporate some of the principles taught by St. John, the acceptance of the incompleteness of all scientific answers will allow them to deal more gracefully with the uncertainties not only of their own lives, but of the lives of their patients.

We will now proceed to a closer look at patients' experience of the dark night of the soul, relating it as well to the experience of the professionals who attempt to walk with them through that experience.

CHAPTER FIVE

PATIENTS AND THE DARK NIGHT

I will begin this chapter with a meditation by John Carmody, a theologian who died in September of 1995 after a three-year struggle with multiple myeloma. He embodies in a vivid way the depth of spirit revealed through an encounter with terminal illness. He was a person with a strongly intellectual, academic background. In the spirit of St. John of the Cross, he faced the reality of death with courage and a decidedly learned detachment. Here is one of his final meditations:

> I do not control your Spirit, so I cannot control my dying. Whenever I feel separated from your Spirit, I lie as though unredeemed in a pit. Animal vitality is passing. Remarkable, cause for praise, always it finally crashes. Spiritual vitality requires crashing, your breaking us apart, our finally realizing we cannot understand you; we have always to journey by faith. In the darkness of that journey, the pain and fear and doom, we learn that you will be what you choose to show us, that you will speak your name only night by night. O God, help me listen for your speaking. Give me the ear of a lover, the collectedness of a disciple. Help me to abide, not squiggle and squirm away. When I run from my death, it nips at my heels. When I abide, it backs away. Yes, you are my final passion, the awfulness of all your otherness. But you are also my bliss and my freedom from all lesser harassments. Be you then also, God, my good death and everlasting life.[1]

Facing a terminal illness cannot truly be understood in the depths of our souls unless we are the one facing it. In this section I will relate some of John Carmody's reflections as examples of the work of someone who for many years was a writer and teacher, solidly trained in theology and philosophy, a former Jesuit priest who left the active ministry to marry. His insights cover a three-year period from the original diagnosis in mid-April of 1992 to the time of his death in September of 1995. The emotions he expresses in his work include the initial shock of the terminal diagnosis, his anger, frustration, despair and depression, as well as his occasional

hope, anticipation, joy at reaching new levels of understanding on both natural and spiritual levels, and his final acceptance of his inevitable death.

Dr. Carmody's reflections speak directly to the core of this chapter,
the experience of contemporary patients in the midst of their own dark night
of the soul. His work refers specifically to John of the Cross on several occasions, and it becomes obvious that what had formerly been intellectual
knowledge and solid academic training was transformed through his living
out of his own final illness. Though he had been a priest for many years,
his choice to leave and to marry had caused him professional and personal
distress. When faced with his impending death, his final writings capture
the full range of emotions experienced by many undergoing the same trials
today. His theological background allowed him to reach back in time to the
dark night experience of St. John of the Cross and make it his own.
Throughout his two final volumes, we can find references to his reliance
on his faith to carry him through his darkest hours. Perhaps his writings
can clarify for us the often unexplainable fears and emotions assailing terminal patients and their families.

ACCEPTANCE, LETTING GO, AND RESOLUTION OF "UNFINISHED BUSINESS"
In an interview for the London Times in June, 1999, Dame Cicely
Saunders, the founder of the modern hospice movement, spoke of the spirit
of hospice. Until her death she remained a primary consultant for St.
Christopher's Hospice in London, passing away at that facility on July 14,
2005. Dr. Saunders's first paper on the hospice movement was written in
1957—its title, "The Care of the Dying." Her years of experience in nurses'
training, as well as her subsequent medical training, came out of her firm
dedication to relieving the pain of those experiencing terminal illnesses. In
her ideal of hospice, she gives the goal for practitioners in the field. "You're
trying to give people the space for them to discover that they are who they
are and that it's all right and not too late."[2] She writes, "Most lives are a
mess of unfinished business: things left unsaid, letters left unwritten, love
left unexpressed. People need to reconcile differences, patch up rifts. There
is the possibility of making good an awful lot of untidiness in life, time to
pack your bags and say goodbye, and sorry, and thank you."[3]

At the point in a person's illness where all extensive treatment has
been forgone, and the main goal of treatment is palliation, the powers of
the psyche may be sorely tested. It may be said that one has reached an
"impasse," a place from which there is no escape, and no turning back.
As Constance FitzGerald states:

Impasse can be the condition for creative growth and transformation *if* the experience of impasse is fully appropriated
within one's heart and flesh with consciousness and consent;
if the limitations of one's humanity and human condition are
squarely faced and the sorrow of finitude allowed to invade
the human spirit with real, existential powerlessness; *if* the
ego does not demand understanding in the name of control
and predictability but is willing to admit the mystery of its
own being and surrender itself to this mystery; *if* the path into
the unknown, into the uncontrolled and unpredictable margins of life, is freely taken when the path of deadly clarity
fades.[4]

Certainly this is the stage where patients with terminal illnesses
find themselves. How each individual copes with arriving here depends on
his or her own personal history and unique approach to life. During the
course of our lives, we very easily construct our images of God out of what
may be familiar to us. Quoting Michael J. Buckley's article "Atheism and
Contemplation," FitzGerald notes, "We make God, or gods, in our own
image. 'Our understanding and our loves are limited by what we are. What
we grasp and what we long for is very much shaped and determined by our
own nature and personality-set.'"[5] What happens at the end of life is a shat-
tering of those images, a failure to withstand the test of our own humanly
created "idols"; FitzGerald states, "John of the Cross is at pains to show
how our images of God are progressively and of necessity changed and
shattered by life experience."[6]

What is often seen in terminally ill patients is an emotional withdrawal from all familiar persons and things, a distancing that is the result
of the natural detachment which occurs during the process of accepting a
terminal diagnosis. FitzGerald comments that it is at the deepest stages of
night that "one sees the withdrawal of all one has been certain of and depended upon for reassurance and affirmation. Now it is a question, not of
satisfaction, but of support systems that give life meaning: concepts, systems of meaning, symbolic structures, relationships, institutions. All supports seem to fail one, and only the experience of emptiness, confusion,
isolation, weakness, loneliness and abandonment remains. . . . The realization that there is *no* option but faith triggers a deep, silent, overpowering
panic, that, like a mighty underground river, threatens chaos and collapse."[7]
Finally, FitzGerald states, "As Americans we are not educated for impasse,

for the experience of human limitation and darkness that will not yield to hard work, studies, statistics, rational analysis, and well-planned programs. We stand helpless, confused, and guilty before the insurmountable problems of our world. We dare not let the full import of the impasse even come to complete consciousness. It is just too painful and too destructive of national self-esteem.[8]

When patients reach this stage, their illness brings about a naturally enforced limitation to independent activity. In the midst of the immediate physical concerns, such as pain control and care of the natural bodily functions, patients undergo a radical awareness of the emotions (or passions, in the words of John of the Cross) of joy, hope, fear, and grief (see *Ascent* I,13). Memories flood into consciousness, of times shared with loved ones and the remembrance of joyous times, which will now have to be relinquished to the unknown. Perhaps the final three emotions overwhelm persons at this stage of illness—fear of the unknown, hope that somehow a reprieve may lurk somewhere not yet discovered, and deep grief that death is inevitable. Again, in the light of the work of John of the Cross, these emotions cause "storms" within us, and in the words of one scholar, the "tiny sphere of the ego is shifted."[9] The sphere of the ego is our human accomplishments, our roles in life, our relationships, and anything else where we have literally invested ourselves during our lifetimes. At the end of life, however, with the diminishment of our human capacities, we are left hanging precipitously on the edge of emotion, and are forced to be still in the face of what perhaps causes great terror in our hearts. I will now explore some of the states of mind and emotions expressed by John Carmody in his final illness.

THEOLOGIAN AND PATIENT: MEETING OF THE MIND AND HEART

In both the earlier meditation by John Carmody and the reflection by Constance FitzGerald, the concepts of John of the Cross are evident. The feeling of abandonment, the realization that all ego-based satisfaction avails nothing in the face of the ultimate relationship with God, and the stripping away of all prior natural satisfactions grip terminally ill patients in what may sometimes feel like an emotional vise.

John Carmody was a serious thinker. The enforced "retreat" into his own thoughts brought him to levels of profound self-reflection which he often had avoided previously. This entailed an intensity, which, for him, was "the ruthless excision of nonessentials."[10]

Like St. John, Dr. Carmody returns repeatedly to Scripture, finding consolation there, especially in Jesus, whom he calls his "model, the sacrament of how I want to live and die."[11] He says, "I must cling to Jesus, dead and risen, if my sense of the God holding me in being is to save me. Clinging to Jesus, I open myself to the Father and the Spirit, through whom Jesus defined himself."[12] As he returns in the depths of his spirit to his lifelong commitment and calls upon his own memory, he likewise reflects on what John of the Cross reminds us, that we need release from whatever emotionally binds us. "Most of what people cling to, of what keeps them from reason and reform, are baubles and bagatelles. Like John of the Cross's tiny cord that holds the sparrow, keeping it from flying free in the heavens, our attachments tend to be ludicrous (*Ascent* I, 11:4)."[13]

One sees in the progression of Dr. Carmody's reflections the growing peace in the midst of episodes of anger and despair. One of the most honest statements he makes, several times in fact, is his disappointment in the friends who fear seeing him in his illness. They seem to him "ever more erratic and inconstant."[14] In the face of terminal illness, people do not know what to "do" for others, because facing one's own death brings on a deep sense of aloneness. Thus, for one who feels this aloneness, the presence of others who do not fear the encounter with a friend in distress can alleviate some of the emotional pain by just being there with them, and those who cannot approach a terminally ill friend miss an opportunity to touch their lives in ways inexpressible in words. "We can't do much for the terminally ill. Sometimes practical things—money, cooking, visiting; more frequently all we can do is care and pray. The ill know this thoroughly as they know that they are always alone. But sometimes care can tame loneliness, milk much of its poison away. So not to care faithfully, regularly, dependably is not to be a significant friend."[15]

Since John Carmody's profession was teaching and writing, his intellectual strengths formed the foundation of what he did for over thirty years. Perhaps this is the reason he closely identifies with the concepts of St. John of the Cross. He states, "This project of coming to grips with a sentence of death is nothing scholarly. The main sources for accomplishing it lie within, in your darkness, my God."[16] Like St. John, he finds it necessary to release all the intense emotions which hinder him from entering into deep relationship with the God who for him is the ultimate relationship. Embracing death for him needs to be God's work within him:

I need my death to be your unmediated action, O God. I need to think of this terminal illness as your touch, your increasingly intimate embrace, your deliberately chosen way of freeing me from bodily limitations so that I might become lost and found in your infinity. . . . Come God, my death. Kill in me all that resists you, who are love. Teach me finally to love my life, my body, my world, now that they are ending. Help me to place them all in your keeping. I want to abandon myself, as all lovers do, even though I am afraid. I cannot do it myself. You must continue to do it for me, in me, as you have been.[17]

As we have already seen in *Ascent of Mount Carmel* and *Dark Night of the Soul*, a progressive "letting go" of all that has formerly given one consolation and emotional solace transpires during the journey toward final union with God. John Carmody vividly describes his own daily growth in ability to release what has given him joy during his own life. His academic credentials, earned by years of study, had conferred upon him a certain status among his peers. Terminal illness significantly changed his perspective. "When we have no health in us, no comeliness to entice the outer world, we lose the power to impress others."[18] He prays,

My consolation, however, comes from contemplating you, my God, and applying my senses to Christ on the cross. There you reknit my bones, even as they fray toward pathological fracture. There you heal the pains most worrying me: my sins of lust, sloth, ingratitude—most of all ingratitude. You have heaped good things upon me. Above all you have given me Christian faith. Yet I have been careless, casual, inadvertent. You have been passionately naked, wholly vulnerable and available, and I have preferred pleasure, success, distraction.[19]

The loss of one's intellectual faculties, for a scholar, seems the ultimate loss prior to an encounter with a terminal illness. At that time, only the patient's intellect and the light of faith can sustain them. "Even the horror of losing my understanding, being driven into unconsciousness, is losing its force. If you need to take away my mind, so be it. I say that more bravely than honestly, because now my mind is my main defense against fear."[20] He sees his dying as a "series of renunciations," realizing that his wife is now picking up more and more of the practical elements of their life together. This is the completion of the "unfinished business" of their day-to-day home life.

> More and more the practical affairs fall to my wife. I used to do the dishes and some of the cleaning, most of the shopping, all the paying of bills and financial planning, most of the deals for the books we wrote. She earned most of our money as a university professor. It was a good arrangement, suiting us both. I was the dreamer with the mind for numbers. She was the teacher with the instinct for politics. Who are we now? What must she become for the future? I want time to work this out, dear God. I don't want to leave her unprepared. Maybe this is male protectionism to the end, but I ask you to let me get our affairs into good order. Of course, if this is not to be, I have to let it go, along with everything else.[21]

Dr. Carmody returns to prayer repeatedly in his book of reflections. Though his career as theologian necessitated his study of many intertwined details and systematic analyses, at the end of his life he finds (as this prayer illustrates), "When we feel the call, we should let go of all thoughts, worries, even joys that take us apart from you. You call me to simplicity. I feel best when resting at my depths, on your buoyancy. . . . Now my body is teaching me stillness."[22] This echoes the stillness of which John of the Cross speaks in the stanzas of "The Dark Night," where, going out alone at night, he knows his soul to be stilled, all emotions calmed by their rest in God. Dr. Carmody's experience is one of uncertainty in the face of what is to come. He says, "At the end of my thoughts, as in the beginning, darkness prevails. It is the dominant spiritual medium as night after night your Spirit broods over waters too primeval for me to sound."[23]

What is apparent in Dr. Carmody's work at this stage of his life is that all his former training and his Christian commitment have become his primary focus. His natural human accomplishments take on their true perspective for him. His reflections on abandonment, the surrender of his own natural human strengths and attributes into the hands of his God, are striking in their constancy throughout his meditations. He says that all his thoughts of former mystics, for example the author of The Cloud of Unknowing, led him to understand that "my life is your doing," and that his deepest instinct is "that you control my fate."[24]

Again referring to St. John of the Cross, Dr. Carmody expresses the understanding that as he rests in God he is able to comprehend John's advice: "Let nothing disturb you." His prayer becomes at that time: "Let us know, as you find best, that we are not alone and meaningless but a part of you, being of your Being. Plunge us into this overwhelming mystery, this ungraspable goodness and love, however we can best stand it, best profit from it."[25]

Part of the natural release experienced by St. John of the Cross in his spiritual journey was the release of a clinging to intellectual concepts, images in the memory, and his own will. As we saw in Chapter Three, St. John did not advocate a total rejection of one's natural intellectual powers, but rather an appreciation of their giftedness and a moving beyond them to relationship with God. Dr. Carmody reflects on this as he views the gifts which science provides him in his illness, appreciating the medical helps he receives for pain control and cancer treatment. As to the perspective in which he holds each, he says,

> Certainly, we ought to use the medical helps that our doctors encourage. God expects us to honor both human intelligence and the regular laws of nature. On the other hand, when we are thrown more nakedly, more directly, upon the divine will, we can tell ourselves that this has the benefit of engaging our faith more profoundly. Then, whether our health prospers or fails can seem to be the will of God immediately, directly. All along, of course, God uses both our actions and the actions of natural agents to fulfill the divine purposes, execute the divine plan.[26]

Patients who have entered into the process of living out a terminal illness may not reach acceptance right away. In fact, there are often periods of anger and depression, well-documented by Elisabeth Kübler-Ross (see Chapter One), which sap the patient's emotional and physical strength repeatedly. The deep spiritual discoveries often come after very painful bouts of anger and resentment. Dr. Carmody notes, "What ought we to say to all the pretty little writers, who go on so preciously about care of the soul? You are not pretty, God, and many of your people are writhing. Sometimes I want to smash those little writers, make sure they at least know rudimentary pain. So free yourself from all of us, us who abuse you. In your terrible transcendence stand far, far apart. Be as different from us as you can be without breaking us into little pieces."[27]

Again he expresses some disappointment in some of his friends, saying, "For a few of you, I have survived for sufficient time to no longer be a news item, a tragedy or curiosity worth your bothering about." But following this he adds, in appreciation, "For far more of you, the will to offer overt support, renewed promises of prayer, has continued strong, much to our benefit and gratitude."[28] Expectations relinquished, reality accepted—these are two elements experienced extensively by terminally ill patients.

Because Dr. Carmody was blessed with a facility for writing, he expressed the wide range of his own emotions well:

> When the body is racked, we can do nothing that feels lovely. You have chosen to tear us apart, slashing the flesh you once formed. In the mysterious ways of your savage love you have become a consuming fire, a cancer holocausting our bones. There is nothing genteel in real suffering, no Calvin Klein blusher or premier cologne. Real suffering is raw, shocking, horrible, knocking "success" into a crumbled cocked hat. . . . Nothing is pure or dependable. All my awareness is slanted. So you must be my awareness, the reality of a faith below taint. When I let go, stop thinking, enter the pain as though it were your arms, I come close to dissolving in your reality.[29]

Here Dr. Carmody expresses emotion similar to St. John's images of being completely one with God as one's own identity is joined, through suffering and purgation, to the Divine. In yet another meditation he echoes once again the sentiment of St. John, woven throughout the entirety of *Ascent of Mount Carmel* and *Dark Night of the Soul*, that it is our desire which causes unrest, and yet our desire which leads us to God: "I knew far too early from precocious wounding that all life is suffering and the cause is desire. But I've never been sure that desire isn't the remedy also, desire made pure by a dazzling beauty, a love that would ask all and on occasion provide all that we or it ever could ask. Can I find this love now in the rotting of my flesh, the throb of my bones, the much greater throb of my angel's heart? Please, please let it be so."[30]

Part of the acceptance of the inevitable final release in death comes when patients realize that any ability they might have had to control the outcome of their disease has vanished. This release of control plays an important part in the peace of soul which facilitates a peaceful death. Dr. Carmody describes it in this way: "The task is to meet the mystery where it presents itself, not where I might like it to be. The call is to let even torpor serve God's purposes, a lumpen benefaction. Maybe some of this is just resting, getting ready for the leopard's roar. Fortunately, it causes little worry. Absent sharp pain, I'm content to wait."[31] The intensity of his own suffering obliterated all ultimate reliance on his former strengths, his writing and teaching, his competence in practical matters—all dissipated in the light of his inability to trust the waning processes of his body.

Pathological fractures, so common in advanced cancer, became a constant threat. His thoughts included, "As my bone marrow gets pounded down, I sometimes feel like Paul's pot, being worked out by the divine potter. I think of clay, ashes, dust—variants of the nothingness of the creature, experienced as liberating. It feels good not to have to matter, except to the mercy of God. It feels fortunate in my bones to escape from the narcissism so thick on the ground, in my past biography."[32]

Dr. Carmody's reflections include the full range of emotion described at length by Elisabeth Kübler-Ross in her descriptions of the stages of grief. What Dr. Carmody possesses is a lifelong gift of faith, in his case the Christian faith that not only led him to his initial vocation to the priesthood, but which upheld him as he lived the transition from priesthood to the life of a layperson, along with his wife, Denise. Fortunately, he was able to continue his deeply loved vocation as teacher and writer. As can be seen in his work, he became almost a psalmist in the last three years of his life. Releasing his dependence on what he "did" for a profound understanding of who he "was" before God, he demonstrates through his final reflections a modern expression of the power of spiritual transformation so emphasized in the works of St. John of the Cross. He says, "Grant to your mature in faith, those who live in the eye of the storm, the grace no longer to reason at length. Let them take their lives like bread from your motherly hand."[33]

ATTACHMENT IN OUR MODERN SOCIETY

The world of modern psychology has appropriated the term "dark night" for any experience without apparent positive elements. We undergo "dark nights of the soul" in uncertain situations where we have not yet reached a satisfactory conclusion. Unfortunately, the full meaning of this term may be submerged in our search for solutions *we* reach, not in our understanding that somehow we are not fully *in control* of our own destiny. "For many today the flood of overly optimistic spiritualities has failed to satisfy, precisely because they so often avoid engaging people on the level of their suffering. There is fresh understanding of our human need to find meaning in our suffering, to engage in the process of grieving if we are to be open to growth in the Lord. In fact we know that it is not possible to embrace tomorrow, to fully engage in the process of change, if we do not grieve."[34]

Too often the solution sought is one which will involve the least amount of pain. Attachment is described as "the beginning of a process of fixing one's desire upon a person, object or situation in such a way as to make it a god."[35] The solutions sought may indeed become "gods" for those seeking relief of emotional distress. For terminally ill patients, seeking a cure may become foremost in their minds. If this goal is unrealistic, spiritual and emotional unrest ensues. The impossibility of living out the concepts taught by St. John is evident in such cases, with often disastrous results. Such patients "fix on a creature in order to escape a feeling of powerlessness and to create a sense of control."[36]

With each turning of hope and expectation on a prospective cure, spirits are raised only to come crashing down again once that hope is dashed. This leads to despair, which in turn leads to sadness and depression. Such attachments are illustrative of the various levels of intellectual and emotional attachments described by St. John of the Cross as hindrances to true spiritual union with God. While there are strong positive elements in seeking a cure—that is, by employing the available medical resources— unrealistic pursuit of these can be detrimental to patients whose illness has reached the incurable stage. At this point, emotional despair may be alleviated by working with these patients toward an acceptance of that fact. Some may reach it; others do not for many reasons. But at the point where medical science has reached its limit, we as practitioners and our patients can benefit from a turning from the concept of "cure" to that of a broader concept of "healing," which includes our spirits.

There appears to be a significant increase in expressed desire for spiritual pursuits in modern society. Forms explored range from nature spiritualities to exploration of Buddhist, Taoist, Native American, and New Age spiritualities. People also migrate between the mainline Protestant and

Catholic churches, and some explore the various forms of Judaism. Choices abound. However, when persons reach the stage of a final illness a certain desperation may be sensed in some patients. This desperation may be described as a "darkness of spirit," which must be faced uniquely by each person and family. "The dark aspect of the night accentuates all the forms of adversity which we undergo in the course of living and being transformed. Much of that adversity arises out of our own inner poverty, from emotional weaknesses, psychological limitations, personal sinfulness, addictions, codependency, attachments, etc. It assails us also from the outside: disease, harsh words, unjust accusations, etc. God integrates all that pain into our night, cooperating with us to convert into good our passage through those diminishments."[37]

Those who work in hospice have seen that we approach a terminal illness as we have lived our lives, with the same attitudes, hopes, fears, and dreams which have accompanied us to where we are. One of the most difficult aspects of "letting go" is acceptance of that place in our lives which includes all our ego-investments, our roles, and any accomplishments on which we have placed significant value. Our final surrender into the plan of our God causes pain at the outset. "The immediate cause of the night is transforming union. The principal cause of its darkness—that is, of the pain—is our immaturity, our resistance, our woundedness, our inner poverty."[38] It would seem that true spiritual release from that pain calls for a surrender of soul that is not effected by us, but rather by the power of God within the soul. In other words, "The going forth is more received in us than performed by us, since it is the Lord who causes us to go forth. He breaks our shackles so that we can move freely out of our attachments . . . more deeply into him."[39]

One example of the process of releasing attachments was a hospice patient I cared for at one point. He was the center of his family's life. This man's role could be described as similar to the hub of a wheel from which radiate all the spokes that support the outer rim. His problem was excruciating pain, radiating from his back down his legs, unrelieved by a tremendous amount of pain medication, the doses of which reached almost astronomical proportions. Even to the day of his death, this gentleman could not let go of his role in the family, and neither could the family release him to a peaceful passing. On doses of pain medication which would immediately have killed a person whose system had not built up tolerance, this man continued to go in and out of the hospital, his family clinging to him in their grief and sadness at losing him. Having refused the option of a surgical procedure which would have eliminated his pain through the implementation of a nerve block, he continued to have his intravenous medications increased, to no avail.

He finally died, in the hospital, his pain seemingly a combination of physical and emotional elements so intertwined that his physicians were at a loss as to how to treat him successfully. Such is the combination of emotional, spiritual, psychological, and social elements which constitute each unique patient. The emotional "storms" of St. John of the Cross become evident today as patients struggle to cling to the known, familiar elements of their lives while attempting to face their fear of the unknown.

Though at the end of his life the patient previously mentioned was no longer in a hospice program, those of us who had been involved in his care experienced a great sense of regret that we had not been able to provide a better situation for him. Part of a hospice program is allowing patients and families free choices about their treatments within hospice guidelines. Throughout the process, the staff listens, each one acting within his or her professional capacity, hopefully supporting and encouraging the entire family while enlisting all possible resources, both medical and spiritual, to facilitate the ease of their last days together.

Certain practitioners, in dealing with the problems of addiction, co-dependency, and attachments have brought the insights of St. John of the Cross to bear on their own work. These spiritually oriented men and women use their own understanding of the principles described by St. John to facilitate their patients' journeys through the difficulties of "letting go" and moving beyond their own personal situations. The "purgation" undergone in such journeys is, as it was in the work of St. John, a combination of active and passive elements.

Active entrance into such programs is freely chosen, the discipline freely embraced. The passive element comes when each person faces his or her own inability to "do it on their own," and subsequently releases natural fears and uncertainties. As with terminally ill patients who withdraw from those they love and enter into a world of their own, all who seek the release of their personal attachments, even to dearly beloved family and friends, find that in time they are mercifully desensitized to the pain, by something quite beyond their own understanding. "God desensitizes us to what we need to transcend. That reversal occurs no matter how providential the creature has been in our life."[40]

Our detachment from all that we love, all that we have accomplished—our "identity" as it is seen in today's society—causes deep pain. We have seen that in the work of John Carmody. The most peaceful hospice patients are those who have completed the task of detachment and who have undergone a transformation not of their own doing. "Transformation always means dying at least partially to what one loves. This dying to self must be all the more complete when we give ourselves to a One-greater-than-ourselves. Therefore, there can be no limits to the uprooting required on our journey in God."[41]

PRACTITIONERS' APPROACHES TO PATIENTS AND FAMILIES IN LIGHT OF THE DARK NIGHT

Dale Larson, in his 1993 volume *The Helper's Journey: Working with People Facing Grief, Loss, and Life-Threatening Illness*, capsulizes the essence of the idealistic desire to "help" which characterizes many health care practitioners. In a reference to the work of George Bernard Shaw, he quotes the playwright: "This is the true joy in life, the being used for a purpose recognized by yourself as a mighty one; the being thoroughly worn out before you are thrown on the scrap heap; the being a force of Nature instead of a feverish selfish little clod of ailments and grievances complaining that the world will not devote itself to making you happy."[42]

Larson explores the motivations leading people into the caring professions. Centering on altruism as a primary factor in motivating people to enter a professional or a volunteer situation, he notes that besides the desire to reach out to help others, people in such professions exhibit a high degree of empathy, the ability to feel with another without becoming overly invested and too subjective in the relationship. Likewise, he examines the problems inherent in too strong an emotional attachment on the part of the health care professionals. Several chapters are dedicated to the professional, in a thorough examination of the processes of "finding the balance" in one's emotions, personal involvement, sense of "burnout," and stress levels.

What such a study emphasizes is that those who work with people facing terminal illnesses, grief, and loss are subject to a number of very natural feelings which must be honestly addressed if caregivers are not to be sidelined by their own inabilities to handle the intensity of the work. Granting the very positive effects of knowing that what one does brings benefit to others, Larson also explores several signs that indicate inordinate stress in a health care practitioner, ranging from apathy and emotional exhaustion to anger, depression, feelings of helplessness, and basic inability to maintain one's normal personal involvements due to an emotional distancing.[43]

We have already seen the experience of two specific practitioners as they strove to integrate their own spirituality with their health care practice (see Chapter Four). In the light of what we have seen in the work of St. John of the Cross, how may we continue to individualize our own response to the intense work of dealing with those in anticipatory grieving stages such as hospice patients and their families? What sorts of people must we be for them? What sorts of people must we be for our fellow workers in the field?

Any approach we take will force us to face our own personal emotional "baggage." This baggage contains both positive and negative elements, which when seen in the overall perspective of our lives will have given us a particular outlook on life. The strengths we have, as well as our weaknesses and personal insecurities—all these elements combine to make us the practitioners we have become, and will continue to become in the lifelong process of personal and spiritual growth.

In an article in the *Kennedy Institute of Ethics Journal*, there appears an analysis of nursing as "moral practice." We as "persons," or "moral agents," have a serious responsibility to go beyond mere technical skill and competence and to integrate our moral selves completely into our practice. What is sought is "the *caring relationship* as a condition of nursing practice, *caring behavior as the integration of virtue and expert activity*, and "*good care*" as the final goal of nursing practice."[44] Seeing the nurse as a person who, through the combination of finely tuned skills and an upright character, specifically exhibits virtues in personal relationships, the authors stress the importance of operating within a spiritual perspective. They set the person in a teleological or goal-oriented profession, which for a nurse is the optimal well-being of his or her patients.[45] This is much like the work of St. John of the Cross, who situates his spirituality in the light of the soul's progression toward its ultimate "end," a final relationship to God.

Likewise, the authors focus on the nursing profession as more than just a "technical art" concerned "exclusively with methods, instruments, strategies, and the like; in short, a science of the means as such."[46] This means that one's practice goes far beyond mere technical efficiency and calls upon the personal resources of moral character which each practitioner possesses. This includes primarily one's ability to relate honestly with another human being in a particular time and place, with a view of the other person as unique, highly valuable, and deserving of the utmost care. This attitude will naturally preclude any treatment of the patient as less than the valuable human person he or she is. "If nurses fail to recognize the *otherness* of the patient, then they are in danger of reducing the patient to a function of themselves or making the patient subservient to their self-development."[47] (We saw a similar concept in Chapter Two when we examined the second formulation of Immanuel Kant's Categorical Imperative. There he stressed that we must never act as though another human being were merely a means to our chosen end. Rather, each human person was to be treated "as an end." Thus he emphasized the value of human persons in themselves.)

The hospice concept, as noted in Chapter One, stresses the respect the professional must have for the entire situation of the patient and his or her family. No matter what one's own personal spirituality may be, a "standing back" is necessary in order to allow each unique person to live out whatever spirituality he or she might have. Respecting one's "otherness" precludes practitioners from imposing their own spirituality on their patients—no "deathbed evangelization," if you will. Rather, it encourages the other to rely for their strength on their *own* spirituality. Care is exercised in this sense when we enter into a smooth flow of interaction with our patients. We perform as professionally trained persons, attempting to integrate our practice with the strength we obtain from our own faith traditions.

Thus, part of the responsibility of practitioners toward patients is their constant awareness of themselves as developing and growing human persons. In a faith context, this will orient practitioners toward their own relationship with God, and may become their spiritual goal, seen as an answer to a call given by God to them as valued by their Creator and thus worthy in themselves to respond to that call. The authors of the article mention nurses' responsibility to develop inner resources, to "care for themselves" responsibly. When they receive personal "rewards" for caring for their patients, these not being monetary rewards, they are in turn given strength to pursue the development of their own inner resources. "Nurses can develop as persons to the degree that they devote themselves to the development of the other. Caring for the other is in fact an important condition for their own development as persons."[48]

Set in the light of the principles of John of the Cross, such a reciprocal relationship is the source of many of the natural consolations we receive as human beings. These may be accepted gratefully, rejoiced in for their giftedness, but never clung to as absolutes. Anyone who honestly analyzes his or her own health care practice knows that at times there will be no apparent positive reward. At these times, one must call upon inner resources. A spiritual orientation will allow practitioners to remember that these resources are grounded in something quite beyond the immediate situation. There are several qualities called for in the relationship between caregivers and patients, which far exceed mere technical skill: "These functions would include, among other things, providing comfort and preserving human dignity in the face of pain and extreme breakdown, presencing (being with a patient), providing comfort and communication through touch, guiding patients through developmental and emotional changes, helping patients to cope with the consequences of the illness for their lifestyle, and interpreting the illness by letting patients themselves verbalize and understand."[49]

Truly responsive and responsible health care practitioners are aware that they possess only human qualities and thus are at times overwhelmed by patients' and families' expectations of them. The qualities of character, steadfast virtue and a realistic view of one's own capabilities will enable those in the caring professions to withstand the onslaughts of emotional exchanges between themselves and those for whom they care. The high level of intensity in situations involving terminal illness draws out of us our very best efforts. If we have not taken the time to replenish our own inner resources, we will be unable to cope with such intensity and will therefore be less than helpful to our patients.

The authors state that "morally virtuous attitudes are an integral part of nursing practice, since this practice takes place within a human relationship where the nurse and the patient are the main actors."[50] It is in this arena where we as practitioners will find the greatest challenge to our professional and our spiritual lives. We may step back from the immediate situation momentarily and take stock of what we are attempting to do in our practice. In the light of St. John's teaching, we stand as total human beings with all our natural qualities and abilities. These are the elements with which we interact with others. Our personal expression of virtuous behavior stems from who we are as human beings, our motivation, and our perception of who we are in a given situation. The authors state, "As we analyze the virtue of care more closely, we can distinguish two dimensions, one cognitive and one affective-motivational."[51]

Taking this at face value, we understand that all our professional skill comes into play as we encounter our patients, but that at the core of our interaction, very much at the level of our human identity, lies whatever motivation leads us to reach out to this other unique individual. Here the elements of surrender of our own will, honesty in our own assessment of ourselves as relational human beings, and willingness to be transformed by such an encounter will hold strong. Our spiritual core will definitely be changed by an encounter with another human being at the depths of his or her acceptance or rejection of a failing state of health. All emotional defenses crumble. We as practitioners are left vulnerable, and if we have not been strengthened at our core, we will be unable to "stand with" that person when he or she needs us most.

If we ask ourselves what will strengthen us at times like this, we might return to St. John of the Cross, as he urges us to relinquish our hold on all the external trappings of our humanness and surrender to the transforming fire of God within us. We recall the image of the log totally enveloped by fire (*Dark Night* II, 10:1),[52] noting that when we are faced with a patient undergoing such emotional turmoil, if we are not strong in our own spirit, we may undermine any remaining strength of spirit the patient possesses. Part of our professional responsibility to our patients is to remain aware of our own state of soul, as far as this is possible with our own human limitations. It is part of the care for ourselves the authors have mentioned. They call nursing "an ethically loaded endeavor, a moral practice primarily geared to making explicit and accomplishing whatever is good for the patient."[53]

Such a view will strengthen our resolve to become persons of upright character, practitioners of virtue in the context of our professional lives. As we have seen in the work of St. John, a person who is able, through the grace of God, to withstand the suffering inherent in personal spiritual purgation, "advances" by that suffering: "First, in suffering, strength is given to the soul by God. In its doing and enjoying, the soul exercises its own weakness and imperfections. Second, in suffering, virtues are practiced and acquired, and the soul is purified and made wiser and more cautious" (*Dark* Night II, 16:9).[54] We might approach this by remembering that when we relinquish the hold on all the external, technical proficiencies of our profession we are thrown back on our own personal resources. Then we discover through the sense of being without apparent support that we are given resources and abilities we might not have imagined. Out of this realization we are led to practice the virtues of which John speaks.

Here our practice will lose any ego-centeredness it may have had. Our pride of accomplishment, so easily clung to in the competitive arena which health care can become, dissipates in the face of our ultimate inability to "do" anything for the other person except give our "presence" to them. Only by our hollowing out our own selves and allowing ourselves to be filled with strength from the ultimate source can we be at all present in a way that will truly benefit the other. In considering nursing as the authors of the article have, as a "moral practice," one may see that the spiritual elements of the teaching of St. John may be beneficial to those in health care, and particularly beneficial to those dealing with patients with terminal illnesses.

Carol R. Taylor responded to the previously mentioned article with a point of view held by many nurses. Her realistic comments echo the earlier thoughts of this study (Chapter Four) when she points out that the ideal for which many of us entered the nursing profession has been drastically altered in recent years. In the competitive world of the profession, qualities of "assertive self-promotion, ruthless efficiency, and a willingness to sacrifice quality to cost containment" exist in many practitioners.[55] For many in the medical world, there exists a "perverted sense of professionalism . . . equated with power, prestige, and self-advancement as nurses individually and collectively seek to secure their survival, security, and advancement in today's cutthroat health care environment."[56] Unfortunately, I have also seen the reality of this statement, which illustrates the challenge involved in rising above such motivations in one's own nursing practice. To go against one's peers, speaking out against injustices committed in these situations, can at times alienate a practitioner from the power structure of many hospitals. Maintaining a virtue-grounded practice calls for a great amount of courage in such situations.

The teaching of St. John of the Cross focused on the purging of the intellect, the memory, and the will. Ms. Taylor's response includes consideration of six elements of nursing practice she believes are essential. Among these six elements are three which fall into the realm of St. John's work: cognition, volition, and imagination. She also includes motivation, which St. John also seriously considers in his analysis of the human soul. For Ms. Taylor, one's cognitive powers are brought into full play in any nursing relationship; all skills and technical knowledge competently practiced remain the tools of the trade. One's volition, corresponding to St. John's concept of the human will, is for her the decision to use one's expertise for the well-being of one's patients.[57] She includes the imagination as "the empathic ability to enter into and share the world of the other sufficiently to understand the other's unique situation and needs."[58] As she considers our motivation, she notes that it is "that which influences the will in a manner that predisposes one to act altruistically to promote patient well-being."[59]

With these points in mind, we may recall the teaching of St. John of the Cross as he urges his spiritual directees to release all ultimate reliance on any of the natural human gifts and attributes, a teaching heavily woven throughout both *Ascent of Mount Carmel* and *Dark Night of the Soul*. It would seem, even if we consider all the above attributes as essential to good nursing practice, or good health care practice in general, that, in the face of terminal illness, even these qualities must be relinquished as ultimate answers. When there are no words and no actions capable of reaching into the soul of a person facing death, all natural abilities fail. In the light of the unspeakable and unknown power of death, practitioners will come to understand the unexplainable nature of another's experience. Then it becomes apparent that the only thing we can do as practitioners is to practice "presence" to the other, in full acceptance of the fact that any perceived "emptiness and aloneness" will be transformed by full release into the ultimate source of spiritual peace.

ADDITIONAL THOUGHTS AND SYNTHESIS FOR PRACTITIONERS

It seems an insurmountable task for those of us schooled in the modern scientific method to release all we have been taught to consider marks of our professionalism to something over which we have absolutely no control. Likewise, the many spiritualities abounding today often stress the "feel-good" qualities of a good spiritual life. Edith Stein, who died in a concentration camp, came to see by her own sufferings that through the darkness of what we do not understand, all "that is hard, sharp, and crude" is made soft, and that the healing which we seek may not be that of our own physical health, but "the health that is God Himself."[60] This is quite a mental shift for many practitioners, since professional identity in the modern setting rises or falls on what can be seen and rewarded. To release that identity is not considered wise. In fact it may seem foolish.

Several years ago a patient asked me why a certain physician "always backs out the door as he is talking to me." It was apparent that the physician did not know he was doing that. He was a man of superior clinical knowledge, but could not deal with the questions posed him by a patient suffering from terminal cancer. Upon discovering that another of his patients had passed away (the patient's wife, though she had been sitting next to him, had not noticed that fact), this physician left the floor obviously emotionally unstrung, again unable to deal with what he had no answers for.

To acquire the ability to stand firm in the face of such occurrences requires that we as practitioners stand aside from our practice at regular intervals, noting "who we are" in relation to it. The qualities of "holy recollection, consisting of internal solitude of spirit and an inner detachment from all that is not God"[61] are vital at times like these, since only by gaining the true perspective on technical/clinical expertise as distinguished from spiritual sensitivity and interrelational ability will such problems be more adequately addressed. Then we, unlike that physician, will find ourselves not needing to flee an encounter with the unexplainable.

St. John was most concerned with the development of the spiritual lives of those he directed. For us, so many centuries later, the need remains though it may be clothed in very different social garb. Our task, first of all, is to become aware of those qualities in ourselves as practitioners which promote unrest within our own hearts and souls. We must, as he encouraged, be brutally honest with ourselves as we notice emotions, tendencies, desires, and motivations which are contrary to an integral and virtue-based practice. Reflecting on the principles taught by St. John, we may recall that he says, "Nothing created or imagined can serve the intellect as a proper means for union with God. . . . All that can be grasped by the intellect would serve as an obstacle rather than a means if a person were to become attached to it" (*Ascent* II, 8).[62] For us in the health professions, this will mean relinquishing our total dependence on the facts we have available to us, though not disparaging them, and falling back on inner resources as together with our patients we face what may be unexplainable and not easily understood.

St. John taught, incorporating the thought of Aristotle, that "two contraries cannot exist in the same subject" (*Ascent* I, 4:2). Practitioners thus cannot be committed to their own self-advancement at the same time as they attempt to maximize the ultimate well-being of their patients. John also described those who are filled with "appetites" (in our society these

could translate as ambitions) as "always dissatisfied and bitter, like someone who is hungry" (*Ascent* I, 6:3). Professional advancement and the desire for recognition may exhibit themselves in such a manner in the modern
hospital milieu. So, for practitioners who succumb to the appeal of advancement and promotion, the pursuit of a practice based in a virtuous character may seem "burdensome and saddening" (*Ascent* I, 11:4).[63] But we
may also take some consolation in John's teaching, echoing St. Thomas
Aquinas (*Summa Theologica* I, 79, 6): "Whatever is received, is received
according to the mode of the receiver" (*Dark Night* 1, 4:2).[64] In this sense,
we may have a gentler hand with our own human weaknesses, which will
also allow us to have the same gentler hand with those who become our
patients.

SUMMARY

This chapter has focused on the experience of patients who, in the
course of a terminal illness, undergo what St. John called the dark night of
the soul. John Carmody's meditations illustrated the journey of a man who
had formerly relied upon his intelligence and training for his livelihood as
he faced his own mortality. The experience of final acceptance, letting go
of all that is familiar, and the resolution of one's "unfinished business" are
all elements of the dying process, faced uniquely by each patient and family
unit. As Dame Cicely Saunders noted, the aim of hospice care is to allow
patients that "space" to complete the emotional tasks. For modern patients,
as well as modern practitioners, the medical milieu may in fact be a very
difficult place to accomplish them, since "cure" may be the focus rather
than the "healing" in a more holistic sense.

Several therapists have also used the theme of the dark night and
the spirituality surrounding it in approaching their patients, helping them
in whatever way possible to come to a spiritual detachment from what
might hinder their spiritual growth. Finally, the tasks of those committed
to helping others in handling grief, bereavement, and terminal illness were
examined in the light of what personal responsibilities emerge—the self-
care, the knowledge of one's own motivations, one's strengths and one's
weaknesses, and how one will relate to others in spite of human inadequacies.

To all the above considerations it seems possible to apply the work
of St. John of the Cross. Specifically, and admittedly in the modern medical
world this seems the most difficult, the passive elements—the emotional

release of all clinging to tangible consolations and discoverable scientific methods—provide an opportunity for spiritual peace to grow and flourish even in the most dire situations. This takes place in very ordinary situations as well. As one author has noted, "Even a genuine contemplative will at times cling to the gifts instead of to God."[65] Accepting that terminal illness is something over which we have no ultimate control calls for a soul-deep release of all unfulfilled hopes and dreams, a "purging" of those elements in our lives. Egan notes,

> Some Christians tend to label every physical and psychological low as a manifestation of the dark night. On the other hand, there is almost no emphasis upon the need for purification in the quest for human authenticity in the many circles in which mysticism has become "trendy." . . . For St. John of the Cross and the Christian tradition, however, the passive dark nights are much more than emotional reactions, the bleak periods between ecstatic experiences, or even psychological breakdown, that is "deautomatization." They are essentially God's loving inflow, which purifies, illuminates, and transforms the entire person. Although they may include the above, the passive nights represent essentially and primarily the *unmediated*, negative experience of the God of love flowing into the person's inner core, reinforced by all sorts of internal and external causes of suffering.[66]

For patients in the final stages of terminal illness, such purgation envelops not only their bodies but also their spirits. If they are able to approach this situation from a faith perspective, looking beyond immediate circumstances to their God, they may discover the capacity to enter into this process deliberately. There is a natural calming of natural appetites and desires as one comes to accept one's illness, corresponding to the natural "annihilation and calming of faculties" in the journey of the "dark night."[67] During this time, all natural "supports"—those personal elements defining one's identity and one's roles in life—are removed, and there is the growing ability to acquire a deep inner peace of soul.[68]

The greatest fear during both the spiritual "dark night" and the final stages of a terminal illness is the "fear of abandonment."[69] For patients, the presence of their loved ones provides some solace. Practitioners may also give solace and encouragement as they employ their skills in obtaining the optimal comfort for each patient according to his or her needs. For practitioners, the fear of abandonment may strike on a professional level as they come to realize that all the technical abilities, necessary as they may be in patient care, pale in comparison to their ability to "be present" to their patients. As Sandra Cronk states, it is at this time that we experience "the crucifixion of all our humanly based understanding."[70]

Precisely at the point where we as practitioners and our patients, as patients, reach a peaceful release of that understanding, the principles taught by St. John of the Cross may be applied. The process is not an easy one, as his work has shown. We also do not accomplish it on our own. Preferably in a supportive spiritual environment such as our own faith traditions, we receive guidance and encouragement. Then we gradually learn to apply it within our professional situations. At the same time, we become more capable of being strong in spirit for those facing serious, perhaps terminal illnesses.

We turn now to the final chapter, where the emphasis will be on our religious traditions as further support for our professional practice. As contemporary health care practitioners, we may lose sight of the validity of a sixteenth-century spirituality for our modern practice. St. John of the Cross and his work are part of a tradition which grounds all human activity in its journey toward God. Though he illustrates one element of that tradition, the *apophatic* (see Chapter Three), we have available some twentieth-century resources on which we may call—specifically, the Documents of Vatican Council II and the *Consistent Ethic of Life* approach advocated by Cardinal Joseph Bernardin in the early 1980s and continuing to the present day. For us as practitioners, it will help to broaden our perspective, as we consider these contemporary spiritual resources.

CHAPTER SIX

SUMMARY AND CONCLUSIONS:
CONTEMPORARY SPIRITUALITY FOR TERMINAL ILLNESS

The Judaeo-Christian tradition, with its historical highs and lows, provides a wealth of spiritual guidance. Likewise, in the Documents of Vatican Council II (1962–65), as well as in *The Consistent Ethic of Life* by Joseph Cardinal Bernardin, there are elements of the tradition applicable to anyone who deals with patients and families in the medical milieu. Though beyond the scope of this particular study, the wealth of spirituality of the Jewish tradition surrounding the sanctity of life broadens the practice of anyone in the field, no matter which faith tradition they claim.

As a final overview of this consideration of St. John of the Cross and the hospice movement (now extended into the broader field of palliative care), the statements of the Christian tradition found in the Vatican Council Documents and Cardinal Bernardin's volume call us to perform our professional tasks with dignity and skill. They also call forth from us a covenant response (see Chapter Two) as we situate ourselves as moral agents within our profession.

GENERAL OVERVIEW

We began this study with a look at the development of the hospice movement. Seeing elements of the solicitous care of the sick as far back as Greek and Roman times, we explored the evolution of care for the dying through the centuries. We then recognized the beginnings of the modern hospice movement in the work of Dame Cicely Saunders in England. Because of various societal pressures and legal actions, the modern hospice approach has been challenged in recent years by the "assisted suicide" and "voluntary euthanasia" movements. This has led to restatement of the original purpose and goal of hospice care, as well as volumes of legal cases stemming from perceived abuses in the health care delivery system.

We also noted the characteristics of those who enter into the hospice profession, as well as the difficult situations which challenge them. We noted as well the personal responsibility inherent in remaining detached yet involved, providing expert care that demands skilled proficiency as well as emotional and psychological support for patients and families. The Hospice Code of Ethics itself provides a framework within which practitioners work. This Code is the essential foundation for any approach to the care of the terminally ill. It clearly delineates the elements of clinical hospice practice as well as the broad concepts of character which form the professional life of physicians, nurses, and allied practitioners.

Chapter Two addressed not only the basic foundational ethical principles involved in health care, but noted that from early days the concept of "virtue ethics" was present. From Aristotle and St. Thomas Aquinas down through history the concept of the virtuous person in pursuit of the "good" has existed. Though submerged a bit in the consciousness of scholars who promoted the foundational principles of ethics in a systematic way, virtue nevertheless remained as a necessary element in the practice of the medical arts. Philosophers such as Kant, Bentham, and Mill added to the mix by their analyses of deontology, utilitarianism, and consequentialism. Focusing on the intellectual powers of humans, their willpower, and their emotions, the study of medical ethics has in recent decades been more inclusive of the idea of virtue ethics, of "what sort of person" becomes a practitioner.

From the mid-1970s to the present, the evolution of the medical-ethical field has moved at an amazing pace. Journals abound in which the specifics of modern cases are analyzed. This has led to an overwhelming sense of responsibility, especially regarding end-of-life issues, with a concomitant realization that we as human agents need more than our skilled professional talents. Spirituality—though in recent years it has become somewhat "trendy"—remains an important element in our practice, providing practitioners an additional framework out of which they may operate.

Chapter Three then addressed one form of spirituality, which may be embraced by today's medical professionals. In the field of hospice and palliative care, a basic experience of what St. John called the Dark Night of the soul may enable professionals to release the notion that medicine can cure all. Accepting the limitations of even the most advanced techniques (excellent in themselves, but sometimes unable to cure advanced disease), these practitioners may find in the work of St. John of the Cross certain helpful spiritual elements. A spirituality of the Dark Night may facilitate the process of letting go of a futile dependence on technology as a final answer.

Chapter Four explored the application of St. John's teachings to the lives of medical professionals. We used the example of a physician and a nurse as they related their own experience of spirituality within today's health care system. We also addressed the issue of how women may encounter a slightly different application of St. John's teachings, in a system which has grown in its appreciation of women's roles within it.

Finally, in Chapter Five we examined the principles of the Dark Night as they apply to patients suffering terminal disease. Through the writings of a theologian who was able to tap in on his own philosophical and spiritual training as well as his experience of his own terminal disease, we applied the teachings of our sixteenth-century scholar and mystic to a person in our own historical time frame. We saw how he called upon his own memory and intellectual skills as he simultaneously had to release them as points of his identity. For patients as well as health care professionals, the appreciation of intellect, personality, emotions, and talents as gifts facilitates the ability to surrender them to the Giver. The Dark Night process teaches both patient and practitioner how to do this, through the gradual stripping away of ego-reliance on any one gift as an ultimate. By focusing on the ultimate source of all life, talent, health, and skill, one gains perspective on the human condition.

Throughout the study, it has been noted that in today's modern world the accomplishments of professionals are rewarded, providing motivation for excellence in one's field. While a spirituality for today does not disparage such striving, in the light of the teachings of St. John of the Cross the rewards are not to be sought as ultimates. They are not proof of our identity. "What we do" is essentially different from "who we are," though a profession skillfully practiced is one statement of that. So it falls to us as professionals to learn "who we are" in the fullest context. Being in tune with our own spiritual nature is a part of that learning. As with our professional study and training, our responsibility as moral agents takes shape within our faith tradition and motivates us to excellence of character.

We have, besides the instructions from St. John of the Cross, encouragement from within our tradition in the form of Church documents and reflective consideration by ecclesiastical and theological leaders. These resources reinforce and contextualize our own personal faith experiences. Our professional practice is strengthened and supported by its grounding in community, and we find inspiration in the thought of our Church and its prayerful leaders. We may now consider two of the many resources available to us in the Roman Catholic tradition.

THE DOCUMENTS OF VATICAN COUNCIL II

Archbishop Rembert Weakland, in his collection of essays entitled *Faith and the Human Enterprise*, makes a strong statement about the need for all of us to internalize the spirit of these Vatican Council Documents. He says,

> We must never forget that the scope or purpose of the conciliar documents is that of increasing our holiness. Their living out should lead to greater personal holiness and to a more loving community of faith. This deeper spirituality cannot be ignored in favor of some external plan or program. Are we a holier people? Are we a more charitable people? Are we a more just people? These are the kinds of questions we must still be asking ourselves. Have the changes remained merely external, or have we truly interiorized them so that they are our very way of thinking and acting?[1]

Papal encyclicals since the time of the Vatican Council have also called persons to respond to the idealistic statements promulgated nearly forty-five years ago. One of the more recent ones has been Pope John Paul II's encyclical *The Gospel of Life* (*Evangelium Vitae*), written in 1995 in response to questions about the sanctity of life. He echoes the spirit of the *Pastoral Constitution on the Church in the Modern World* (*Gaudium et Spes*), which was originally promulgated in 1965 and remains a solid statement on the dignity of the human person in the world.

If we as health care practitioners claim the Roman Catholic faith as our tradition, we have a responsibility to translate that into action in our increasingly pluralistic society. Recalling our consideration of the natural law, we note that several popes focused on that ability of humans to discern their own dignity and that of others through their natural reasoning. These include John XXIII in *Pacem in Terris* (1963) and Paul VI in *Populorum Progressio* (1967). This ability crosses all denominational barriers, as does our practice.

Whatever spirituality we claim, our essential identity as human persons serves as our link to others, no matter of what faith tradition. As *Gaudium et Spes* says, "The joy and hope, the grief and anguish of the men of our time, especially of those who are poor or afflicted in any way, are the joy and hope, the grief and anguish of the followers of Christ as well. Nothing that is genuinely human fails to find an echo in their hearts."[2] For those of us in the hospice and palliative care professions, addressing grief and pain are daily occurrences.

Over four decades ago, the Council was aware of the tremendous effect of technological advances on the world:

> The spiritual uneasiness of today and the changing structure of life are part of a broader upheaval, whose symptoms are the increasing part played on the intellectual level by the mathematical and natural sciences (not excluding the sciences dealing with man himself) and on the practical level by their repercussions on technology. The scientific mentality has wrought a change in the cultural sphere and on habits of thought, and the progress of technology is now reshaping the face of the earth and has its sights set on the conquest of space.[3]

Like St. John of the Cross, the Church focused on Christ as the way to our destiny. "The Church believes that Christ, who died and was raised for the sake of all, can show man the way and strengthen him through the Spirit in order to be worthy of his destiny: nor is there any other name under heaven given among men by which they can be saved."[4] Like St. John too, the document focuses on the essential unity of the human being, composed of body and soul, which was to be celebrated, not condemned.[5]

This document will resonate with those of us who have been trained in the scientific method as well, since it speaks of the dignity of the intellect, of truth, and of wisdom. "Man, as sharing in the light of the divine mind, rightly affirms that by his intellect he surpasses the world of mere things. By diligent use of his talents through the ages he has indeed made progress in the empirical sciences, in technology, and in the liberal arts."[6] It recognizes the far-reaching efforts of our intellects and states that "his intellect is not confined to the range of what can be observed by the senses. It can, with genuine certainty, reach to realities known only to the mind, even though, as a result of sin, its vision has been clouded and its powers weakened."[7]

More importantly, for the considerations of this study, the document affirms the capacity in the human person to "discover a law which he has not laid upon himself but which he must obey. Its voice, ever calling him to love and to do what is good and to avoid evil, tells him inwardly at the right moment: do this, shun that. For man has in his heart a law inscribed by God. His dignity lies in observing this law, and by it he will be judged. His conscience is man's most secret core, and his sanctuary. There he is alone with God whose voice echoes in his depths."[8]

Going further to describe the effects of this inner conscience in all of human activity, both between individuals and between nations, *Gaudium et Spes* speaks of the sanctity of that activity as it affects the world. Because it is a part of the plan of God (section 34) human activity moves the world toward God. "Far from considering the conquests of man's genius and courage as opposed to God's power as if he set himself up as a rival to the creator, Christians ought to be convinced that the achievements of the human race are a sign of God's greatness and the fulfillment of God's mysterious design."

For all who practice a profession, the accomplishments within that profession serve as landmarks in a dedicated life calling. Even St. John of the Cross recognized the need for humans to return on occasion to aspects of their spiritual discipline which had provided help in previous stages, as we noted in Chapter Three. In a modern spiritual approach to the practice of health care, then, infusing our practice with an awareness of something beyond the immediate situation gives us a much-needed perspective on difficult challenges. The Council's *Decree on the Apostolate of Lay People* (*Apostolicam Actuositatem*) expressed the Church's position on the need for lay persons practicing professionally in the world to ground their activities in Christ and in His Church.[9] It is in this document that we find encouragement and support for living a spiritual life in the midst of what the document calls "the temporal order."[10] It states, "Christ, sent by the Father, is the source of the Church's whole apostolate. Clearly then, the fruitfulness of the apostolate of lay people depends on their living union with Christ; as the Lord said himself: 'Whoever dwells in me and I in him bears much fruit, for separated from me you can do nothing' (Jn. 15:5). This life of intimate union with Christ in the Church is maintained by the spiritual helps common to all the faithful, chiefly by active participation in the liturgy."[11]

As in the teaching of St. John of the Cross, our personal union with Christ will form the foundation of our practice, shaping our decisions and guiding us to an ever-increasing ability to discern the proper mode of action within given situations. This document also calls forth everyone, not just members of the presbyterate of the Church and vowed religious, but every person who exercises a Christian calling within the world. "This lay spirituality will take its particular character from the circumstances of one's state in life (married and family life, celibacy, widowhood), from one's state of health, and from one's professional and social activity. Whatever the circumstances, each one has received suitable talents and these should be cultivated, as should also the personal gifts [he] has from the Holy Spirit."[12]

We have considered the balance necessary between the respect for human intellect and talents and the need to release our dependence on them in the face of futile medical situations. The Decree also addresses the importance of proper valuing of such professional talents, while integrating them within a virtuous life. "They should also hold in high esteem professional competence, family and civic sense, and the virtues related to social behavior such as honesty, sense of justice, sincerity, courtesy, moral courage; without them there is no true Christian life."[13] Finally, the entire Decree situates the professional lives of Christian lay persons within the greater context of the world itself, stressing the importance of the "renewal of the temporal order" through both individual and community efforts. It provides a much needed level of guidance and instruction for practitioners seeking to integrate their spiritual and professional lives today.

THE CONSISTENT ETHIC OF LIFE

The Consistent Ethic of Life, a collection of addresses by the late Cardinal Joseph Bernardin, calls for a focused awareness on the sanctity of life, from conception to natural death. In view of the controversies surrounding abortion and euthanasia, this collection of his talks provides hospice and palliative care practitioners with yet another framework in which they may ground their practice. We will now consider this volume.

In 1983, Joseph Cardinal Bernardin gave the first of his formal lectures on a consistent ethic of life at Fordham University. He had been invited to speak on the U.S. Catholic Bishops' pastoral letter, "The Challenge of Peace: God's Promise and Our Response." But he broadened the scope of his address because of his belief that the university setting was one in which the relationship between the Catholic moral vision and American culture could be seriously considered.[14] Since the Bishops' Peace Pastoral focused on the linkage of the issues of war and abortion as assaults on human life, Cardinal Bernardin sought through his address to include consideration of the sanctity of human life from conception to natural death. For this reason, he included the issues of euthanasia and capital punishment in the broad spectrum of his analysis.

As a Roman Catholic Cardinal, Joseph Bernardin was aware of the role the Catholic Church played in the development of public policy. He said, "It is the lessons we can learn from the policy impact of the pastoral which are valuable today. The principal conclusion is that the Church's social policy role is at least as important in *defining* key questions in the public debate as in *deciding* such questions."[15] Bernardin's point in this first address on "the consistent ethic of life" is that the Bishop's pastoral letter is a starting point for developing the broader view of the sanctity of life, but that, in order to include the wider issues, we need to be aware of what he calls a "shift in perspective" of Catholic moral teaching in the thirty years prior to the letter. What he called the traditional Catholic teaching on the taking of human life was that "there should always be a *presumption* against taking human life, but in a limited world marked by the effects of sin there are some narrowly defined *exceptions* where life can be taken."[16]

Bernardin saw the teaching as retaining its validity in resolving "extreme cases of conflict when fundamental rights are at stake," but he added that in the light of the last thirty years "the presumption against taking human life has been strengthened and the exceptions made ever more restrictive."[17] He interpreted this on two levels, the first on the level of principle and the second on the level of pastoral practice.

The first level, that of principle, was related to the original "Just War" theory, which found its rationale in the idea of defense, recovery of property, and punishment. Those three reasons had undergone a transformation and synthesis into the "defense of the innocent and the protection of those values required for decent human existence."[18] Moreover, without denying the original teaching of St. Thomas Aquinas, Bernardin noted that even though it had originally been taught that capital punishment was justified in order to protect the state, the more modern approach was to search for more humane methods of defending society. Such a shift called for a broader outlook on the sanctity of life, and it was what Bernardin labeled "a consistent ethic of life." This was grounded in the belief that all life was sacred and to be protected.

In the health care professions, specifically in the hospice and palliative care arena, the issue of the sanctity of life becomes very important at the end of life. Medical advances have been phenomenal, and the ability to sustain life beyond previously imagined limits has brought a level of uncertainty to the moral decision-making process. Bernardin states it in this way:

The technological challenge is a pervasive concern of Pope John Paul II, expressed in his first encyclical, *Redemptor Hominis*, and continuing through his address to the Pontifical Academy of Science last month when he called scientists to direct their work toward the promotion of life, not the creation of instruments of death. The essential question in the technological challenge is this: In an age when we *can* do almost anything, how do we decide what we *ought* to do? The even more demanding question is: In a time when we can do anything technologically, how do we decide morally what *we should never do*?[19]

Cardinal Bernardin realized that one of the major tasks of the Catholic Church as teacher was to be a credible influence in our pluralistic society. He also realized that there was much work to be done in finding the balance between issues. He said, "The spectrum of life cuts across the issues of genetics, abortion, capital punishment, modern warfare and the care of the terminally ill. These are all distinct problems, enormously complicated, and deserving individual treatment.[20] His main thrust in the Fordham address was to call for an "attitude or atmosphere in society which is the pre-condition for sustaining a consistent ethic of life. . . . Attitude is the place to root an ethic of life, but ultimately ethics is about principles to guide the actions of individuals and institutions."[21]

Cardinal Bernardin emphasized the need for civility in discussions in the public arena. He was aware that sometimes acrimonious disputes arise, and because of his own personal approach to dealing with adversity, advocated a genteel approach between people. Such an approach would facilitate even the most difficult discussions.

Bernardin's discussion included four levels, woven together in what he termed the "seamless garment" of the broad issue of the sanctity of life. These levels began with a single principle which was the prohibition against attacks on innocent life. Again covering the issues previously mentioned, this principle is central to Catholic teaching and serves as the foundational element in his approach.

Second on Bernardin's list was the distinction between various cases rather than what made them similar. Aware that several moral principles were needed to analyze different issues, he called for discernment regarding the particular moral insight applicable in any given situation.

The Cardinal's third level questioned the way we translated our personal commitment to our public witness of life. He stressed that no one person could be responsible for doing everything, but that each was responsible for doing something, in tune with his or her talents and abilities.

Finally, Bernardin's fourth level encompassed the relationship between moral principles and concrete political choices. In his mind, the consistent ethic of life was needed to provide "a coherent linkage among a diverse set of issues, and would serve to test political party platforms, public policies, and political candidates."[22] His emphasis was on the possibility of living out a personal ethic of life in a public manner, recognizing that all such commitments "are applied concretely by the choice of citizens."[23]

Cardinal Bernardin drew on *Gaudium et Spes* as well as on the teachings of Pope John Paul II. He ended his address by noting, "The pastoral life of the Church should not be guided by a simplistic criterion of relevance. But the capacity of faith to shed light on the concrete questions of personal and public life today is one way in which the value of the Gospel is assessed. . . . It is a significant opportunity for the Church to demonstrate the strength of a sustained moral vision."[24]

FURTHER REFLECTIONS ON *THE CONSISTENT ETHIC OF LIFE*

In their volume, *Fullness of Faith: The Public Significance of Theology*, Michael J. Himes and Kenneth R. Himes, O.F.M., devote an entire chapter to the topic "Grace and a Consistent Ethic of Life." In it, they respond to a statement in the book *Modernity on Endless Trial*, by Leszek Kolakowski, in which he says that Christianity, out of fear of losing its unique identity in an increasingly secularized world, had taken on "frenzied efforts at mimicry"[25] in order to stay afloat. The authors analyze the question of whether or not there is actual hostility between the two domains—secular and sacred. They reach the conclusion that indeed there is not as drastic a separation as Kolakowski indicates.

Rather, in light of the New Testament, wherein Jesus Christ entered into the human world as fully God and fully human, there is no complete division of the realms of sacred and secular. The authors point out that, in the Christian tradition, the belief is that God has offered the "gift of self" to human beings, and that the world which we inhabit is the arena in which we are capable of either accepting or rejecting that offer. Grace, which is God's free gift, plays a central role in the work of St. John of the Cross, as we saw in Chapter Three. So the authors of *Fullness of Faith* note that we, as humans with the God-given freedom of soul, in our very choices for good or for evil demonstrate the goodness of God's creation.[26]

Throughout this study we have said that our response in any given situation is basically our response to the guidance of God within our hearts and souls. Noting that the propensity of the scientific world is to ask for proofs, we also recognized that the natural response for many practitioners is to look for signs and proofs, cures and closure for themselves as well as for their patients. Within the medical milieu, the tension between what is seen as secular and what is personally held as sacred is strong. Quoting David Tracy, the authors note that in *Gaudium et Spes* the world "is truly affirmed without being canonized."[27]

> But the statement that the sacred and the secular are not and cannot be opposed realms within the world, a statement which seems to follow necessarily from the Catholic doctrine of grace, is not equivalent to the claim that the sacred and secular cannot be distinguished. . . . The action of God and the natural causal network of creation are distinguished modally, not substantively: certain things are not caused by God and others by natural factors; *everything* is caused by God *one hundred percent* and caused by natural forces within the world *one hundred percent*. . . . A far truer statement of the relationship between the two elements recognizes that everything depends on God yet everything depends on one-self—from two different perspectives.[28]

Following along with the teachings of St. John of the Cross, we may then appreciate all we see around us in the natural world, and in the tremendous technological discoveries with which we work. But in the realm of the sacred, we may also appreciate the Source beyond the imme-diate and place ourselves in relationship to It. By appreciating creation, and humanity's part in that creation, we are freed from ultimate reliance on its external trappings.

Thus, within the medical milieu, we as practitioners in the Chris-tian tradition are enabled to carry on our work with a view which applauds and appreciates the wonders of modern technology. But more than that, we ground our practices in our faith traditions, realizing that "God's grace un-dergirds all being, supports every human act, holds in being and gives ef-fectiveness to every choice and undertaking, brings to its conclusion every relationship. It is not confined to certain spheres of activity, certain kinds of acts or relations. The locus of grace is everywhere, not some circumscribed domain of experience. Yet all human acts, private and social, are free human acts truly originating in human beings motivated by their own ends good and evil, agapic and selfish, wise and foolish."[29]

Practitioners in the health care field have their feet in two distinct realms from the start, taking their professional identities from one while grounding their personal identities in family and faith traditions. So it is from all these backgrounds and traditions that we as moral agents find ourselves functioning in our work.

> Because we are social beings, our sense of identity, our language and the ways of viewing the world which are built into it and therefore into us, our continuity in time with past and future generations, our willingness to give ourselves to tasks which may not see completion in our lifetime, our reception of values and standards of beauty from a cultural tradition, all tie us in to communities. And the survival and well-being of these communities are *our* survival and well-being. The life, the choices, the success and the failure of our community support or threaten us on the deepest level of our being.[30]

St. John of the Cross made a point of proclaiming his loyalty to the Church, as we saw in Chapter Three. He was also the product of a definite historical time and place—the sixteenth-century spiritual and literary world of Spain. Within that culture and out of that spiritual tradition he formed his spiritual life. For those of us in the modern world, the culture and historical circumstances are quite different. Practitioners face questions daily which never would have entered the world of St. John. Choices he could never have imagined are placed before us as well. We have the technological ability to extend life to limits previously thought impossible. This gives us tremendous responsibility for making solid, spiritually wise medical decisions which encompass the psychological, social, and spiritual levels of patients' and families' lives. Besides that responsibility, practitioners must remain faithful to their own spiritualities within these situations.

So it is that each health care professional, especially in the realms of hospice and palliative care, has the opportunity to discover the source of graced wisdom. It is as the Himes brothers note,

If everything which exists is rooted in the gracious self-communication of God, grasping anything in its depth, in the foundations of its being, in the full conditions of its actuality, is the discovery of grace. Every human act, precisely because it is the act of a free and creative human being, is grounded in the free agapic act of God. No domain of human activity, private or public, is secular, if secular means remote from or unrelated to the action of grace, independent of divine action. But every human act can implicitly or explicitly either affirm or deny its rootedness in the freedom of God.[31]

The Decree on the Apostolate of the Laity obliges all who are of the Roman Catholic tradition to respond within their life situations in a truly Christian manner.[32] This means, for those who practice in the health professions, actions performed in the line of duty have the capacity to proclaim by their essence the grace of each unique situation. The transformation not only of the individual committed person but also of the community in which he or she practices is at times quite visible. "Believers must engage in transformative conversation and action so that human political, social and economic communities become what they are but so often obscure, the locus of the agape of God."[33]

In what can be perceived as a totally secular situation, practitioners in today's medical milieu have a unique opportunity to act as a sacramental presence to those around them. This is not to say that they engage in work-time evangelization in the negative sense of becoming oppressive, preachy presences to their co-workers. Rather, in the spirit of Cardinal Bernardin, their own integrity will speak as a strong witness for their inner convictions. In the Catholic tradition, the seven sacraments engage each one of us on the level of both the specific event of sacrament itself and the reality to which each points. "All reality is not only potentially a medium of God's self-gift but no element of the created order can be truly itself *unless* it is a symbolic expression of the divine. Creation is in the image of the creator, and the very integrity of the creature is to be itself, an entity brought forth, maintained and loved by God."[34]

The authors refer to Langdon Gilkey's 1974 article in *Theological Studies*, "Symbols, Meaning, and Divine Presence." They expand on the idea of persons within "secular" contexts being sacramental presences to one another. Gilkey notes the interrelationship of the holy within our lives with the moral decisions we humans are called upon to make: "It is the holy as it permeates our entire life as creatures, and at every level of that life, to which worship primarily responds: the holy that founds our being, inspires our creativity, that cements and deepens our relationships, elicits and demands our moral judgments, and directs our common efforts to recreate and liberate the world."[35]

The authors include Cardinal Bernardin's work in their reflections as well. In summarizing his approach they say, "The consistent ethic of life is meant to articulate the graced nature of all life and the value of human life too often obscured by various forces in modern society."[36] To his approach they attribute four main characteristics. They state that it is analogical, comprehensive, dialogical, and consistent.[37]

Echoing what we noted in the previous section, they point out that the "similarity amidst difference" forms the basis for searching out the consistent ethic amid all the varied situations presented to us today. Despite the obvious differences in unique situations and issues such as euthanasia, abortion, capital punishment, and nuclear war, the foundational element remains the belief that all life is sacred and is to be protected.

As a comprehensive theory, the authors note that a consistent ethic of life is "comprehensive in its concern for all significant threats to the sacredness of human life."[38] As did Bernardin, the authors stress the many ways life is threatened in today's society. Importantly, then, they go on to reemphasize the dialogic nature of any conversation about these issues.

As with Cardinal Bernardin's work, they maintain that "precisely because the sanctity of life is a moral experience available to all persons, the voices and insights of many contributors to public discussion must be heard. The Catholic community ought not to act as if its practical strategies for promoting human life are the only useful and valid ones available within society."[39]

Finally, they echo the point that "a consistency in value is required."[40] With a strong reference once again to the tradition of the Church, the authors draw us back to a commitment to the values exhibited by Jesus Christ in his earthly life:

> An understanding of God's purposes for human life has been manifested in the life and ministry of Jesus. In his teaching Jesus emphasized the value his Father placed on human life and the extent of God's concern which embraced all people irrespective of distinctions such as class, race, gender or nationality. . . . Catholic theology's major contribution is not to

be expected at the level of concrete moral choices. Instead, the understanding of grace found in the Catholic tradition provides an orientation, a perspective from which to analyze and address specific moral dilemmas. It highlights the sacredness of all human life and serves as a counterpoint to the biases of a culture such as the American tendency to adopt a functionalist mentality when assessing human life.[41]

Reflecting the teaching of Thomas Aquinas, whose teachings we considered in Chapter Two, the authors have noted that overarching moral principles cannot cover all specific instances encountered in today's health care environment. So it would seem that the general orientation and perspective which they mention is a valuable tool for practitioners as they confront these situations. They call for discernment, the potential for which lies within each individual: "Moral vision orientates ethical reflection but does not replace such reflection. A consistent ethic of life roots itself in a moral vision, but moral principles must be developed which can guide decision-making and action. Principles are derived from the moral vision not so much by deductive logic as through discernment of those which 'fit' with the overall vision."[42]

St. John noted — throughout his *Ascent of Mount Carmel* and *Dark Night of the Soul* — the importance of validating one's spiritual discoveries within one's own spiritual community. Such a practice tends to eliminate wild flights of fancy by tempering them with the insights of others. Such a process seems important today as well. The authors note,

> In our culture, debates about private and public morality take place in a climate heavily weighted toward privacy. Lacking an appreciation for the communal nature of our lives, individualism promotes the removal of more and more issues from the public arena. Guided by the impoverishing vision of individualism, a society finds less and less reason to see moral issues, especially intensely personal ones, as also having public significance. When community and society seem vague and unidentifiable, the only reality is the individual. A consistent ethic of life encourages a sensitivity to the public nature of life and death issues and opposes the privatizing tendencies of an individualistic culture.[43]

For those of us practicing in the health care field, it thus seems apparent that we are not alone with our decisions. As we discern our own unique roles as practitioners in the modern world of medicine, validation is available to us not only with our fellow professionals but within our own faith traditions. Hospice and palliative care workers deal with those "intensely personal" moments in patients' and families' lives. It is the nature of the work itself. But in the midst of that work, there are both medical and faith communities which support our medical-ethical and faith-based decisions. If we are to integrate these decisions into what Bernardin called the "seamless garment" of a consistent ethic of life for our professional lives, we may tap in to those resources. They provide us with strong professional and spiritual pillars to shore up our sometimes fragmented societal approach to morality.

We saw in earlier chapters that the call to be an ethical person within the medical milieu has been present from the beginning of the medical professions. Though the settings are vastly different, the underlying principles as well as the call to be a virtuous person in the midst of complex life situations have remained constant, though at times more indirectly stated than at others. We are called to appreciate the intellectual gifts of humanity as it seeks ever more complicated technological answers. We are also called to develop a clearer perspective of the limitations of those very capacities. The awareness of the limitations of human qualities as "ultimates" brings a sense of acceptance, through the God-given grace of discernment.

Like St. John in the midst of his dark night of the soul, we experience the deep pain of clinging to what we can see or prove, things on which we in the health care professions are trained to rely. But at times we sit at the bedside of a dying person who has accepted that the disease itself has moved beyond the powers of medical science to cure. At these times, we may also be gifted with the sense that the peace toward which the dying move is in itself far beyond the limits of our human understanding. St. John experienced this himself and wrote about it in later works such as *The Spiritual Canticle* and *The Living Flame of Love*. In those works, he expresses in vivid terms his love for the gifts of creation and rounds out what many label as morbid and negative in *Ascent of Mount Carmel* and *Dark Night of the Soul*.

For a final thought on St. John of the Cross, I will look to Pope John Paul II's Apostolic Letter on the occasion of the fourth centenary of the saint's death. The Pope's great devotion to this saint as expressed in this letter provides another resource for today's health care professionals who seek to permeate their practice with a faithful living-out of committed spirituality.

THE POPE SPEAKS

In reference to the influence of St. John on the Church, the Pope said this: "The Church finds joy in attesting to the abundant fruits of holiness and wisdom that this her son continues to bear through the example of his life and the light of his writings. Indeed, his person and his teachings draw the interest of people from the most diverse religious and cultural surroundings. He understands them and speaks to the deepest aspirations of the human person and the believer."[44]

The Pope wrote of his own personal devotion to St. John from the earliest days of his own priestly formation. Noting that today's world is "filled with risks and temptations in the sphere of faith,"[45] he pointed out that his doctoral thesis was on the subject of *faith according to St. John of the Cross*. He outlined the need for the gift of faith in living out a true Christian life today: "I felt . . . that John . . . had set forth Christian life in terms of such basic aspects as communion with God, the contemplative dimension of prayer, the strength that apostolic mission derives from life in God, and the creative tension of the Christian life lived in hope . . . the message of a vigorous, living faith which seeks and finds God in His Son Jesus Christ, in the Church, in the beauty of creation, in quiet prayer, in the darkness of night, and in the purifying flame of the Spirit."[46]

Pope John Paul thus expressed his belief that the spirituality of St. John was applicable to the modern world. Including a reference to *Gaudium et Spes* (section 21) he stated that the witness of the Church today "is brought about chiefly by *the witness of a living and mature faith, namely, one that is so well formed that it can see difficulties clearly and overcome them.*"[47]

Such is the faith needed for the increasingly complex decisions in the medical world. Especially in decisions at the end of life, an appreciation of the dignity of human life comes through a belief in the giftedness of the human condition. The Pope pointed to the contemplative life as a source of fulfillment for today's Christian.[48] He pointed to our capacity to 'discover His presence and His love in all circumstances, whether favorable or unfavorable, in moments of fervor and in periods of apparent abandonment.'"[49]

The Apostolic Letter echoed what we have already noted, that the gift of faith governs all human actions in relation to God. It is nothing we attain by our own efforts, but rather it is the gift of God's guidance freely offered at all times. Quoting St. John in his *Ascent of Mount Carmel* (III, 17:2) the Pope said, "The will should rejoice only in what is for the honor and glory of God, and the greatest honor we can give Him is to serve Him according to evangelical perfection; anything not included in such service is without value to man."[50]

Moving into the value of St. John's words for us today, the Pope went on to say that he would highlight two aspects of that God-given faith which are especially applicable. These are the relationship between natural reason and faith, and living out that faith through interior prayer.[51]

We saw in Chapter Three that in St. John's mind there was not a discrepancy between an appreciation of human intellect and the surrender of that intellect to God in a relationship of love. The Pope stated, "Rational man's superiority to the rest of mundane reality should not lead to pretensions of earthly dominion. Instead it ought to guide him toward his most proper end, union with God, to whom he is similar in dignity. For that reason, faith does not justify scorning human reason. Nor is human rationality to be regarded as opposed to the divine message. On the contrary, they work together in intimate collaboration: '*A person can get sufficient guidance from natural reason, and the law and doctrine of the Gospel* (*Ascent* II, 21:4).'"[52]

He went on to say that in today's world the constant concern of the Church is for the cultural and theological development of the faithful "so that their interior life may grow deep and they may be able to give an account of what they believe."[53] He noted that encountering God "in mystery" is the means to the growth in the interior life. Referring to the fact that the expression "dark night" is now used in all aspects of life and not just in regard to the spiritual life, John Paul noted that our age has experienced what it calls "the silence or absence of God."[54] Human suffering on the moral, physical, and spiritual levels threatens faith. But the teachings of St. John call forth from the spiritual searcher a recommitment to a sense of gratitude for God's love and mercy. Even amid the uncertainties of human life, such a sense allows humans to exercise their freedom by their choice not to "depend on pleasant or unpleasant feelings" as ultimate guides.[55]

Again summoning our awareness of Jesus Christ as our role model, the Pope recalled St. John's treatment of Jesus' sense of abandonment on the Cross. He wrote that "Christians who live by faith habitually make the cross of Christ their point of reference and norm of living. Paraphrasing St. John, he advised: "When something distasteful or unpleasant comes your way, remember Christ crucified and be silent (*Ascent* II, 7:11)."[56]

Concluding his reflections John Paul pointed to the universal impact the teachings of St. John might have for us today. Appealing to "mystics and poets, philosophers and psychologists, representatives of other religious creeds, men and women of culture and plain folk,"[57] he described several levels on which John's writings might touch modern men and women:

> Some turn to him because they are attracted by the humanistic values he represents, for instance: language, philosophy and psychology. He speaks to us all of the truth of God and of the surpassing vocation of man. For this reason many who read his writings only for the profundity of his poetry consciously or unconsciously assimilate his teachings. . . . But he is also the guide of those within the holy Church who seek greater intimacy with God. The theologian "called to intensify his life of faith and ever unite scientific investigation and prayer (*Living Flame of Love* III, 30ff)" can learn from him, and so can directors of conscience, for whom he wrote many spiritually clear-sighted pages.[58]

Finally, addressing the Church of Spain specifically in words applicable to the medical community as well, the Pope described how we today can bring about the integration of the spirituality John exemplified with our own professional lives: "[By promoting] a suitable harmony between *the Christian message and the values of culture* . . . [which] means stirring up an open and living faith which carries the new lifeblood of the Gospel to the various areas of public life. This synthesis must be brought fully into practice by committed Christian lay people in the different sectors of culture. For this deep interior renewal of community and culture, John of the Cross offers the example of his life and the wealth of his writings."[59]

The Pope's Apostolic Letter illustrated his devotion to St. John of the Cross and offered his readers access to the spiritual teachings of this sixteenth-century poet and mystic. Addressing the question frequently posed in the medical milieu of the balance between the scientific (and provable) and the spiritual (personally experienced and less easily proven) worlds, he gives modern men and women insights on their own spiritual search in a highly pluralistic world. For practitioners today, his words serve as yet another resource accessible to those exploring the world of St. John's *Ascent of Mount Carmel* and *Dark Night of the Soul*, fully expressive of the faith tradition of the Church, yet applicable to those of other traditions and cultures.

CONCLUSION

Chapters One through Five led us through the world of hospice and palliative care, the philosophical and theological worlds which have served as the basis for the evolution of the field of biomedical ethics, the life and teachings of St. John of the Cross, and the experiences of practitioners and patients as they addressed end-of-life issues. Our final chapter has given an overview of some of the traditions and teachings of the Roman Catholic Church for today's world.

Because of the pluralism both of cultures and religious backgrounds, any spirituality for modern health care practitioners must be able to reach the level of soul-transformation and moral integrity. The surrender of spirit which does not negate the God-given gifts of intellect, talent, and professional skill must find its source in a faith commitment elicited by grace. Such a commitment evolves through both natural reasoning and human faith in an absolute Being who draws us near. It speaks of a loving self-gift which touches us on the level of our own disposition and ability to receive it. For this reason, each individual will search out his or her own way of responding in any given situation.

St. John of the Cross wrote out of the experiences of his own life and times. We today will live out our spiritualities in a very different world. Science and technology add undeniable complexity to our decisions, for while appreciating them as valid expressions of the human spirit of exploration, we as practitioners in the hospice and palliative care field deal daily with questions of the Ultimate. When all medical resources have been exhausted, there remains the question of what one's life has meant. It is this question which leaves us standing face-to-face with another human being as he or she faces the unknown, the unprovable, and that which defies easy explanation. Death, to many, is likened to the darkness, the abyss, of which St. John wrote.

Within this world of choices and decisions, we stand as moral agents faced with not only the medical decisions involved in a plan of medical treatment, but also the spiritual questions of the meaning of our lives and what we shall do for ourselves and our families at the end of those lives.

The spirituality of St. John may provide us with a depth of wisdom and spiritual peace, much as it did for him and for those he taught. Though it is far from an easy thing to understand in our modern scientific and technologically advanced world, it is also, as Pope John Paul II pointed out, something to which we may turn confidently. Within our own hearts, we will discover its unique application. Our professional lives may then develop a greater depth of integrity and moral commitment that reflects the image of the transformation of the log in the fire of God's transforming love. It is an image which St. John's teachings describe so vividly for us, and it is still applicable for us today. Understanding it will transform not only our spiritual lives, but also our professional lives in a very complex, ever-evolving world.

NOTES

CHAPTER ONE: HOSPICE CARE

[1] Amenta and Bohnet, *Nursing Care of the Terminally Ill*, 49.
[2] Ibid., 50.
[3] Ibid., 51.
[4] Stoddard, *The Hospice Movement: A Better Way of Caring for the Dying*, 26–27.
[5] Ibid., 39.
[6] Ariès, *The Hour of Our Death*, 201.
[7] Ibid., 107.
[8] Stoddard, *The Hospice Movement*, 80.
[9] Ibid., 81.
[10] Ibid., 80.
[11] Amenta and Bohnet, *Nursing Care of the Terminally Ill*, 51.
[12] Ibid., 52.
[13] Stoddard, *The Hospice Movement*, 85.
[14] Ibid., 87.
[15] Ariès, *The Hour of Our Death*, 585.
[16] Amenta and Bohnet, *Nursing Care of the Terminally Ill*, 28.
[17] Ibid.
[18] Ibid., 37.
[19] Ariès, *The Hour of Our Death*, 613.
[20] Amenta and Bohnet, *Nursing Care of the Terminally Ill*, 49.
[21] Ibid.
[22] Ibid., 50.
[23] Amenta and Bohnet, *Nursing Care of the Terminally Ill*, 55.
[24] Kübler-Ross, *The Wheel of Life: A Memoir of Living and Dying*, 142.
[25] Ibid., 144.
[26] Amenta and Bohnet, *Nursing Care of the Terminally Ill*, 57.
[27] Stoddard, *The Hospice Movement*, 76.
[28] Ibid., 141.
[29] Amenta and Bohnet, *Nursing Care of the Terminally Ill*, 31.
[30] Ariès, *The Hour of Our Death*, 587.
[31] Ibid., 586.
[32] Ibid., 614.
[33] Ibid.

[34] Ibid., 591.

[35] Stoddard, *The Hospice Movement*, 48.

[36] Ibid., 126.

[37] Amenta and Bohnet, *Traits of Hospice Nurses Compared with Those Who Work in Traditional Settings*, 415.

[38] Byock, *Dying Well: The Prospect for Growth at the End of Life*, 206.

[39] Salerno and Willens, eds., *Pain Management Handbook*, 467.

[40] Ibid.

[41] Ibid., 468.

[42] Ibid.

[43] Ibid.

[44] Ibid., 470.

[45] Ibid., 45.

[46] Callahan, *The Troubled Dream of Life: In Search of a Peaceful Death*, 127.

[47] Randall and Downie, *Palliative Care Ethics: A Good Companion*, ix.

[48] Ibid., 7.

[49] Ibid., 15.

[50] Ibid., 81.

[51] Ibid., 91.

[52] Kübler-Ross, *On Death and Dying*, 38–137.

[53] National Hospice Organization Ethics Committee, 1993–1994, *Hospice Code of Ethics*, Item Number 713024.

[54] Ibid., 1.

[55] Ibid., 2.

[56] Benjamin and Curtis, *Ethics in Nursing*, 72.

[57] Downie and Calman, *Healthy Respect: Ethics in Health Care*, 166.

[58] Ibid.

[59] Ibid., 3.

[60] Ibid.

[61] Ibid., 4.

[62] Ibid.

CHAPTER TWO: ETHICAL CONSIDERATIONS AND THEIR DEVELOPMENT

[1] Kelly, *The Emergence of Roman Catholic Medical Ethics in North America: An Historical, Methodological, Bibliographical Study*, 104–05.

[2] Aristotle, *The Ethics of Aristotle: The Nichomachean Ethics*, 10.

[3] Ibid.

[4] Ibid., 12.

[5] Ibid., 15.

[6] Ibid., 17.

[7] Copleston, *A History of Philosophy*, Volume I, 74.

[8] Aristotle, *The Ethics of Aristotle: Nichomachean Ethics*, 30.

[9] Aristotle, *The Complete Works of Aristotle*, 1729: (*N.E.*1:1094.1a).

[10] Ibid., (*Nichomachean Ethics*, 1:1094.6).

[11] Copleston, *A History of Philosophy*, Volume I, 74.

[12] Aristotle, *The Ethics of Aristotle*, 27.

[13] Ibid.

[14] Ibid.

[15] Ibid., 19.

[16] Ibid., 20.

[17] Ibid., 21.

[18] Aristotle, *The Complete Works of Aristotle,* Volume II, 1742.

[19] Aristotle, *The Ethics of Aristotle: Nichomachean Ethics*, 91.

[20] Aristotle, *The Complete Works of Aristotle,* Volume II, 1800.

[21] Copleston, *A History of Philosophy*, Volume I, 86.

[22] Ibid., 85.

[23] Aristotle, *The Complete Works of Aristotle,* Volume II, 1800.

[24] Aristotle, *The Ethics of Aristotle: Nichomachean Ethics*, 120.

[25] Wadell, *The Primacy of Love: An Introduction to the Ethics of Thomas Aquinas*, 12.

[26] Ibid., 21.

[27] Bourke, "Thomistic Ethics," in *The Westminster Dictionary of Christian Ethics*, 623.

[28] Ibid.

[29] Aquinas, *Summa Theologica*, Vol. I-II, 583.

[30] Selman, *St. Thomas Aquinas: Teacher of Truth*, 84.

[31] Davies, *The Thought of Thomas Aquinas*, 220.

[32] Aquinas, *Summa Theologica*, I-II, 583.

[33] Ibid., 596.

[34] Ibid.

[35] Bourke, "Thomistic Ethics," 624.

[36] Davies, *The Thought of Thomas Aquinas*, 225.

[37] Ibid., 226.

[38] Aquinas, *Summa Theologica*, Vol. I-II, 794–95.

[39] Davies, *The Thought of Thomas Aquinas*, 240.

[40] Ibid.

[41] Aquinas, *Summa Theologica*, Vol. II-II, 1320, 1389, 1434.

[42] Selman, *St. Thomas Aquinas: Teacher of Truth*, 84.

[43] Wadell, *The Primacy of Love*, 106.

[44] Ibid., 113.

[45] O'Meara, "Virtues in the Theology of Thomas Aquinas," 265.

[46] Ibid., 278–79.

[47] Ibid., 274.

[48] Hauerwas, "Virtue," in *The Westminster Dictionary of Christian Ethics*, 649.

[49] Aquinas, *Summa Theologica*, I-II, 1008ff.

[50] Ibid., 407: (*Summa Theologica*, I-I, 79, 12).

[51] Ibid., 1000.

[52] O'Meara, "Virtues in the Theology of Thomas Aquinas," 258.

[53] Ibid., 274.

[54] Ibid., 281.

[55] Mappes and Zembaty, eds., *Biomedical Ethics*, 53.

[56] Fletcher, "The Hippocratic Oath," in *The Westminster Dictionary of Christian Ethics*, 268.

[57] Mappes and Zembaty, eds., *Biomedical Ethics*, 53.

[58] Ibid.

[59] Fletcher, "The Hippocratic Oath," 268.

[60] Ibid., 269.

[61] Childress, "Paternalism," in *The Westminster Dictionary of Christian Ethics*, 449.

[62] Ibid.

[63] Ibid., 450.

[64] Mappes and Zembaty, eds., *Biomedical Ethics*, 4.

[65] Ibid., 5.

[66] Macquarrie, "Deontology," in *The Westminster Dictionary of Christian Ethics*, 151.

[67] Mappes and Zembaty, eds., *Biomedical Ethics*, 6.

[68] Ibid., 17.

[69] Ibid.

[70] Beauchamp and Childress, *Principles of Biomedical Ethics*, 57.

[71] Mappes and Zembaty, eds., *Biomedical Ethics*, 17.

[72] Ibid., 18.

[73] Ibid.

[74] Beauchamp and Childress, *Principles of Biomedical Ethics*, 56.

[75] Ibid., 60.

[76] Ibid., 47.

[77] Hare, "Utilitarianism," in *The Westminster Dictionary of Christian Ethics*, 641.

[78] Beauchamp and Childress, *Principles of Biomedical Ethics*, 48.

[79] Hare, "Utilitarianism," 641.

[80] Beauchamp and Childress, *Principles of Biomedical Ethics*, 48.

[81] Ibid, 112, n.5.

[82] Mappes and Zembaty, eds., *Biomedical Ethics*, 7.

[83] Ibid., 8.

[84] Ibid.

[85] Ibid.

[86] Beauchamp and Childress, *Principles of Biomedical Ethics*, 50.

[87] Mappes and Zembaty, eds., *Biomedical Ethics*, 12.

[88] Ibid., 15.

[89] Aristotle, *The Ethics of Aristotle: Nichomachean Ethics*, 31.

[90] Mappes and Zembaty, eds., *Biomedical Ethics*, 21–22.

[91] Ibid., 22.

[92] Ibid.

[93] Ibid.

[94] Ibid.

[95] Ibid., 23.

[96] Beauchamp and Childress, *Principles of Biomedical Ethics*, 73.

[97] Albert R. Jonsen, in the Foreword to DuBose et al., eds., *A Matter of Principles: Ferment in U.S. Bioethics*, x.

[98] Ibid., xi.

[99] Ibid., xii.

[100] Ibid.

[101] Ibid.

[102] Ibid., xiv.

[103] Ibid., xv.

[104] Beauchamp, "Principlism and Its Alleged Competitors," 181.

[105] Jonsen, in the Foreword to DuBose et al., eds., *A Matter of Principles*, xvi.

[106] Beauchamp, "Principlism and Its Alleged Competitors," 184.

[107] Ibid.

[108] Ibid., 182.

[109] Jonsen, in the Foreword to DuBose et al., eds., *A Matter of Principles*, xiv.

[110] Beauchamp and Childress, *Principles of Biomedical Ethics*, 120.

[111] Childress, "Autonomy," in *The Westminster Dictionary of Christian Ethics*, 52.

[112] Ibid.

[113] Beauchamp and Childress, *Principles of Biomedical Ethics*, 124.

[114] Childress, "Autonomy," 53.

[115] Beauchamp and Childress, *Principles of Biomedical Ethics*, 123.

[116] Ibid., 125.

[117] Ibid., 189.

[118] Ibid.

[119] Frankena, *Ethics*, 47.

[120] Beauchamp and Childress, *Principles of Biomedical Ethics*, 190.

[121] Ibid., 191.

[122] Ibid., 195.

[123] Ibid., 259.

[124] Ibid.

[125] Ibid., 260, emphasis theirs.

[126] Ibid., 262.

[127] Ibid., 272–73.

[128] Ibid., 327.

[129] Ibid., 330.

[130] Werpehowski, "Justice," in The Westminster Dictionary of Christian Ethics, 330.

[131] Ibid.

[132] Allen, "Covenant," in *The Westminster Dictionary of Christian Ethics*, 136.

[133] May, *Testing the Medical Covenant: Active Euthanasia and Health Care Reform*, 53.

[134] Ibid.

[135] Ibid., 54.

[136] Ibid., 4.

[137] Ibid., 11.

[138] Ibid., 55.

[139] Ibid.

[140] Ibid., 56.

[141] Ibid., 58, 61.

[142] Ibid., 63.

[143] Werpehowski and Crocco, eds., *The Essential Paul Ramsey: A Collection*, 168.

[144] Ibid., 170, emphasis his.

[145] Ibid.

[146] Häring, *Free and Faithful in Christ*, Volume I, 237.

[147] Pellegrino, *The Virtues in Medical Practice*, xi.

[148] Murdoch, *The Sovereignty of Good*, quoted in Meilaender, *The Theory and Practice of Virtue*, 75.

[149] Meilaender, *The Theory and Practice of Virtue*, 4.

[150] Ibid., 8.

[151] Hauerwas, "Virtue," 648.

[152] Wadell, *The Primacy of Love*, 111.

[153] Ibid., 116.

[154] Pellegrino and Thomasma, *The Virtues in Medical Practice*, 84.

[155] Ibid.

[156] Ibid., 28.

[157] Ibid., 87.

[158] Pellegrino, "Toward a Virtue-Based Normative Ethics for the Health Professions," 253.

[159] Ibid., 254.

[160] Ibid., 260.

[161] Ibid., 263.

[162] Ibid., 264.

[163] Ibid., 266.

[164] Pellegrino and Thomasma, *The Virtues in Medical Practice*, xiii.

[165] Pellegrino, "Toward a Virtue-Based Normative Ethics for the Health Professions," 270.

[166] Ibid., 271.

[167] Hauerwas, "Virtue," 650.

[168] Ibid.

[169] Pellegrino, "Toward a Virtue-Based Normative Ethics for the Health Professions," 272.

[170] Häring, *Free and Faithful in Christ*, Volume III, 326.

CHAPTER THREE: DARK NIGHT OF THE SOUL

[1] Payne, "The Influence of John of the Cross in the United States: A Preliminary Study," 167ff.

[2] Egan, *Christian Mysticism: The Future of a Tradition*, 1.

[3] Ibid.

[4] Ibid.

[5] Ibid., 2.

[6] Ibid.

[7] Ibid., 3.

[8] Ibid.

[9] Ibid., 4.

[10] Ibid.

[11] Ibid., 31.

[12] Ibid.

[13] Ibid., 165.

[14] Ibid., 166.

[15] Ibid., 5.

[16] Ibid.

[17] Ibid.

[18] Ibid., 7.

[19] Ibid., 9–10.

[20] Rodriguez, "Origins: The Yepes Family," in *God Speaks in the Night*, 5.

[21] Ibid., 56.

[22] Ibid., 40.

[23] Ibid., 52.

[24] Ibid., 70.

[25] Ibid., 80.

[26] Ibid., 171.

[27] Ibid., 168.

[28] Ibid., 28.

[29] Ibid.

[30] Cummins, *Freedom to Rejoice: Understanding St. John of the Cross*, 53.

[31] Ibid., 55.

[32] Ahlgren, *Teresa of Avila and the Politics of Sanctity*, 9.

[33] Ibid., 10.

[34] Ibid., 14.

[35] Ibid.

[36] Ibid.

[37] Ibid., 19.

[38] Rodriguez, "Origins: The Yepes Family," in *God Speaks in the Night*, vi.

[39] Ibid., viii.

[40] Nieto, *Mystic, Rebel, Saint: A Study of St. John of the Cross*, 21.

[41] Ibid., 22.

[42] Ibid.

[43] Ibid., 24.

[44] Ibid., 35.

[45] Ibid, 24.

[46] Ibid., 29.

[47] Nieto, *Mystic, Rebel, Saint: A Study of St. John of the Cross*, 41.

[48] Cummins, *Freedom to Rejoice*, 126.

[49] St. John of the Cross, *Dark Night of the Soul*, 50–52.

[50] Ibid., 41.

[51] Ibid.

[52] Ibid., 42.

[53] Ibid., 33.

[54] Ibid., 35.

[55] Egan, *Christian Mysticism*, 171.

[56] Ibid., 172.

[57] Nieto, *Mystic, Rebel, Saint: A Study of St. John of the Cross*, 122.

[58] Ibid.

[59] Collings, *The Way of the Christian Mystics: John of the Cross*, 155.

[60] Cummins, *Freedom to Rejoice*, 78.

[61] Ibid., 15, 149.

[62] Nieto, *Mystic, Rebel, Saint: A Study of St. John of the Cross*, 63.

[63] Nieto, *Mystic, Rebel, Saint: A Study of St. John of the Cross*, 122.

[64] St. John of the Cross, *Dark Night of the Soul*, 102.

[65] Nieto, *Mystic, Rebel, Saint: A Study of St. John of the Cross*, 122, n.19.

[66] Ibid., 123.

[67] St. John of the Cross, *Dark Night of the Soul*, 124.

[68] Egan, *Christian Mysticism*, 192.

[69] St. John of the Cross, *Dark Night of the Soul*, 102.

[70] Ibid.

[71] Ibid., 143.

[72] Cummins, *Freedom to Rejoice*, 48.

[73] Nieto, *Mystic, Rebel, Saint: A Study of St. John of the Cross*, 58.

[74] Egan, *Christian Mysticism*, 181.
[75] Cummins, *Freedom to Rejoice*, 32.
[76] St. John of the Cross, *Ascent of Mount Carmel*, 138.
[77] Ahlgren, *Teresa of Avila and the Politics of Sanctity*, 17.
[78] St. John of the Cross, *Ascent of Mount Carmel*, 206.
[79] Ibid., 368.
[80] Ibid., 224.
[81] Egan, *Christian Mysticism*, 168.
[82] Ibid., 181.
[83] Ibid., 176; St. John of the Cross, *Living Flame of Love*, 684.
[84] Kübler-Ross, *On Death and Dying*, 38–137.
[85] Cummins, *Freedom to Rejoice*, 132–33.
[86] St. John of the Cross, *Ascent of Mount Carmel*, 156.
[87] Ibid., 116.
[88] Cummins, *Freedom to Rejoice*, 82.
[89] Collings, *The Way of the Christian Mystics: John of the Cross*, 66.
[90] Ibid., 63.
[91] Cummins, *Freedom to Rejoice*, 120.
[92] Ibid., 84; St. John of the Cross, *Ascent of Mount Carmel*, 144.
[93] Ibid., 87.
[94] Cummins, *Freedom to Rejoice*, 85; St. John of the Cross, *Ascent of Mount Carmel*, 148.
[95] St. John of the Cross, *Ascent of Mount Carmel*, 149.
[96] Ibid.
[97] Ibid., 148.
[98] Ibid., 151.
[99] Cummins, *Freedom to Rejoice*, 88.
[100] St. John of the Cross, *Ascent of Mount Carmel*, 150–51.
[101] Egan, *Christian Mysticism*, 176.
[102] Ibid., 175–76.
[103] Cummins, *Freedom to Rejoice*, 48, 94, 118.
[104] Ibid., 118.
[105] Ibid., 94.
[106] St. John of the Cross, *Ascent of Mount Carmel*, 329, n1.
[107] Egan, *Christian Mysticism*, 179; St. John of the Cross, *Ascent of Mount Carmel*, 118–30.
[108] St. John of the Cross, *Ascent of Mount Carmel*, 154.
[109] Cummins, *Freedom to Rejoice*, 98.

[110] Ibid., 97.

[111] St. John of the Cross, *Ascent of Mount Carmel*, 199.

[112] Collings, *The Way of the Christian Mystics: John of the Cross*, 128.

[113] Ibid., 127; St. John of the Cross, *Ascent of Mount Carmel*, 268.

[114] Cummins, *Freedom to Rejoice*, 104.

[115] Ibid., 108.

[116] St. John of the Cross, *Ascent of Mount Carmel*, 289.

[117] Cummins, *Freedom to Rejoice*, 117.

[118] Ibid., 118, 121.

[119] Ibid., 120; St. John of the Cross, *Ascent of Mount Carmel*, 293.

[120] Cummins, *Freedom to Rejoice*, 124; St. John of the Cross, *Ascent of Mount Carmel*, 293.

[121] Cummins, *Freedom to Rejoice*, 125; St. John of the Cross, *Ascent of Mount Carmel*, 314–15.

[122] Cummins, *Freedom to Rejoice*, 125.

[123] Ibid., 48t, 127, 144.

[124] St. John of the Cross, *Ascent of Mount Carmel*, 354.

[125] Ibid.

[126] Ibid., 361.

[127] Cummins, *Freedom to Rejoice*, 36.

[128] Ibid., 127.

[129] Collings, *The Way of the Christian Mystics: John of the Cross*, 72.

[130] Ibid., 73.

[131] St. John of the Cross, *Ascent of Mount Carmel*, 377.

[132] Ibid., 378–80.

[133] Ibid., 381.

[134] Ibid., 382.

[135] Ibid., 385–92.

[136]. Ibid., 394.

[137] Egan, *Christian Mysticism*, 180.

[138] St. John of the Cross, *Ascent of Mount Carmel*, 384–85.

[139] Cummins, *Freedom to Rejoice*, 48.

[140] Ibid., 144.

[141] Ibid., 145.

[142] St. John of the Cross, *Dark Night of the Soul*, 416.

[143] Ibid., 437.

[144] Cummins, *Freedom to Rejoice*, 148–49.

[145] St. John of the Cross, *Dark Night of the Soul*, 439.

[146] Ibid., 440–45.

[147] Ibid., 445.

[148] Ibid., 446.

[149] Ibid., 445–48.

[150] Ibid., 448–49.

[151] Payne, *John of the Cross and the Cognitive Value of Mysticism*, 16.

[152] Ibid., 17.

[153] Hardy, "Embodied Love in John of the Cross," 141.

[154] Ibid.

[155] Ibid., 142.

[156] Ibid., 143.

[157] Ibid., 144.

[158] Ibid., 153.

[159] Ibid.

[160] Payne, *John of the Cross and the Cognitive Value of Mysticism*, xi.

[161] Ibid., x.

[162] Ibid., 2–3.

[163] Ibid., 6.

[164] Ibid., 17.

[167] Mallory, *Christian Mysticism: Transcending Technique*, 6.

[166] Ibid., 13.

[167] Payne, *John of the Cross and the Cognitive Value of Mysticism*, 24.

[168] Ibid., 26.

[169] Ibid., 28.

[170] Ibid., 29.

[171] Ibid., 25.

[172] Mallory, *Christian Mysticism: Transcending Technique*, 149.

[173] Ibid.

[174] Ibid., 150.

[175] Payne, *John of the Cross and the Cognitive Value of Mysticism*, 30.

[176] Ibid., 31.

[177] Ibid., 32.

[178] Egan, *Christian Mysticism*, 189.

[179] Ibid., 398, n.18.

[180] Collings, *The Way of the Christian Mystics: John of the Cross*, 101.

[181] Ibid., 102.

[182] Ibid.; St. John of the Cross, *Ascent of Mount Carmel*, 166.

[183] Ibid., 103.

[184] Egan, *Christian Mysticism*, 188.
[185] St. John of the Cross, *Ascent of Mount Carmel*, 316.
[186] Egan, *Christian Mysticism*, 207.
[187] St. John of the Cross, *Ascent of Mount Carmel*, 397.
[188] Ibid., 431.
[189] Egan, *Christian Mysticism*, 206.
[190] Ibid., 207.
[191] St. John of the Cross, *Ascent of Mount Carmel*, 215.
[192] Egan, *Christian Mysticism*, 14.
[193] Ibid.
[194] Ibid., 16.
[195] Ibid., 215.
[196] Ibid.
[197] Ibid., 218.
[198] Ibid.
[199] Ibid., 221.
[200] Ibid., 223.
[201] Ibid., 218.
[202] Carr, *Transforming Grace: Christian Tradition and Women's Experience*, 186, and 240–41, note 13.
[203] Lerner, *The Creation of Patriarchy*, 45.
[204] Saiving, "The Human Situation: A Feminine View," 8.
[205] Ibid., 13.
[206] Ibid.
[207] Conn, "Restriction and Reconstruction," 11.
[208] Ibid.
[209] Ibid., 12.
[210] Lerner, *The Creation of Patriarchy*, 206.
[211] Ibid., 207, with reference to Aristotle's *De Generatione Animalium*.
[212] Ibid., 224.
[213] Ahlgren, *Teresa of Avila and the Politics of Sanctity*, 7.
[214] Weber, *Teresa of Avila and the Rhetoric of Femininity*, 17.

CHAPTER FOUR: PRACTITIONERS AND THE DARK NIGHT

[1] Annas, et al., eds., *American Health Law*, 3.
[2] Ibid., 374.
[3] Ibid., 375.

⁴ Ibid., 377.

⁵ Ibid., 383–87.

⁶ Ibid., 400.

⁷ Nieto, *Mystic, Rebel, Saint: A Study of St. John of the Cross*, 125.

⁸ Cummins, *Freedom to Rejoice*, 78.

⁹ Ibid., 44.

¹⁰ Ibid., 108.

¹¹ Kavanaugh and Rodriguez, eds., *The Collected Works of John of the Cross*, 199.

¹² St. John of the Cross, *Dark Night of the Soul*, 286.

¹³ Ibid., 429.

¹⁴ Egan, *Christian Mysticism*, 212.

¹⁵ Collings, *The Way of the Christian Mystics: John of the Cross*, 92.

¹⁶ Ibid., 125.

¹⁷ Gula, *Reason Informed by Faith: Foundations of Catholic Morality*, 220.

¹⁸ Ibid., 241.

¹⁹ Ibid.

²⁰ Ibid., 242.

²¹ Ibid.

²² Ibid., 242–43.

²³ Ibid., 243–46.

²⁴ St. John of the Cross, *Ascent of Mount Carmel*, 234.

²⁵ Gula, *Reason Informed by Faith: Foundations of Catholic Morality*, 245.

²⁶ Ibid., 251.

²⁷ Ibid., 124.

²⁸ Ibid., 223.

²⁹ Sulmasy, *The Healer's Calling: A Spirituality for Physicians and Other Health Care Practitioners*, 7.

³⁰ Ibid., 9.

³¹ Ibid., 15.

³² Ibid., 33.

³³ Ibid., 34.

³⁴ Ibid., 43.

³⁵ Ibid., 44.

³⁶ Ibid., 45.

³⁷ St. John of the Cross, *Ascent of Mount Carmel*, 268.

[38] Sulmasy, *The Healer's Calling*, 75.

[39] Ibid., 83.

[40] Ibid., 86.

[41] Ibid., 87.

[42] Ibid., 106.

[43] Ibid., 114.

[44] Ibid., 99–100.

[45] St. John of the Cross, *Dark Night of the Soul*, 385.

[46] Ibid., 277.

[47] Sulmasy, *The Healer's Calling*, 118.

[48] Kavanaugh and Rodriguez, eds., *The Collected Works of John of the Cross*, 387.

[49] Sulmasy, *The Healer's Calling*, 114.

[50] Annas, et al., eds., *American Health Law*, 701–10.

[51] St. John of the Cross, *Dark Night of the Soul*, 118.

[52] Ibid., 125.

[53] Ibid., 147.

[54] Ibid., 164.

[55] Ibid., 151.

[56] Ibid.

[57] Ibid., 133.

[58] Reverend James P. Holland, Parochial Vicar, St. Anne's Parish, Castle Shannon, Pennsylvania. Interviewed by author, June 15, 1999.

[59] Stoddard, *The Hospice Movement: A Better Way of Caring for the Dying*, 125.

[60] Ibid., 190.

[61] Ibid., 233.

[62] Dumm, *Cherish Christ Above All: The Bible in the Rule of Benedict*, 32.

[63] Ibid., 40.

[64] Ibid., 39.

[65] Häring, *The Virtues of an Authentic Life: A Celebration of Spiritual Maturity*, 17.

[66] Ibid., 167.

[67] Ibid., 18.

[68] Ibid.

[69] St. John of the Cross, *Ascent of Mount Carmel*, 206.

[70] Häring, *The Virtues of an Authentic Life: A Celebration of Spiritual Maturity*, 118.

[71] Ibid., 135.

[72] St. John of the Cross, *Ascent of Mount Carmel*, 231.

[73] Häring, *The Virtues of an Authentic Life: A Celebration of Spiritual Maturity*, 137.

[74] Ibid., 139.

[75] Ibid., 140.

[76] Gula, *Reason Informed by Faith: Foundations of Catholic Morality*, 316.

[77] Ibid.

[78] Ibid.

[79] Ibid., 317.

[80] Ibid., 321.

[81] Wright, *A Theology of Christian Prayer*, 31.

[82] Gula, *Reason Informed by Faith: Foundations of Catholic Morality*, 319.

[83] Ibid., 323.

[84] St. John of the Cross, *Ascent of Mount Carmel*, 171.

[85] Ibid., 129.

[86] Ibid., 276–77.

[87] Stoddard, *The Hospice Movement*, 267.

[88] Harkness, *The Dark Night of the Soul*, 28–29.

[89] Ibid., 163.

[90] Ibid., 116.

[91] Cassidy, "Together in the Darkness," 2.

[92] Thompson, *Fire and Light: The Saints and Theology*, 85.

[93] Ibid., 87.

[94] Slattery, ed., *St. John of the Cross: A Spirituality of Substance*, 89.

[95] Ibid., 97.

[96] Ibid., 103.

[97] Ibid., 109.

[98] Cronk, *Dark Night Journey: Inward Re-Patterning toward a Life Centered in God*, 52–53.

[99] Ibid., 35.

[100] Ibid.

[101] FitzGerald, "Impasse and Dark Night," 292.

[102] Ibid., 293.

[103] Kavanaugh, "Faith and the Experience of God in the University Town of Baeza," 51.

[104] Culligan, "Qualities of a Good Guide: Spiritual Direction in John of the Cross's Letters," 65–67.

[105] Read, "John of the Cross for Carpenters: The Ordinary Way of the Dark Night of Faith," 88.

CHAPTER FIVE: PATIENTS AND THE DARK NIGHT

[1] Carmody, *God Is No Illusion: Meditations on the End of Life*, 121.
[2] *The Times* (London), 8 June, 1999, 19.
[3] Ibid.
[4] FitzGerald, "Impasse and Dark Night," 290.
[5] Ibid., 294.
[6] Ibid.
[7] Ibid., 297–98.
[8] Ibid., 299.
[9] Egan, *Christian Mysticism*, 14.
[10] Carmody, *Cancer and Faith*, 11.
[11] Ibid., 52.
[12] Ibid., 83.
[13] Ibid., 103; St. John of the Cross, *Ascent of Mount Carmel*, 143.
[14] Carmody, *God Is No Illusion*, 99.
[15] Ibid.
[16] Carmody, *Cancer and Faith*, 35.
[17] Ibid., 4–5.
[18] Ibid., 119.
[19] Ibid., 7.
[20] Ibid., 22.
[21] Ibid., 18–19.
[22] Ibid., 28.
[23] Ibid., 39.
[24] Ibid., 40.
[25] Ibid., 32–33.
[26] Ibid., 65.
[27] Carmody, *God Is No Illusion*, 62.
[28] Ibid., 63.
[29] Ibid., 113.
[30] Ibid., 65.
[31] Ibid., 92.

[32] Ibid., 81.

[33] Ibid., 59.

[34] Wagner, "Women and Prayer," in Slattery, ed., *St. John of the Cross*, 113.

[35] Nemeck, and Coombs, *O Blessed Night: Recovering from Addiction, Codependency and Attachment Based on the Insights of St. John of the Cross and Pierre Teilhard de Chardin*, 9.

[36] Ibid., 10.

[37] Ibid., 71.

[38] Ibid., 74.

[39] Ibid., 76.

[40] Ibid., 81.

[41] Ibid., 87.

[42] Larson, *The Helper's Journey: Working with People Facing Grief, Loss, and Life-Threatening Illness*, 2.

[43] Ibid., 35.

[44] Gastmans et al., "Nursing Considered as Moral Practice: A Philosophical-Ethical Interpretation of Nursing," 44.

[45] Ibid., 45.

[46] Ibid., 46.

[47] Ibid., 49.

[48] Ibid., 50.

[49] Ibid., 52.

[50] Ibid., 53.

[51] Ibid., 54.

[52] St. John of the Cross, *Dark Night of the Soul*, 416.

[53] Gastmans et al., "Nursing Considered as Moral Practice," 58.

[54] St. John of the Cross, *Dark Night of the Soul*, 433.

[55] Taylor, "Reflections on 'Nursing Considered as Moral Practice,'" 72.

[56] Ibid.

[57] Ibid., 78.

[58] Ibid.

[59] Ibid.

[60] Stein, *The Science of the Cross: A Study of St. John of the Cross*, 26, 103.

[61] Cummins, *Freedom to Rejoice*, 39.

[62] St. John of the Cross, *Ascent of Mount Carmel*, 173.

[63] Ibid., 141.
[64] St. John of the Cross, *Dark Night of the Soul*, 368.
[65] Egan, *Christian Mysticism*, 206.
[66] Ibid., 209–10.
[67] St. John of the Cross, *Dark Night of the Soul*, 400.
[68] Ibid., 413–14.
[69] Ibid., 425.
[70] Cronk, *Dark Night Journey*, 158.

CHAPTER SIX: SUMMARY AND CONCLUSIONS:
CONTEMPORARY SPIRITUALITY FOR TERMINAL ILLNESS

[1] Weakland, *Faith and the Human Enterprise: A Post-Vatican II Vision*, 15–16.
[2] Flannery, gen. ed., *Vatican Council II: The Conciliar and Post-Conciliar Documents*, New revised edition, Vol. I, 903.
[3] Ibid., 906.
[4] Ibid., 911.
[5] Ibid., 915.
[6] Ibid.
[7] Ibid., 916.
[8] Ibid.
[9] Ibid., 769.
[10] Ibid., 773.
[11] Ibid., 770.
[12] Ibid., 771.
[13] Ibid.
[14] Bernardin, *Consistent Ethic of Life*, 1.
[15] Ibid., 3.
[16] Ibid., 5.
[17] Ibid.
[18] Ibid.
[19] Ibid., 7.
[20] Ibid.
[21] Ibid.
[22] Ibid., 17–18.
[23] Ibid., 18.
[24] Ibid., 18–19.

[25] Himes and Himes, *Fullness of Faith: The Public Significance of Theology*, 74.

[26] Ibid., 77.

[27] Ibid., 78.

[28] Ibid., 78–79.

[29] Ibid., 79.

[30] Ibid., 80.

[31] Ibid., 81–82.

[32] Flannery, gen. ed., *Vatican Council II*, 771.

[33] Himes and Himes, *Fullness of Faith*, 84.

[34] Ibid., 85.

[35] Ibid., 86.

[36] Ibid., 90.

[37] Ibid.

[38] Ibid.

[39] Ibid., 91.

[40] Ibid.

[41] Ibid., 92, and 201, note 35 [from Richard McCormick's "Theology and Bioethics," in *Hastings Center Report* 19 (1991): 5–10].

[42] Ibid., 93.

[43] Ibid., 95.

[44] Pope John Paul II, "John of the Cross, Master of the Faith," in *The Pope Speaks* 35(1990), 217.

[45] Ibid., 218.

[46] Ibid.

[47] Ibid., emphasis his.

[48] Ibid., 220.

[49] Ibid., 221.

[50] Ibid., 223.

[51] Ibid.

[52] Ibid., emphasis his.

[53] Ibid.

[54] Ibid., 224.

[55] Ibid., 225.

[56] Ibid.

[57] Ibid., 226.

[58] Ibid.

[59] Ibid., 227, emphasis his.

REFERENCES CONSULTED

Ahlgren, Gillian T.W. *Teresa of Avila and the Politics of Sanctity*. Ithaca, NY: Cornell University Press, 1996.

Allen, Joseph L. "Covenant," in Childress and Macquarrie, eds. *The Westminster Dictionary of Christian Ethics*. Westminster, 1967, 1986.

Amenta, Madalon O'Rawe, and Nancy L. Bohnet. *Nursing Care of the Terminally Ill*. Boston: Little, Brown, 1986.

———. "Traits of Hospice Nurses Compared with Those Who Work in Traditional Settings." *Journal of Clinical Psvchology* 40 (March 1984): 414–421.

Annas, George J., et al., eds. *American Health Law*. Boston: Little, Brown, 1990.

———. "How We Live." Special Supplement, *Hastings Center Report* 25:6 (November-December 1995): S12–S14.

Aquinas, Thomas. *Summa Theologica*. Volume I–II. New York: Benziger Brothers, 1947.

———. *Summa Theologica*. Volume II–II. New York: Benziger Brothers, 1947.

Ariès, Philippe. *The Hour of Our Death*. New York: Oxford University Press, 1981.

Aristotle. *The Complete Works of Aristotle,* Volume II. Edited by Jonathan Barnes. Princeton, NJ: Princeton University Press, 1984.

———. *The Ethics of Aristotle: Nichomachean Ethics*. Translated by J. A. K. Thomson. London: Penguin, 1953, 1976.

Arras, John D., and Bonnie Steinbock, eds. *Ethical Issues in Modern Medicine*. Fourth edition. Mountain View, CA: Mayfield, 1995.

Ashley, Benedict, O.P., and Kevin O'Rourke, eds. *Healthcare Ethics: A Theological Analysis*. St. Louis: The Catholic Health Association of the United States, 1989.

Beauchamp, Tom L. "Principlism and Its Alleged Competitors." *Kennedy Institute of Ethics Journal* 5:3 (September 1995): 181–198.

————, and James F. Childress, eds. *Principles of Biomedical Ethics*. Fourth edition. New York: Oxford University Press, 1994.

Benjamin, Martin, and Joy Curtis. *Ethics in Nursing*. Third edition. New York: Oxford University Press, 1992.

Beresford, Larry. *The Hospice Handbook*. Boston: Little, Brown, 1993.

Bernardin, Joseph Cardinal. *The Consistent Ethic of Life*. Kansas City, MO: Sheed and Ward, 1988.

Berwick, Donald M. "The SUPPORT Project: Lessons for Action." Special Supplement, *Hastings Center Report* 25: 6 (November-December 1995): S21–S22.

Bourke, Vernon J. "Thomistic Ethics," in Childress and Macquarrie, eds. *The Westminster Dictionary of Christian Ethics*.Westminster, 1967, 1986.

Branson, Roy. "Virtues, Obligations, and the Prophetic Vision." *Kennedy Institute of Ethics Journal* 6:4 (December 1996): 361–365.

Brody, Howard. "The Best System in the World." Special Supplement, *Hastings Center Report* 25:6 (November-December 1995): S18–S20.

Burns, Sister Sharon. "The Spirituality of Dying: Pastoral Care's Holistic Approach is Crucial in Hospice." *Health Progress* (September 1991): 48–54.

Byock, Ira, M.D. *Dying Well: The Prospect for Growth at the End of Life*. New York: Riverhead, 1997.

————. "The Hospice Clinician's Response to Euthanasia/Physician-Assisted Suicide." First National Conference on Clinical Hospice Care/Palliative Medicine, February 20–23, 1994. San Francisco: 1994.

Callahan, Daniel. "Once Again, Reality: Now Where Do We Go?" *Hastings Center Report* 25:6 (November-December 1995): S33–S36.

————. *The Troubled Dream of Life: In Search of a Peaceful Death*. New York: Touchstone, 1993.

Callanan, Maggie, and Patricia Kelley. *Final Gifts: Understanding the Special Awareness, Needs, and Communication of the Dying*. New York: Bantam, 1992.

Campbell, Courtney S., Jan Hare, and Pam Matthews. "Conflicts of Conscience: Hospice and Assisted Suicide." *Hastings Center Report* 25:3 (May-June 1995): 36–43.

Cantor, Norman L., and George C. Thomas III. "Pain Relief, Acceleration of Death, and Criminal Law." *Kennedy Institute of Ethics Journal* 6:2 (June 1996): 107–127.

Capron, Alexander Morgan. "Abandoning a Waning Life." *Hastings Center Report* 25:4 (July-August 1995): 24–26.

Carmody, John Tully. *Cancer and Faith: Reflections on Living with a Terminal Illness*. Mystic, CT: Twenty-Third Publications, 1994.

————. *God Is No Illusion: Meditations on the End of Life*. Valley Forge: Trinity, 1997.

Carr, Anne E. *Transforming Grace: Christian Tradition and Women's Experience*. San Francisco: Harper and Row, 1988.

Cassidy, Sheila. "Together in the Darkness." *The Tablet* (December 1, 1997): 1.

Chambers, Tod. "From the Ethicist's Point of View: The Literary Nature of Ethical Inquiry." *Hastings Center Report* 26:1 (January-February 1996): 25–32.

Childress, James F. "Autonomy," in Childress and Macquarrie, eds. *The Westminster Dictionary of Christian Ethics*. Westminster, 1967, 1986.

————. "Paternalism," in Childress and Macquarrie, eds. *The Westminster Dictionary of Christian Ethics*.

————, and John Macquarrie, eds. *The Westminster Dictionary of Christian Ethics*. Philadelphia: Westminster, 1986.

Clouser, K. Danner. "Common Morality as an Alternative to Principlism." *Kennedy Institute of Ethics Journal* 5:3 (September 1995): 219–236.

Collings, Ross, O.C.D. *The Way of the Christian Mystics: John of the Cross* (Volume X). Collegeville, MN: The Liturgical Press, 1990.

Conn, Joann Wolski. "Restriction and Reconstruction." *Women's Spirituality: Resources for Christian Development*. Edited by Joann Wolski Conn. New York: Paulist Press, 1986.

Connors, Russell B., Jr., and Martin L. Smith. "Religious Insistence on Medical Treatment: Christian Theology and Re-Imagination." *Hastings Center Report* 26:4 (July-August 1996): 23–30.

Copleston, Frederick, S.J. *A History of Philosophy*. Volume I: Greece and Rome. New York: Doubleday Image, 1962.

Crigger, Bette-Jane. "Where Do Moral Decisions Come From?" *Hastings Center Report* 26:19 (January-February 1996): 33–38.

Cronk, Sandra. *Dark Night Journey: Inward Re-Patterning toward a Life Centered in God*. Wallingford, PA: Pendle Hill, 1991.

Culligan, Kevin, O.C.D. "Qualities of a Good Guide: Spiritual Direction in John of the Cross's Letters." *Carmelite Studies*. Volume VI. *John of the Cross: Conferences and Essays by the Members of The Institute of Carmelite Studies*. Edited by Steven Payne, O.C.D. Washington, DC: ICS Publications, 1992.

Cummins, Norbert, O.C.D. *Freedom to Rejoice: Understanding St. John of the Cross*. London: HarperCollins Religious, 1991.

Curran, Charles. *The Living Tradition of Catholic Moral Theology*. Notre Dame, IN: University of Notre Dame Press, 1992.

Davies, Brian. *The Thought of Thomas Aquinas*. Oxford: Clarendon, 1992.

DeBlassie, Paul, III. *Deep Prayer: Healing for the Hurting Soul*. New York: Crossroad, 1990.

DeCaussade, Jean-Pierre. *The Sacrament of the Present Moment*. San Francisco: HarperSanFrancisco, 1982.

Downie, R. S., and K. C. Calman. *Healthy Respect: Ethics in Health Care*. Oxford: Oxford University Press, 1994.

DuBose, Edwin R., Ron Hamel, and Laurence J. O'Connell, eds. *A Matter of Principles: Ferment in U.S. Bioethics*. Valley Forge, PA: Trinity, 1994.

du Boulay, Shirley. *Cicely Saunders: Founder of the Modern Hospice Movement*. New York: Amaryllis, 1984.

Dumm, Demetrius, O.S.B. *Cherish Christ Above All: The Bible in the Rule of Benedict*. New York: Paulist Press, 1996.

Egan, Harvey, S.J. *Christian Mysticism: The Future of a Tradition*. New York: Pueblo, 1984.

Emanuel, Linda L. "Reexamining Death: The Asymptotic Model and a Bounded Zone Definition." *Hastings Center Report* 25:4 (July-August 1995): 27–35.

————. "Structured Deliberation to Improve Decision-Making for the Seriously Ill." Special Supplement, *Hastings Center Report* 25:6 (November-December 1995): S14–S18.

FitzGerald, Constance, O.C.D. "Impasse and the Dark Night." In *Women's Spirituality: Resources for Christian Development*, edited by Joann Wolski Conn. New York: Paulist Press, 1986.

Flannery, Austin, O.P., general editor. *Vatican Council II: The Conciliar and Post-Conciliar Documents*. New revised edition. Volume I. Northport, NY: Costello, 1998.

————, general editor. *Vatican Council II: More Post-Conciliar Documents*. Collegeville, MN: The Liturgical Press, 1982.

Fleming, Ursula. *Grasping the Nettle: A Positive Approach to Pain*. London: Fount Paperbacks, 1990.

————. "John and Pain." Rolheiser, Ron, OMI, ed. *A Fresh Approach to St. John of the Cross: Growth through Pain and Sexuality*. St. Paul's Press, 1993.

Fletcher, Joseph. "The Hippocratic Oath," in Childress and Macquarrie, eds. *The Westminster Dictionary of Christian Ethics*. Westminster, 1967, 1986.

Frankena, William. *Ethics*. Second edition. Englewood Cliffs, NJ: Prentice-Hall, 1973.

Fry, Sara T., Aileen R. Kellen, and Ellen M. Robinson. "Care-Based Reasoning, Caring, and the Ethic of Care: A Need for Clarity." *The Journal of Clinical Ethics* 7:1 (Spring 1996): 41–47.

Gallagher, John A. *Time Past, Time Future: An Historical Study of Catholic Moral Theology*. New York: Paulist Press, 1990.

Gastmans, Chris, Bernadette Dierckx de Casterle, and Paul Schotsmans. "Nursing Considered as Moral Practice: A Philosophical-Ethical

Interpretation of Nursing." *Kennedy Institute of Ethics Journal* 8:1 (1998): 43–69.

Gaucher, Guy. *The Passion of Thérèse of Lisieux*. New York: Crossroad, 1990.

Gula, Richard M., S.S. *Euthanasia: Moral and Pastoral Perspectives*. New York: Paulist Press, 1994.

————. *Reason Informed by Faith: Foundations of Catholic Morality*. New York: Paulist Press, 1989.

————. *What Are They Saying About Moral Norms?* New York: Paulist Press, 1982.

Guroian, Vigen. *Life's Living Toward Dying*. Grand Rapids, MI: William B. Eerdmans, 1996.

Gustafson, James F. *Protestant and Roman Catholic Ethics: Prospects for Rapprochement*. Chicago: University of Chicago Press, 1978.

Hardwig, John. "Is There a Duty to Die?" *Hastings Center Report* 27:2 (March- April 1997): 34–42.

————. "SUPPORT and the Invisible Family." Special Supplement, *Hastings Center Report* (November-December 1995): S23–S25.

Hardy, Richard P. "Embodied Love in John of the Cross." *Carmelite Studies*, Volume VI. *John of the Cross: Conferences and Essays by Members of The Institute of Carmelite Studies and Others*. Edited by Steven Payne, O.C.D. Washington, DC: ICS Publications, 1992.

Hare, R. M. "Utilitarianism," in Childress and Macquarrie, eds. *The Westminster Dictionary of Christian Ethics*.

Harkness, Georgia. *The Dark Night of the Soul: From Spiritual Depression to Inner Renewal*. New York: Abingdon-Cokesbury, 1945.

Häring, Bernard. *Free and Faithful in Christ.* 3 vols. New York: Seabury Press, 1978–1981.

————. *The Virtues of an Authentic Life: A Celebration of Spiritual Maturity.* Ligouri, MO: Ligouri Publications, 1997.

Hauerwas, Stanley. "Virtue," in Childress and Macquarrie, eds. *The Westminster Dictionary of Christian Ethics.* Westminster, 1967, 1986.

Hendin, Herbert. "Selling Death and Dignity." *Hastings Center Report* 25:3 (May-June 1995): 19–25.

Himes, Michael J., and Kenneth R. Himes, O.F.M. *Fullness of Faith: The Public Significance of Theology.* Mahwah, NJ: Paulist Press, 1993.

Holland, Reverend James P., Parochial Vicar, St. Anne's Parish, Castle Shannon, PA. Interviewed by Author, June 15, 1999.

Hopkins, Patrick D. "Why Does Removing Machines Count as 'Passive' Euthanasia?" *Hastings Center Report* 27:3 (May–June, 1997): 29–37.

Hospice Code of Ethics. National Hospice Organization Ethics Committee, 1993–1994. Arlington: 1995.

Husted, Gladys L., and James H. Husted. *Ethical Decision-Making in Nursing.* St. Louis: Mosby-Year Book, 1991.

Irish, Donald P., Kathleen F. Lundquist, and Vivian Jenkins Nelson, eds. *Ethnic Variations in Dying, Death, and Grief: Diversity in Universality.* Washington, DC: Taylor and Francis, 1993.

Jones, Cheslyn, Geoffrey Wainwright, and Edward Arnold, eds. *The Study of Spirituality.* New York: Oxford University Press, 1986.

Jonsen, Albert. "Casuistry: An Alternative or Complement to Principles." *Kennedy Institute of Ethics Journal* 5:3 (September 1995): 237–252.

Kavanaugh, Kieran, O.C.D. "Faith and the Experience of God in the University Town of Baeza." *Carmelite Studies VI: John of the Cross: Conferences and Essays by Members of The Institute of Carmelite Studies*. Edited by Steven Payne, O.C.D Washington, DC: ICS Publications, 1992.

————, and Otilio Rodriguez, O.C.D., translators. *The Collected Works of St. John of the Cross*. Washington, DC: ICS Publications, 1991.

Kaveny, M. Cathleen. "Assisted Suicide, Euthanasia and the Law." *Theological Studies* 58:1 (March 1997): 124–148.

Keating, James. "The Good Life: An Invitation to Holiness." *Church* (Summer 1995): 15–20.

————. "Listening to Christ's Heart: Moral Theology and Spirituality in Dialogue." *Milltown Studies* 39 (Summer 1997): 48–65.

————. "Prayer and Ethics in the Thought of Hans Urs von Balthasar." *Irish Theological Quarterly* 62:1 (1996–1997): 29–37.

————, and John Corbett, O.P. "Euthanasia and the Gift of Life." *Linacre Quarterly* 63 (August 1996): 33–41.

Kelly, David F. *Critical Care Ethics: Treatment Decisions in American Hospitals*. Kansas City, MO: Sheed and Ward, 1991.

————. *The Emergence of Roman Catholic Medical Ethics in North America: An Historical, Methodological, Bibliographical Study*. New York: Edwin Mellen, 1979.

Kilner, John F., Arlene B. Miller, and Edmund D. Pellegrino, eds. *Dignity and Dying: A Christian Appraisal*. Grand Rapids, MI: William B. Eerdmans, 1996.

Kramer, Kenneth. *The Sacred Art of Dying: How World Religions Understand Death*. New York: Paulist Press, 1988.

Kübler-Ross, Elisabeth. *Death: The Final Stage of Growth*. Englewood Cliffs, NJ: Prentice-Hall, 1975.

———. *Death is of Vital Importance: On Life, Death, and Life After Death*. Barrytown, NY: Station Hill, 1995.

———. *On Death and Dying*. New York: Macmillan, 1969.

———. *On Life After Death*. Berkeley: Celestial Arts, 1991.

———. *Questions and Answers on Death and Dying*. New York: Collier, 1974.

———. *The Wheel of Life: A Memoir of Living and Dying*. New York: Scribner, 1997.

Kukse, H. "The Fears of the Dying." (Letter; comment.) *Hastings Center Report* 23:4 (1993): 42:1.

Larson, Dale G. *The Helper's Journey: Working with People Facing Grief, Loss, and Life-Threatening Illness*. Champaign, IL: Research Press, 1993.

Lauritzen, Paul. "Ethics and Experience: The Case of the Curious Response." *Hastings Center Report* 26:1 (January-February 1996): 6–15.

Lerner, Gerda. *The Creation of Patriarchy*. New York: Oxford University Press, 1986.

Lo, Bernard. "End of Life Care after Termination of SUPPORT." Special Supplement, *Hastings Center Report* 25:6 (November-December 1995): S6–S8.

MacIntyre, Alasdair. *After Virtue: A Study in Moral Theory*. Notre Dame, IN: University of Notre Dame Press, 1984.

Macquarrie, John. "Deontology," in Childress and Macquarrie, eds. *The Westminster Dictionary of Christian Ethics*. Westminster, 1967, 1986.

Mahoney, John. *The Making of Moral Theology: A Study of the Roman Catholic Tradition*. Oxford: Clarendon, 1987.

Mallory, Marilyn May. *Christian Mysticism: Transcending Technique*. Amsterdam, Van Gorcum Assen, 1977.

Maloney, George A., S.J. *In Jesus We Trust*. Notre Dame, IN: Ave Maria, 1990.

Mappes, Thomas, and Jane S. Zembaty, eds. *Biomedical Ethics*. Third edition. New York: McGraw-Hill: 1981, 1986, 1991.

Marshall, Patricia A. "The SUPPORT Study: Who's Talking?" Special Supplement, *Hastings Center Report* 25:6 (November-December 1995): S9–S11.

May, William F. *Testing the Medical Covenant: Active Euthanasia and Health Care Reform*. Grand Rapids, MI: William B. Eerdmans, 1996.

McCormick, Richard. "Theology and Bioethics." *Hastings Center Report* 19 (1991): 5–10.

Meilander, Gilbert. *The Limits of Love: Some Theological Explorations*. University Park: The Pennsylvania State University Press, 1987.

———. *The Theory and Practice of Virtue*. Notre Dame, IN: University of Notre Dame Press, 1984.

Merton, Thomas. *The Ascent to Truth*. San Diego: Harcourt, Brace, 1981.

———. *Contemplative Prayer*. New York: Doubleday, 1996.

Midgley, Mary. "Visions, Secular and Sacred." *Hastings Center Report* 25:5 (September-October 1995): 20–27.

Miles, Steven H. "Physician-Assisted Suicide and the Profession's Gyrocompass." *Hastings Center Report* 25:3 (May-June 1995): 17–19.

Miller, Franklin G., and Howard Brody. "Professional Integrity and Physician-Assisted Death." *Hastings Center Report* 25:3 (May-June 1995): 8–17.

Miller, M., et al., eds. *Dictionnaire de Spiritualité*, Volume X. Paris: Beauchesne, 1982.

Moskowitz, Ellen H., and James Lindemann Nelson. "The Best Laid Plans." Special Supplement, *Hastings Center Report* 25:6 (November-December 1995): S3–S6.

Murdoch, Iris. *The Sovereignty of Good*. London: Routledge and Kegan Paul, 1970.

National Hospice Organization Ethics Committee, 1993–1994. *Hospice Code of Ethics*. Jeanne Maguire Brenneis, et al., eds. Arlington, VA: National Hospice Organization, 1995.

Nelson, Hilde Lindemann. "Death and Kantian Dignity." *The Journal of Clinical Ethics* 7:3 (Fall 1996): 215–221.

Nemeck, Francis Kelly, OMI, and Marie Theresa Coombs, Hermit. *O Blessed Night: Recovering from Addiction, Codependency and Attachment Based on the Insights of St. John of the Cross and Pierre Teilhard de Chardin*. New York: Alba House, 1991.

Nieto, José. *Mystic, Rebel, Saint: A Study of St. John of the Cross*. Geneva: Librairie Droz, 1979.

Nouwen, Henri. *Our Greatest Gift: A Meditation on Dying and Caring*. San Francisco: HarperSanFrancisco, 1994.

Nuland, Sherwin B. *How We Die*. New York: Vintage Books, 1995.

O'Brien, David J., and Thomas A. Shannon, eds. *Catholic Social Thought: The Documentary Heritage*. New York: Orbis, 1992.

O'Donnell, Thomas J., S.J. *Medicine and Christian Morality*. Second edition. New York: Alba House, 1991.

O'Meara, Thomas F. "Virtues in the Theology of Thomas Aquinas." *Theological Studies* 58:2 (June 1997): 254–285.

Overberg, Kenneth, S.J., ed. *Mercy or Murder: Euthanasia, Morality, and Public Policy*. Kansas City, MO: Sheed and Ward, 1993.

Paguio, Erlinda. "Thomas Merton and the Saints of Carmel." *Spiritual Life* 42:2 (Summer 1996): 74–86.

Patrick, Anne E. *Liberating Conscience: Feminist Explorations in Catholic Moral Theology*. New York: Continuum, 1996.

Payne, Steven. O.C.D. "The Influence of John of the Cross in the United States: A Preliminary Study." *Carmelite Studies*. Volume VI. *John of the Cross: Conferences and Essays by Members of The Institute of Carmelite Studies and Others*. Edited by Steven Payne, O.C.D. Washington, DC: ICS Publications, 1992.

————. *John of the Cross and the Cognitive Value of Mysticism: An Analysis of Sanjuanist Teaching and its Philosophical Implications for Contemporary Discussions of Mystical Experience*. Dordrecht: Kluwer Academic, 1990.

Pellegrino, Edmund. "Clinical Ethics: Balancing Praxis and Theory." *Kennedy Institute of Ethics Journal* 6:4 (December 1996): 347–350.

————. "Toward a Virtue-Based Normative Ethics for the Health Professions." *Kennedy Institute of Ethics Journal* 5:3 (September 1995): 253–277.

————. "The Virtuous Physician and the Ethics of Medicine." *Ethical Issues in Modern Medicine*. Edited by John D. Arras and Bonnie Steinbock. Mountain View, CA: Mayfield, 1995.

————, and David C. Thomasma. *The Virtues in Medical Practice*. New York: Oxford University Press, 1993.

Pope John Paul II. *The Gospel of Life: An Encyclical Letter on Abortion, Euthanasia, and the Death Penalty in Today's World.* New York: Random House, 1995.

———. "John of the Cross, Master of the Faith." *The Pope Speaks* 35 (1990): 217–228.

———. *The Splendor of Truth.* Boston: St. Paul Books and Media, 1993. *Proactive Responses to the Assisted Suicide/Euthanasia Debate.* National Hospice Organization Ethics Committee 1995–1996. Arlington, VA: 1996.

Ramsey, Paul. *The Essential Paul Ramsey.* Edited by William Werpehowski and Stephen D. Crocco. New York: Yale University Press, 1994.

———. *The Patient as Person.* New Haven, CT: Yale University Press, 1970.

Randall, Fiona, and R. S. Downie. *Palliative Care Ethics: A Good Companion.* Oxford: Oxford Medical, 1996.

Read, Denis, O.C.D. "John of the Cross for Carpenters: The Ordinary Way of the Dark Night of Faith." *Carmelite Studies.* Volume VI. *John of the Cross: Conferences and Essays by Members of The Institute of Carmelite Studies.* Edited by Steven Payne, O.C.D. Washington, DC: ICS Publications, 1992.

Rodriguez, José Vicente. "Origins: The Yepes Family." *God Speaks in the Night: The Life, Times, and Teaching of St. John of the Cross.* Federico Ruiz, O.C.D., Project Director. Washington, DC: ICS Publications, 1991.

St. John of the Cross. *Ascent of Mount Carmel.* In *The Collected Works of Saint John of the Cross*, revised edition. Kieran Kavanaugh, O.C.D., and Otilio Rodriguez, O.C.D., eds. Washington, DC: ICS Publications, 1991.

———. *Dark Night of the Soul.* In *The Collected Works of Saint John of the Cross*, revised edition. Kieran Kavanaugh, O.C.D., and Otilio Rodriguez, O.C.D., eds. Washington, DC: ICS Publications, 1991.

————. *Living Flame of Love*. In *The Collected Works of Saint John of the Cross*, revised edition. Kieran Kavanaugh, O.C.D., and Otilio Rodriguez, O.C.D., eds. Washington, DC: ICS Publications, 1991.

Saiving, Valerie. "The Human Situation: A Feminine View." *Readings in Ecology and Feminist Theology*. Edited by Mary Heather MacKinnon and Moni McIntyre. Kansas City, MO: Sheed and Ward, 1995.

Salerno, Evelyn, and Joyce Willens, eds. *Pain Management Handbook*. St. Louis: Mosby-Year Book, 1996.

Saunders, Dame Cicely. "In Britain: Fewer Conflicts of Conscience." *Hastings Center Report* 27:1 (January-February 1997): 27–28.

Scher, Jeffrey S. *Scripture and Ethics: Twentieth-Century Portraits*. New York: Oxford University Press, 1997.

Schneider, Carl E. "Making Sausage: The Ninth Circuit's Opinion." *Hastings Center Report* 27:1 (January-February 1997): 27–28.

Selman, Francis John. *St. Thomas Aquinas: Teacher of Truth*. Edinburgh: T. and T. Clark, 1994.

Slattery, Peter, O. Carm., ed. *St. John of the Cross: A Spirituality of Substance*. New York: Alba House, 1994.

Smith, David H., and Robert M. Veatch, eds. *Guidelines on the Termination of Life-Sustaining Treatment and Care of the Dying*. Indianapolis: Indiana University Press, 1987.

Solomon, Mildred Z. "The Enormity of the Task: SUPPORT and Changing Practice." Special Supplement, *Hastings Center Report* 25:6 (November-December 1995): S28–S32.

Sparks, Richard C. *Contemporary Christian Morality: Real Questions; Candid Responses*. New York: Crossroad, 1996.

Spohn, William C. "The Return of Virtue Ethics." *Theological Studies* 53 (1992): 60–75.

———. "Spirituality and Ethics: Exploring the Connections." *Theological Studies* 58:1 (March 1997): 109–123.

Stein, Edith. *The Science of the Cross: A Study of St. John of the Cross*. Chicago: Henry Regnery, 1960.

Stoddard, Sandol. *The Hospice Movement: A Better Way of Caring for the Dying*. New York: Vintage Books, 1978.

Sulmasy, Daniel P., O.F.M., M.D. *The Healer's Calling: A Spirituality for Physicians and Other Health Care Practitioners*. New York: Paulist Press, 1997.

Taylor, Carol R. "Reflections on 'Nursing Considered as Moral Practice.'" *Kennedy Institute of Ethics Journal* 8:1 (1998): 71–82.

Thompson, Joyce E., and Henry O. Thompson. *Bioethical Decision-Making for Nurses*. Lanham, MD: University Press of America, 1992.

Thompson, William M. *Fire and Light: The Saints and Theology*. New York: Paulist Press, 1987.

Vaux, Kenneth L. *Death Ethics: Religious and Cultural Values in Prolonging and Ending Life*. Philadelphia: Trinity, 1992.

Veatch, Robert. "Abandoning Informed Consent." *Hastings Center Report* 25:2 (March-April 1995): 5–12.

———. "The Dying Cancer Patient." *Ethical Issues in Modern Medicine*. Fourth edition. Edited by John D. Arras and Bonnie Steinbock. Mountain View, CA: Mayfield, 1995.

————. "Resolving Conflicts among Principles: Ranking, Balancing, and Specifying." *Kennedy Institute of Ethics Journal* 5:3 (September 1995): 199–218.

Wadell, Paul J., C.P. *The Primacy of Love: An Introduction to the Ethics of Thomas Aquinas*. New York: Paulist Press, 1992.

Wagner, Sonia, SGS. "Women and Prayer." *St. John of the Cross: A Spirituality of Substance*. Edited by Peter Slattery, O. Carm. New York: Alba House, 1994.

Weakland, Archbishop Rembert, O.S.B. *Faith and the Human Enterprise: A Post-Vatican II Vision*. Maryknoll, NY: Orbis, 1992.

Weber, Alison. *Teresa of Avila and the Rhetoric of Femininity*. Princeton, NJ: Princeton University Press, 1990.

Werpehowski, William. "Justice," in Childress and Macquarrie, eds. *The Westminster Dictionary of Christian Ethics*.

————, and Stephen D. Crocco, eds. *The Essential Paul Ramsey: A Collection*. New Haven, CT: Yale University Press, 1994.

Wright, John, S.J. *A Theology of Christian Prayer*. New York: Pueblo, 1979.

INDEX

spiritual community, 205
"spiritual housekeeping" *(oikonomia),*
    153
spiritual searching, in health care system,
    141–145
St. Anne's Parish, 146
St. Christopher's Hospice, 5, 8–10
St. Luke's Hospice, 5, 14
standards of disclosure, 26–27
Stein, Edith, 186
Stoddard, Sandol, 4–5, 11, 15, 16, 158
stoicism, 13
subjective standard of disclosure, 27
substantive moral judgments, 50
suffering, 144, 184, 208–209
Sulmasy, Daniel, 141–145
Summa Theologica (Aquinas), 52–56
support, absence of, 14
support staff, 42
suspicion awareness system, 7
"Symbols, Meaning, and Divine Pres-
    ence" (Gilkey), 203–204
sympathy, 159

T

Taylor, Carol R., 185
teaching hospitals, 9
technology and faith, 201–202
teleological perspective, 49
Ten Commandments, 75
Teresa of Avila, St., 88–89, 92, 100, 131–
    132
Theology of Christian Prayer, A (Wright),
    156
Thomasma, David C., 79
Thompson, William, 160
time frame, patient's need to set, 18
timely delivery of services, 34
titles and positions, 163
Tracy, David, 201
transfer of care, 37
Transforming Grace: Christian Tradition

and Women's Experience (Carr), 128–
    129
Trobisch, Ingrid, 132
trust, 24
truth-telling, 25–26
twilight sleep, 18

U

Underhill, Evelyn, 89–90
unfinished business, 168–170, 173
University of Pittsburgh, 147
"unknowing," 88
utilitarianism, 62–64

V

Valdés Index of Prohibited Books, 94–95
Vatican Council II, 194–197
via affirmativa, 88
via negativa, 88
virtue, Aquinas on, 54–55
virtue and contemplation, 123–125
virtue ethics, 22, 79–84
Virtues of an Authentic Life, The (Häring),
    152
vocabulary of ethics, 67–68, 79
volition, 185–186
volunteers, 42
von Stein, Baron, 5
vulnerability, 30, 35–36

W

Weakland, Rembert, Archbishop, 194
*Well-Being: It's Meaning, Measurement
    and Moral Importance* (Griffin), 63
will, purging of, 109–110, 112, 124, 184,
    185
Willens, Joyce, 19, 20
Williamson, Marianne, 132
Winter, Miriam Therese, 132
women, in health care settings, 132, 150–
    151